BRITISH CHIMNEY SWEEPS

BRITISH
CHIMNEY SWEEPS

FIVE CENTURIES OF CHIMNEY SWEEPING

BENITA CULLINGFORD

NEW AMSTERDAM BOOKS

IVAN R. DEE, PUBLISHER

CHICAGO

Published in Great Britain by The Book Guild, Ltd.

Library of Congress Cataloging-in-Publication Data:
Cullingford, Benita, 1939–
    British chimney sweeps : five centuries of chimney sweeping / Benita Cullingford.
        p. cm.
        Includes bibliographical references and index.
        ISBN 1-56663-345-1 (alk. paper)
1. Chimney sweeps–Great Britain. 2. Chimneys–Cleaning–Great Britain–History. I.
Title.
GT5960.C552 G73 2001
697'.8—dc21

00-045253

CONTENTS

ACKNOWLEDGEMENTS

In the past, chimney sweeps had no guild and their trade was difficult to research. I am grateful, therefore, to Kathleen Strange for her study of sweeps' apprentices, *The Climbing Boys* (1982), also to staff at Abbeyhouse Museum, Kirkstall. The Abbeyhouse Folk Museum held a unique library of over 1500 books and prints containing references to chimney sweeps, the result of a 35-year dedication to 'sweepiana' bequeathed to the museum by Dr Sydney Henry in 1955. (Dr Henry's collection has recently been moved to Armley Mills, Leeds.) Mention must also be made of Professor George Lewis Phillips, of San Diego State College, California, for his pamphlets on the subject.

I found valuable references in the Guildhall Library and The British Library, and I should particularly like to record my thanks to staff in the Guildhall print room. My gratitude is also due to Lord Salisbury and archivist Robin Harcourt-Williams of Hatfield House and other owners of homes, large and small who let me explore their rooftops. I am also grateful to Sonia Addis-Smith, Joan Neal, and Percy Pearce for information about chimney-sweeping ancestors. I acknowledge help from: Brother Jonathan, Mount St Bernard's Abbey; Cheltenham Museum; London Patent Office; Marylebone Library; The Royal Society of Arts; and The Le Strange Estate.

Information about Scottish chimney sweeping from Michael McLenaghan was most useful. I am greatly indebted to Founder Member, David Mitchell and Martin Glynn, President of The National Association of Chimney Sweeps, and to Derek Blake, Guild of Masters Sweeps, for their help and friendship. Finally, and most importantly, I thank my husband Pip, for illustrations and proof reading, and my daughters Sharon and Natasha, for indexing and much appreciated support.

BENITA CULLINGFORD

FOREWORD

This book fills a gap in British social history as it is the first to chronicle the history of chimney sweeps. As the author reveals, the sweeping of chimneys has been an important trade for over five centuries. Quite apart from their obvious role of keeping flues clean, sweeps came to play other important roles; as preventers of fires, as early fire-fighters, as 'night men' who emptied outside lavatories. The book is written in a clear way and is well researched. The text is enlivened by anecdotes and intriguing glimpses of a sweep's life.

G.D.M. FRIZELLE M.Sc.
University of Cambridge

FOREWORD

BRITISH CHIMNEY SWEEPS

1

CHIMNEYS AND SWEEPS (12TH–17TH CENTURY)

There are few employments so indispensably
necessary to human comfort and convenience,
nor any profession but we could find a better
substitute for than a chimney-sweeper.

David Porter, *Master Sweep*, 1792.

A Smoky Problem

When our ancestors left communal caves to build dwellings of their
own, the fire was placed in a central hearth shared by all the family.
Pre-historic hearths can still be seen at Skara Brae on the Scottish Isle
of Orkney. It was here, around 3000BC (before the Egyptian pyramids
were completed) that the local community built their homes. Each
family lived in a circular interconnecting chamber. At the centre of
each chamber was a square stone-lined hearth.

For many centuries, whether in castle, manor, or more humble
dwelling, the central hearth remained the focus of family life. In the
Great Hall of the manor, where lords, land-workers and servants lived
together as one extended family, the hearth was raised a little above
the ground. At night, logs would be propped against andirons, (later
known as fire-dogs) and left to burn. Above the hearth, roof timbers
became blackened with smoke.[1]

During the Norman period the hearth was moved closer to the end
of the hall where the lord sat with his family. To produce enough
draught at floor level to keep the fire blazing two doors were placed
opposite each other, one in the front wall of the house, the other at
the back. This arrangement was known as a 'cross-passage'. It was
popular in country cottages, particularly in Ireland, when the front
door was used regularly and the back reserved for days when the wind
blew 'contrary'.

Unfortunately, exposed fire causes the aggravation of a smoky

1

atmosphere because smoke when heated drifts upwards. There may have been compensations, however. Smoke helped with hygiene when there was no sanitation, and as the Reverend William Harrison pointed out:

> The smoke in those daies [pre-chimneys] was supposed to be sufficient hardening for the timber of the house, so it was reputed to keepe the good man and his familie from the quake or pase.[2]

Smoke escaped through rafters and gaps in walls, but from the 13th century, when horn was inserted in window spaces, special exits had to be made. Openings in the roof ranged from simple holes to louvres placed in the roof ridge directly over the hearth. Hexagonal louvres had fitted boards at the sides that could be opened by pulling a rope. Eventually though, lifestyles became more sophisticated and greater comfort was called for. Somehow, smoke had to be confined and then assisted to the air outside.

The creation of 'smoke chambers' effectively isolated the hearth in a

Hearth with wattled smoke-canopy, County Armagh. (Sketch by P N Cullingford after *Irish Folk Ways*)

2

narrow corridor. They were made by placing two partitions across the width of the hall. Reaching from floor to rafters these were timber-framed and plastered on the inside. Heat radiated into the hall through a space in one side. A smoke chamber reduced the size of the hall and made an additional room behind the hearth.

The next step was to fashion a 'smoke hood' above the fire. Fourteenth-century hoods and canopies varied, but all tapered towards the roof. Some were capped by a 'headless barrel', (a wooden barrel with top and bottom removed).

In castles, the smoke problem was solved by cutting a funnel-shaped flue through the wall to the outside. Edward King, describing the medieval flue in Tunbridge Castle (1782), noted that it started in the upper state room then rose upwards, sloping backwards 'within the thickness of the wall' until it reached 'the loop of exit'. Vertical flues were successful because smoke was less likely to drift backwards.

The earliest chimneys as we know them were made of stone. Many castles had circular chimneys built into their battlements, though few survive. A remarkable stone chimney can still be seen in Boothby Pagnell, Lincolnshire. In the village is a tiny Norman manor – believed to be a 'Camera', a chamber-block where the lord and his family could retire. Crafted from limestone, around 1200, the chimney's tall circular shaft is supported on the outside by a gabled buttress. In the hall on the first floor the spacious fireplace has a stone hood.

Brick Chimneys (15th–17th Century)

As towns expanded in the 15th century, houses several storeys high with overhanging gables were packed closely together. Because the houses were built of timber, there was an ever-present danger of fire. Stone chimneys might be built within, but chimneys had to be tall enough to extend well above roof thatch. Stone masons were highly paid craftsmen and stone was expensive to quarry and transport. Fortunately, a solution was at hand. English brick-making was coming into its own.

Some fine examples of early brick-making are extant. Chenies Manor, on the Hertfordshire–Buckinghamshire border was constructed of red brick in the 1460s and its splendid twisted chimneys can still be seen. The Old Palace, Hatfield, (Hertfordshire) where Elizabeth I spent her childhood, was brick-built between 1480 and 1490.

Bricks could be made cheaply and locally and were easy to work with, especially after 1571, when their size was regulated.[3] Many timber-framed houses were rebuilt and brick chimneys were inserted in the cross-passage, resulting in a considerable reduction in fire risk. Houses thereafter were designed with an integrated chimney shaft extending through the roof.

When large brick chimneys known as 'stacks' were placed inside the house in a central position the design of the house was completely altered. Because of the support afforded by the stack additional floors could be added above ground level, and areas either side of the stack made into rooms. Every room was given a fireplace each with its own flue. Wherever possible fireplaces were placed back to back. By this means, many flues could share the same stack. Flues were narrowed and gathered together towards the top, where the chimney extended through the roof. Chimney tops were either square or octagonal, depending on the number of flues. (For a section on chimney pots, see Chapter 3.)

Chimneys thus became an important feature of a house and much attention was paid to their appearance. In large houses they displayed fine brickwork in ornamental patterns and mouldings and were often set at angles. The chimney had become a status symbol.[4]

James I inherited Elizabeth's Old Palace at Hatfield. In 1608 he decided to exchange it for 'Theobalds', the home of Robert Cecil (1st Earl of Salisbury). Robert Cecil, who was fond of building, immediately dismantled three quarters of the Old Palace and used the bricks to build an impressive new mansion close by. Hatfield House took five years to build and Robert Cecil died just before its completion in 1612.

Hatfield House still possesses 83 splendid brick chimneys. Grouped in ranks, their tall eight-sided shafts form an impressive roof-top display. Each chimney top is enclosed by an ornamental brick 'cap'. There are large holes around the circumference and eight protruding pipes – altogether an unusual and ingenious way of dealing with smoke.

On a more modest scale was the 'double pile' house, which became popular during the 17th century. The house was double fronted with four partitioned rooms on the ground floor and a similar arrangement on the floor above. Sometimes a single-storey extension was added. All rooms had fireplaces. The plan of an Exeter shipowner's town house in 1675 shows that three flues were contained in each of the three chimneys in the external walls, and the first-floor internal stack housed two flues; eleven fireplaces altogether.

In country areas – such as Devon and Wales – to save space inside, yeoman farmers built large chimneys on the outside wall of their cottages. Towards the end of the century chimneys generally became plainer and more compact.

A row of twelve bedroom chimneys on the west wing of Hatfield House. (Reproduced by kind permission of Lord Salisbury)

Chimney Sweeping (Early Methods)

Although chimneys became essential to the home, they also presented householders with an inbuilt problem that was never-ending. Smoke could be directed – more or less successfully (see Chapter 3, section on chimney doctors) – but its very containment in a chimney caused a sooty residue to form throughout the entire length of the flue. Smoke from a well lit fire travels up a hot flue until it reaches an outlet. But when the fire dies down, the flue cools; cold air rushes in and smoke fumes thicken and congeal, forming soot.

Before the extensive use of coal, there were many ways of sweeping chimneys. Methods differed because chimneys varied in shape and size and the assorted fuel that was burned produced different kinds of soot.

Wide chimneys that were straight and single storey in height – either from ground or first floor – could be cleaned by standing in the open fireplace with a long-handled broom. The broom, made of birch twigs tied together with thong, was inserted up the chimney. It loosened the soot which could be swept down the flue and collected. A household servant probably carried out the task.

If the flue was slightly longer, a bundle of rushes on the end of a pliable pole was used. It was pushed up from the fireplace, then down from the chimney top, (see Mulled Sack's Portrait, Chapter 8).

A country method for tall narrow chimneys was to place a bundle of straw or driftwood inside the chimney then raise and lower it by means of a rope. Depending on the flue's width, a small holly bush or fir tree was adequate. The tree was taken to the chimney top attached to a rope. A stone was fastened to the other end of the rope and lowered down the flue until it reached the hearth. Then the rope was grasped from the fireplace and the tree slowly pulled down. A similar top-to-bottom technique was carried out with a long pole. This was rammed down the chimney to dislodge impacted lumps of tar. Lastly, a bundle of twigs tied to the end brushed the chimney clean.

Another approach involved the use of birds. A report from Ireland[5] reveals that geese were used in cleaning cottage chimneys. The large bird would be dropped down the flue from the roof, then pulled back up again by a rope attached to its neck. Its powerful wings would loosen the soot as it struggled (the blacker the bird, the cleaner the chimney). In large farmhouse chimneys in Cork and County Kerry, turkeys proved useful. Pushed down from the top, their wings scraped the sides as they descended and they emerged from the fireplace unharmed. Mr E.E. Evans,[6] on his journeys through Ireland, remembers seeing a heron's wing hanging up on the mantle. This would have been used to dust the hearth. Ducks were helpful chimney sweeps as well, and the practice was by no means confined to Ireland.

Many flues had to be scraped. This was because wood – due to its water content – produced soot, which clumped together and hardened into a tar-like crust (see Chapter 4). On the Isle of Man and other districts with stone cottages, chimneys were deliberately set on fire to burn off the soot. Straw was lit in the hearth or the chimney was 'fired' by letting off a shotgun up the flue. Chimneys were often constructed with this incendiary method in mind. In Ayot St Lawrence, Hertfordshire, the end wall chimney of The Brocket Arms – an inn dating from the 16th century – was reputed to have been cleaned by this method until the late 1970s.

English Sweeps (16th Century)

Houses higher than a single storey required the services of a professional sweep. To clean efficiently the sweep had to climb inside the chimney flue and remove soot with a scraper. Poking the flue with a long-handled broom dislodged accessible soot but compacted portions

6

remained in niches and bends. Continual prodding loosened plaster and bricks. This created draught holes that could fan a mild chimney fire into a roaring blaze.

Early reference to professional chimney sweeps is difficult to trace. The trade – unlike its counterparts abroad – had no guild, and there appear to be no official records until the 16th century. Documented evidence of a professional sweep was first discovered in Norfolk. During the reign of Henry VIII, when Sir Thomas Lestrange was Sheriff of Norfolk, the *Household and Privy Purse Accounts* of Hunstanton Manor, show that payment was made to a local sweep. During the first week in December, 1519, chimney sweep John Scott was paid 2d for 'swepyng of ye Kechyn chymnye'. John Scott, or John the Scotsman, came from Ringstead village, a few miles east of Hunstanton.

By comparison, the same accounts for Sir Thomas's 12th-century ancestral manor show that 2d was paid for felling two loads of wood, and 2d paid out for 'ale for Mrs Lestrange'. Lady Lestrange may have watched her chimney being swept. During its Tudor Period, the kitchen at Hunstanton had a wicket in the upper part, 'where the lady of the house might inspect the proceedings of the servants'.

In 1558 a lesser fee was paid by Nottingham town council. According to *The Chamberlain's Accounts* for the Guild Hall, the sum of 1d was paid for 'sweppyg and dresyng' the chimney. Who received this payment or which chimney was swept is unknown.

Chimney sweep Michael Muns was employed in 1589 to sweep the chimneys of a large country house at West Horndon. Michael Muns lived in the village of Fryerning, Essex. He swept seven chimneys: the nursery chimney; the kitchen range; the bake-house chimney; the dairy chimney; the porter's chimney; the Great Room chimney, in the gatehouse; the outer gatehouse chimney. He was paid 2d each for five of the chimneys, and 14d for the two large chimneys: a total of two shillings (10p).

In Lancashire, the Steward's *Household Accounts* of the ancient manor of Smithills record that in December 1591 the sum of 1s.4d was paid to a chimney sweep for 'Dressinge of privies and swypinge of chimnes for onne holl yere'. This entry indicates that more than one chimney was swept during the year and that the sweep was also paid for another more sanitary service (see Chapter 3).

Smithills is situated two miles northwest of Bolton. The old manor was once the home of the Shuttleworth family of Gawthorpe Hall (now owned by the National Trust). Chimneys at Smithills may have been swept by a travelling sweep. During the 16th century many wanderers or 'vagabonds' skilled in different trades roamed the

Smithills Hall, Lancashire.

countryside in search of work. Later, when the Shuttleworth family lodged near London, they rented a house from Henrie Iremonger in Islington. Household accounts[7] at that time showed that a sum of 3½d was paid for 'sweepings of two chymneys'.

In Hertfordshire nearly 40 years later, George Smith was paid one year's allowance for 'sweepeing chymneis' and 'killing rats and mice' at Hatfield House. Housekeeper's bills do not state the sum paid. But at Quickswood, a smaller house on Lord Salisbury's estate, we know that Kadwalader Morgan was paid £1 on 9th October 1647, for sweeping chimneys and washing 'bucks' (rags).

London Sweeps (17th Century)

> The man that sweeps the chimneys,
> with the brush of thornes:
> And the one his neck a truss of poles,
> tipped al with hornes.[8]

During the reign of James I (1603–1625) there were approximately 150,000 inhabitants in London. Although the number of dwellings is

8

unknown, all homes had chimneys, and in most cases more than one. The City's most important marketplace was Cheapside. Extending (as it still does) from St Paul's Cathedral to King William Street, running parallel to the Thames, it was full of merchant traders. Their narrow timber-framed shops were sandwiched together on either side of the thoroughfare. Rich and poor dwelt side by side. The poorest lived in one room in upper storeys, while wealthy traders owned substantial properties. Premises three to six storeys high had tall vertical chimneys.

Cheapside was well provided with chimney sweeps. Many of them lived just north of Cheapside in Old Street and Rotten Row. Life was hard for poorer sweeps at the beginning of the century, and they petitioned the King: the *Petition of the Poor Chimney Sweepers of the City of London to the King*, alleged that there were 200 of them who, 'by the almost general neglect by Householders of their own and the City's safety, were ready to be starved for want of work.' They prayed

that an overseer might be appointed, by Letters Patent, for thirty-one years, with authority to enter houses and compel persons to afford to the sweepers access to their chimneys to sweep the same, and to pay the usual charge for such services, or in default of payment their goods to be distrained. The overseer and his deputies to be paid for their services by the delivery to them of the soot gathered.

On 8th July 1618, Sir Robert Nauton (Secretary of State) wrote to the Lord Mayor, informed him that His Majesty had read the Chimney Sweeps' Petition, and judged its contents to be 'well grounded for the safety of the City and suburbs from casualty by fire',[9] and commanded the Lord Mayor and Recorder, 'to consider the same and certify their opinion thereon'. Furthermore, the King proposed that someone well known and respected in the city should 'oversee those allowed for the purpose'.

In reply a letter from the Lord Mayor to Sir Robert Nauton stated that the Recorder, Sir Anthony Benne, and himself 'had considered the Chimney Sweeps Petition', but decided that such an appointment would be 'troublesome' and costly. There were enough

officers annually sworn to oversee all chimneys etc., and take care that they were sufficiently made and kept against peril of fire, both as to the decay of the brick or stonework, and also as to their foulness by soot; and that as to the proposed additional number of one hundred chimney-sweepers being permitted, the present number could not live by their labour.

9

Addidit criticum virtuti vuinus honorem
Ipsa cicatrias gloria major eric. Le. Sh.

Engraved by R. Cooper from a rare Print by Pass

Sir Robert Nauton.

Consequently, and despite the King's sympathetic response, the chimney sweepers' plea came to nothing.

The Eleanor Cross

Dominating the centre of Cheapside was a monument that far outshone all others, the Eleanor Cross (see Appendix). During the 15th and 16th centuries it became the favourite meeting place for street traders. Foremost among these were the chimney sweepers. The imposing presence of the 'Great Cross', as it was known, acted as their 'Guildhall'. It was their meeting place, their place of rest and, above all, it was where any mistress or maidservant could find them if they needed their chimneys swept.

Unfortunately for the chimney sweeps, the cross was so violently abused by Puritans in 1641 that it was eventually removed:

> On the 2nd May 1643, the Cross was pulled down. At the fall of the top cross drums beat, trumpets blew, and multitudes of caps were thrown in the air, and a great shout of people with joy...

Cheapside Cross, as it appeared on its erection in 1606.

The chimney sweepers felt no joy. The loss of their monument caused so much anguish that 20 years later, in 1663, their feelings were poignantly expressed in two works of fiction: *The Learned Conference* and *The Chimney-Sweepers Sad Complaint*. Although both tracts were written anonymously and are obvious parodies, they do reveal many interesting facts about the London sweeps' way of life.

The Learned Conference was set at 'Chimney-Sweepers' Hall' in Old Street. Those present were Masters, Wardens and Assistants of 'The Company of Chimney-Sweepers', who were 'richly clothed in their black robes and hoods of the same'. The proceedings of the conference were written in the form of a play with principal characters Messrs Black, Smut, Broom, and Trumpeter, together with Assistants and Journeymen in minor roles.

Mr Black, acting as chairman, explained that the chimney sweeping trade had declined because the Cross had been removed, and that a 'speedy way' was needed to replace it. Mr Smut suggested they might draw up a petition and present it to the City of London. Mr Broom agreed, saying, 'That's the direct way to a cow's thumb.' (A 'cow' in

11

the slang of the period means a thousand pounds.) The Assistants grumbled about the loss of soot:

...We are at a loss if we do not get a Patent to hinder the coffee-men from sweeping their own chimneys, (which is now their constant practise) saving the sut [soot] to mix with that hellish Berry to colour their cursed liquor, which is a great hindrance to those of our occupation, who are deprived of their Sailes which they sold to the Dyers, and gain'd a fine benefit, it being very good both for the Dyers of Blacks, and all manner of other colours.

Mr Black pointed out that the first step would be to get a new 'constant place of standing', so that other matters could be sorted out. He asked if anyone could suggest a witness for their cause. Trumpeter volunteered to support them, even promising to 'lock up his conduit', so that the water carriers could help as well, for he had noticed the chimney-sweepers' dwindling trade from his vantage point (on top of the conduit):

I have stood and watched the city round, viewing all passages day and night, where instead of hundreds of your occupation, who used formerly to rise every morning out of the tops of chimneys like break of day, now I can see but one, two or three in a fortnight, so that you must of necessity have a dead time of trade, though my Water-bearers have ever since had full employment.

Mr Collier, the Clerk, then 'drew up the petition', and gave it to Mr Black who read it to the assembled company:

To the Honourable and Famous and Renowned City of London.
The humble *Petition* of the Mr Wardens, and Assistants with the rest of the brotherhood of the noble Company of Chimney-Sweepers. Humbly shewe that the ... monument of the Cheapside Cross was not only a graceful ornament to this famous city; but also ... a place to which our occupation was much advanced, we having liberty to wait there every morning for imployment, whither the London Lasses and Virgins of the City repaired upon all occasions ... to make clean their chimneys, and sweep the sut and dust out ... Whereby we enjoyed not only good wages but many a good breakfast of beef, bread, and beer,

12

before their Mrs. were up, in such plenty, that our trade was as beneficial as most occupations about the city.

That by the loss of this rich monument ... our occupation totally distroyed, we have ever since been ... forced to wander up and down like hackneys day after day, and week after week to little or no purpose ... In tender consideration of these our great grievances, our humble desires are,

First, that some trusty messengers may be employed to discover and find out those persons who were Abettors ... of this ... unparallel'd Villany...

Third, that all those who are well-wishers ... will freely contribute to the rebuilding of this stately ornament...

Fourthly, that the work being finished, we may again have the freedom as formerly, to take up our standing there for the advancement of our occupation, and the preservation of our wives and families from utter ruin.

The reading of the petition was applauded. Then a copy of the *Resolution of the Maidens of London*, was read (see Appendix), and 'signed by the many thousand maids in and about the City of London'.

Three years after publication of *The Learned Conference*, on Saturday 1st September 1666, a small fire, reputedly in a baker's chimney in Pudding Lane, caused the City's most devastating conflagration. The fire started at about 10 pm, and burned for four days and nights. More than 13,000 houses were destroyed and 200,000 people made homeless. Samuel Pepys, whose home was saved, described the scene at Moorfields where a massive refugee camp had been set up to shelter the homeless:

Drank there, and paid twopence for a plain penny loaf; thence homeward, having passed through Cheapside and Newgate market, all burned.

It appears that the City sweeps eventually found a new trading position. They chose the Little (or Pissing) Conduit near St Paul's. Obsolete since the Great Fire, the conduit now served a useful purpose. It became a prop for the chimney sweeps' shovels and brooms and a meeting place while they waited to be hired.

Local sweeps were a common sight to Edward 'Ned' Ward. Ned was a tavern keeper and writer of coarse humorous prose. Between 1698 and 1700 he wrote a popular monthly tract chronicling the daily observations of a scholar from the country and his cockney companion. It was called *The London Spy*. The following passage describes a scene outside St Paul's church-yard at 'about three a clock' in the afternoon:

> Came to the Cheapside Conduit, pallisade'd in with chimney-sweeper Brooms, and guarded with such an infernal crew of Soot-colour'd Funnel-Scourers, that a Countryman seeing so many black attendance waiting at a Stone-Hovel, took it to be one of Old Nick's tenements, and ask'd a shopkeeper, why they would suffer the Devil to live in the Heart of the City?

Sweeps' Appearance

We first learn something about chimney sweeps' appearance from contemporary dramatists Shakespeare and Ben Jonson. In 17th-century literature, chimney sweeps were portrayed with soot-blackened features. Their 'funereal' appearance is alluded to in Shakespeare's play *Cymbeline* written around 1609. The 'unbeknown' sons of King Cymbeline chant the following lament for their sister Imogen, who is believed dead:

Fear no more the heat o' the sun,
Nor the furious winter rages,
Thou thy worldly task hast done,
Home art gone, and ta'en thy wages;
Golden lads and girls all must,
As chimney-sweepers come to dust.

Shakespeare contrasts the golden looks of Imogen (who is disguised as a boy) with the grimy appearance of chimney sweeps, yet implies that all are equal in death.

In the same year, Ben Jonson's comedy *Epicene* was produced for the first time. Truewit and Clerimont openly gossip about Morose, their friend's uncle, who 'can endure no noise'. (The sweeps would not sign an agreement to make less noise.)

> TRUEWIT: They say he has been upon divers treaties with the fishwives and orange-women, and articles propounded between them. Marry, the chimney-sweepers will not be drawn in.

The action of the play takes place near the Strand, the Law Courts, and the Thames. Ben Jonson must have been acutely aware of the bustle and noise of London street traders as they competed for

14

custom. Fishwives and costermongers (fruit sellers) could attract customers by the smell of their goods, but chimney sweepers could only advertise their trade by cries of 'Soot-Sweep-O'.

Their appearance is mentioned again when Truewit taunts Morose by making fun of the barber, Cutbeard:

TRUEWIT: Or, that he never be trusted with trimming of any but chimney-sweepers.

The implication is that it wouldn't matter to chimney sweepers whether they had a clean shave or not.

An early woodcut print of a chimney sweep, 'Tom' (1620)[10] clearly depicts the clothes and equipment of his trade. He is shown clean-faced with a trimmed beard and drooping moustache. His black hat with small feather and narrow hat band is turned down at the brim. He wears a loose long-sleeved shirt and ragged knee-length trousers. On his feet are short boots. He carries a small sack and a bundle of long brooms. Under the print are the words:

Chimny sweep chimny sweep hear maid;
To cleanse Sooty chimnies is Tom's trade;

A woodcut from 1620 showing a sweep.

A woodcut of a chimney sweep from 1640.

Though base it be held, I think it no scorn
A living to get by broom and by horn.
Ile clean your foul holes; rouz from sleep,
Let in Black Tom, your chimnies to sweep.

A later print (1640) shows a sweep with soot-blackened face and hands and up-turned hat. Compared with other traders who wear breeches and jackets cut to the hips, this particular sweep is clothed in a protective outer garment. It is long-sleeved and loose-fitting, with a tie at the waist probably of cord or rope. Over his left shoulder he carries a soot sack and a bundle of tightly bound rods. Protruding from the end of one of the rods is a stiff brush. In his left hand he holds a long-handled scraper, the head of which is small and triangular.

An engraving, 'Seyley and his boy',[11] printed in 1687, shows two sweeps: Master Sweep Seyley and his young apprentice. The two are on their way to work. Seyley carries a pointed pole on one shoulder and a bundle of birch brooms on the other. Hooked over his belt is a scraper. Unlike chimney sweep Tom 60 years before, he wears a short tunic with a belt over leggings. The leggings have a fashionable tie below each knee and overlap his shoes. Both sweeps carry large sacks and wear wide-brimmed hats with collapsible crowns. Though shabbily dressed they have clean faces and hands. The young boy holds a short long-bristled hand brush. He wears a laced-up jerkin with sewn-in sleeves and breeches – torn at the knee through climbing – and thin-soled pumps. His shoes could easily be kicked off before ascending a chimney.

The Reverend J. Granger, Vicar of Sheptake, Oxfordshire, reported that 'The bass and treble voice of Seyley and his boy were generally heard in the streets, about 6 o'clock in the morning.'[12]

Scottish Chimney Sweeping (17th Century)

At the beginning of the 17th century many tall tenements were built in the city of Edinburgh. In contrast to single-roomed stone cottages, where chimneys were rare, the city tenements rose 12 to 14 storeys. Their chimneys were such a great height that local sweeps devised a special method for sweeping them. The technique required two sweeps. 'The roper', who needed to be agile and unafraid of heights, operated from the chimney top, while 'the bottomer' worked from the fireplace inside. Equipment was simple: a length of rope, lead weight, short ladder, bunch of twigs and a sheet.

After climbing the stairs the roper entered the garret through a small

An engraving from 1687 of Seyley and his boy. (Marcellus Lauron)

17

door and used the ladder to reach a hatch in the roof. First the steep slated roof had to be negotiated, then the ridge at the top, and finally the stone face of the chimney stack. Sometimes long nails had to be driven into the stones, to assist the final climb to the chimney pots – a vertical distance of 25 feet.

Inside the room containing the fireplace all furniture was removed. This was necessary in case an avalanche of soot descended the flue. The fireplace opening was then covered by a large sheet. Sweeping began when the roper at the top had located the correct flue. This could be a difficult task when upwards of 20 pots were simultaneously discharging smoke. The procedure for finding the flue involved a series of pre-arranged calls. The bottomer first shouted 'Ah, Hee ... Hee ... Hee' up the chimney, and then listened. If correct, the response would be 'He, He, He.' The roper, having tied the weight to one end of the rope, lowered it down the flue to the fireplace. The bottomer removed the weight, pulling down more rope until they both had the same amount. He then tied on the bundle of twigs and indicated that all was ready by shouting 'He – up, He – up.' The twigs were hauled up to the top by the roper, then pulled down again by the bottomer, continuing until the bottomer was satisfied by the fall of soot. Sweeping was stopped by calling 'He, He, He...'[13]

In London, following the Great Fire and the devastation of Cheapside, the City was quickly rebuilt. It expanded dramatically both to the north and west. In 1682 speculative builders such as Nicholas Barbon started building brick houses arranged in terraces. By the end of the 17th century most of the principal streets and squares had been built, and such an increase in chimneys greatly benefited the chimney sweeping trade.

Notes

[1] Seen in Ludwick Hall, Hertfordshire, proof that (before the chimney was built) the old hall had both louvre and smoke chamber.

[2] *Descriptions of England* (1577).

[3] Regulation size (9" x 4" x 2¼") *Pattern of English Building*, A. Clifton-Taylor, 1972.

[4] Chimneys remain as monuments. Outside the Hertfordshire village of Sandridge is a lone chimney stack. It is known as the 'John Bunyan Chimney'. An inscription on the buttress reads: 'John Bunyan is said by tradition to have preached and occasionally to have lodged in the cottage of which this chimney was a part.'

[5] *Niles Register*, 27th April 1844.

[6] *Irish Folk Ways*, E.E. Evans, 1957.

[7] Hunstanton records, February 1609.

[8] *The Pepysian Garland* (1612), edited by G.H.E. Rollins.

[9]Records, City of London, *Remembracia* (1579–1664).
[10]*England, Cries and Itinerant Trades.* 1620
[11]*Biographical History of England*, Reverend J. Granger, 1769
[12]*London Street Criers and Hawkers*, Marcellus Lauron & Karen Beall. 1687
[13]Acknowledgements: Michael McLenaghan, *Old Reekie Chimney Sweeps*, Colinton, Edinburgh.

2

FUEL AND THE SOOT TRADE

PART 1: FUEL

Early Fuels

When wood was plentiful, chimney sweeping was less of a problem for the wealthy who could obtain hard wood such as oak, which burned slowly. In manors and other large residences, logs were cut to fit the size of the fireplace. Fires remained alight almost continuously and because the flue stayed hot, the build-up of soot was minimal.

For the poor it was a different matter. Logs were heavy, and without conveyance most people had to make do with inferior wood that could be bundled and carried by one person. To make thin dry wood burn longer it was sprinkled with dampened earth. Consequently, smoke lingered in the flue creating more soot. As forests become thinner, a Cheminage Tax dissuaded people from felling trees close to the roadside. Citizens were also required by law to cover their fires at night. This was known as the 'Curfew'.

During the 16th century when wood for ship-building become scarce, Elizabeth I forbade any oak, ash or beech that grew within 14 miles of the sea (or any navigable river) to be used as domestic fuel.

Other sources of fuel were faggots, charcoal and peat. Faggots cut from the Common and mixed with vegetable peelings were popular with cottagers. Peelings were dried at the back of the fireplace and then brought forward. This produced a 'woolly soot',[1] described by Master Sweep William Duck as adhering together 'like rags'. It burned like pitch and blackened the chimney top. Chimney sweeps often removed encrustations an inch thick from the sides of the flue.

Charcoal produced a good heat with hardly any ash and no smell. Furthermore, it was smokeless. Unfortunately, charcoal manufacture required vast amounts of wood. 'In 1475, Sir John Soy's manors round Little Berkhampstead are stated to have sent 62 loads of charcoal to London.'[2]

Peat had a strong smell and produced a lot of smoke. It smouldered rather than blazed so that fires could be kept in all night. Similarly, the burning of turf in the Fen district caused local sweep Alfred

20

Wiseman to complain that it clothed the walls of the chimney with a 'sticky substance like black treacle'.[3]

Seacoal

Coal contained more heat-giving energy[4] per unit of weight than wood or charcoal. Seacoal was transported by barge from Newcastle and offloaded at landing places in Fleet Ditch. At first, it could only be used in forges and kilns. The smoke it produced was so intolerable that Elizabethan chairs were purpose-built with short legs to avoid the fumes. William Harrison, in *Descriptions of England* (1577), speaks of the 'multitude of chimneys ... marvellously altered for the worse'. He remembers that when he was young only religious houses, manors and great parsonage had chimneys: 'Now', he remarks, 'we have many chimneys ... our tenderlings complain of rheums, catarrhs, and poses.' When Elizabeth I agreed to the use of coal for domestic fires, she made it illegal to burn coal in London during Parliamentary sessions. This was in response to a country Member who complained that:

Many brewers, smiths and other artificers of London had ... taken to the use of pitcoal for their fires, instead of wood; which fills the air with noxious vapours and smoke, very prejudicial to health.

By the end of the 16th century, coal was in general use throughout the metropolis, with 200 ships employed in the London trade and 200,000 caldrons being imported annually.

A coalfire needed a good draught to keep burning and it became necessary to reduce the size of the fireplace. Sir Hugh Platt not only redesigned the fireplace but also suggested improvements to seacoal. He maintained that the fireplace should be reduced by inserting a false back and sides, and that this should be carried high enough to narrow the flue opening, thereby increasing the draught. His publication *A New Cheape and Delicate Fire of Cole-Balles* (1603), reads:

First I do hold it an infallible rule to know a good cole by viz. if the same being held over a candle, or rather a flaming fire, do melt, and as it were drop or frie ... but if the same grow hard and drie over the flame, it is a signe of a lean and hungrie cole ... of which kind are the Sunderland Coles, whereof the poores wharfe in London can give a sufficient testimony...

21

Sir Hugh recommended the 'firing' of seacoals into 'boles', proposing that loam and sawdust should be mixed with coal which 'maketh a sweete and pleasing fier'.

Coal fires were also difficult to start and coal-men who made house deliveries often lit fires as well. Coal was kept below ground level, tipped into cellars through a hole in the pavement. An iron lid known as a 'man-hole' protected the circular opening. When countryman John Yeoman visited the City in 1774, he was amazed at the London coalholes:

> The contrivance they have in London is a maviell to one who never saw a City before. In the foot Road, which is all Paved with fine White Stone, Under the which every one has a cole house. Over the Same theres a Round hole about Nine inches over cover'd with a Plate of Iron even with the Pavement. So they take up this Iron plate, the coals are Throne down without going into peoples Houses.

The iron lids were frequently stolen and night watchmen had to make extra patrols to keep down the thefts.

In country areas – until the 1860s and the spread of railways – coal was expensive to use. Counties such as Hertfordshire, where coal had to be fetched by pony and trap from depots such as Boxmoor and Hatfield, were burdened with coal levies. Within a radius of 20 miles from the General Post Office, St Martin's-le-Grand, taxes were payable in each of the five counties surrounding London. Boundary markers, in the form of stone obelisks determined the limit.

London Coal Traders

As trade in coal increased, larger ships were needed and Billingsgate became the main landing place for coal. Behind Billingsgate wharf was a large piece of common land known as Roomland. It was used as a trading place for coal until the Coal Factors Society was formed in 1769. The Society bought two houses on the north side of Thames Street and the new enterprise became The Coal Exchange.

During the 18th century five families dominated the London coal trade: Horne, Wright, Dale, Wood and Sells (see Appendix). The families eventually combined and became two Merchant companies. Towards the end of the century, John Charrington started trading at Chadwell. When John was born (1767), his grandfather Thomas Charrington was a farmer at Leigh in Surrey. John had often seen farm wagons loaded with country produce going to London and

22

Coal boundary marker in Hertfordshire.

returning with coal, and he decided to become a coal merchant. In 1790, he leased a wharf and dwelling house from the Dean and Chapter of St Paul's. It was situated at 58 Lower Shadwell. The street, known as Codpeie Row and The Old Orchard, connected Bell wharf and Shadwell dock. Coal was either stored on the wharf or transported by barge inland via canals and riverways. This led to John's seven-year partnership with Daniel Cloves, a barge builder. (At one time Charringtons operated up to 100 barges.)

John Charrington's enterprise led to five successive generations of Charringtons. In 1859, when one quarter of the general trade on the Thames was taken up with coal, The Dale Company and Sells merged with John Charrington to become 'Charringtons'.

PART 2: SOOT

Soot had many uses. It was difficult to remove, smelled offensively and could – in certain circumstances – endanger health (see elsewhere). Yet, this smutty deposit was much sought after:

There is scarcely any rubbish which cannot be converted ... even the soot ... is ... sold for manure. Or perhaps they are carrying it to the dyers, who use it for a kind of dun colour.[5]

Many of the poorer classes stained their floors with soot to cover the dirt and it was commonly thought that soot could whiten teeth. This mistaken belief greatly amused the sweep, whose teeth only appeared white because of the contrast with their blackened features.

From the beginning of the 18th century, there was an abundance of soot. The removal of soot from London (and other cities) led to a lucrative trade that benefited both chimney sweep and farmer for over 200 years. Revenue from the sale of soot made up a substantial part of the chimney sweeps' income. The quantity of soot sold in London was estimated to be 500,000 bushels per annum.

A bill for a large amount of soot (1782) from Master Sweep Robert Edwards (High Holborn) to Sq[r] Radecliffe shows that soot cost ½d per bushel and customers paid in instalments:

		£	s	d
	left to pay	2	12	0
March 22	louded 160 Bushels	5	0	0
" 26	louded 160 Bushels	5	0	0
" 29	louded 160 Bushels	5	0	0
April 5	louded 160 bushels	5	0	0
	louden		10	0
		£22	2	0

June 7 1782

Re[d] in part of This Bill
fourteenpounds to me Robert Edwards

Agriculture (18th Century)

Soot was valued most as a fertiliser. Soot contains ammonia salts and is nitrogenous manure, which acts as an effective stimulant. Soot was sold by the bushel and its quality and consistency varied. As a rule 'the lighter the soot the higher its nitrogen content and the greater its common value.'[6]

There were three main types. 'Best soot' was produced from pure

24

coal. Of less value was soot obtained from the poorer classes, who burned coal with a mixture of potato peelings. This, however, weighed three times as much as pure coal soot. Wood soot, which had little value as a fertiliser (and was often mixed with coal soot), was nearly ten times heavier.

Although soot was sold loose, it was more usual to buy an estimated five bushels per sack. Costs to the farmer in 1730 were 2d per bushel in spring and 12d later in the year. Depending on the type of crop, farmers top-dressed their soil at different times of the year. For cereals it was Christmas to April, when up to 25 bushels were used per acre. At the beginning of March, 'barley was harrowed in' and 'sooted' on top. The grain had 'no less than three dressing'. Soil was also top-dressed at the end of the year to encourage new growth.[7] Because soot tended to 'burn' crops if used too quickly, it had to be stored. Large mounds were heaped on straw then left in fields enclosed by hurdles. Sometimes the hurdles were thatched.

More soot was used in Hertfordshire and to a lesser extent Bedford-shire, than in any other county. The frequent use of best soot helped to transform Hertfordshire's chalky boulder clay into a highly fertile state. William Ellis (1733) wrote:

If the harvest is backward, those farmers who live within thirty miles of London, and whose land is proper for it ... send their teams thither as many do in our parts (Little Gaddesden), for this noble manure ... and that it may come cheaper home, we commonly carry up chaff, corn, wood, flour, or timber, and fetch, in return, soot in sacks, or loose, in a cart or wagon ... above all other single dressings, does the London soot excel in this soil.

This was still true in 1795 when D. Walker, in his *General View of Agriculture in Hertford* wrote: 'Herts is deemed the first corn country in the Kingdom.'

Soot Adulteration

Some people were apprehensive about the way soot was obtained. *The Morning Chronicle* (London, 11th January 1775) reported that a correspondent had overheard a chimney-sweeper's boy pleading with his neighbour, 'For God's sake he might be permitted to sweep the chimneys for the soot', for if he did not carry home a bushel he should be 'half murdured'. After making inquiries, the correspondent had found the boy's report in general to be true. Farmers, ever mindful of their crops, began to suspect that their 'best' soot was being adulterated. An appeal was made to London Master Sweep, David Porter (see Chapter 8). Mr Porter might appear an unlikely champion of their cause, but this astute campaigner acted on behalf of master sweep and farmer alike.

In 1792, David Porter published his *Considerations on the Present State of Chimney Sweepers*. He was particularly scathing about certain aspects of the soot trade:

> ...Of all the various acts of deception and fraud which are practised without control none are equal in their lassitude to those used by chimney sweeps and dealers in soot.

Farmers were given short measure through the smallness of their sacks and the art of filling them. Soot was adulterated by sifting coal ashes and wetting them, mixing soot with smith's forge dust, or by adding sweepings of burnt cork.

David Porter suggested the following remedies for the situation:

- Chimney-sweepers residing in the City of London and Borough of Southwark should form a company controlled by 12 annually appointed persons. The Lord Mayor and an Alderman to act as Head and Deputy.
- A penalty be imposed for the adulteration of soot.
- All soot should be properly measured by the bushel.
- Licensed 'meters' (inspectors) to be appointed for the trade.
- Costs offset by the buyer for metage and loading – 8d for every 5 bushels.
- Accounts kept, with names and amounts recorded.
- Tickets and receipts issued.
- The Company to impose a 1d per bushel tax.

There were many other worthy recommendations, but little notice was taken.

Artful dodges

Sixty years later, Master Sweep George Elson testified that some sweeps were still earning a good living from devious soot practice. When George and his brother were country climbing boys in the 1840s (see Chapter 4) they met a group of rascally sweeps. The sweeps' favourite trick was to:

26

tread the soot down hard in the strike-measure until it was half-full and caked; then the loose soot added on top would be all that would run from the measure, affecting a saving of half a strike of soot each time.[8]

This fraud was carried out so successfully that several of the sweeps began trading solely as soot dealers and doubled their profits for years. Eventually a farmer, 'not quite so dull as others', found them out. Their ruse was discovered when he 'stuck his pen-knife into the bottom of the strike-measure' and found that it was being carried upside down, with 'only a covering of soot on the surface and none inside'.

The two lads were present on this occasion. When a constable was sent for they 'all jumped into the cart and galloped away'. As no payment had been given for the soot, in George Elson's words, it was really a case of 'biter bitten'. He adds, though, that as soon as they were out of the neighbourhood the sweeps tried the trick with other farmers, and succeeded.

George also relates an amusing incident with a goose. Just before Christmas, while George was working for Northampton Master Sweep Tom Bale (see Chapter 5), they delivered some soot to a local farmer. It was common practice for farmers who bought small quantities of soot to store it in the dovecote. Tom had tipped one sackful into the dovecote and was returning from his cart with a second when he saw 'the object of his Christmas dreams – a fine fat goose'.

The goose was peering into the dovecote. Now, whether Tom accidentally chased the goose into the soot-filled dovecote or whether the snow-white creature, terrified by Tom's black appearance, fled inside of its own accord, can only be guessed at. The goose, however, after much floundering around in the soot-heap, set up such a screeching that 'brought out the farmer'. When the goose scrambled out, now black instead of white, the farmer laughed. Then he saw how lame it was. Tom pointed out that the goose was no longer fit for market.

'Tell you what I'll do,' said Tom seizing his opportunity, 'I'll stan yer two shillings for her, the missis could do with er goose at Christmas.' The farmer agreed and Tom gleefully bore the hapless goose away.

19th-Century Soot Trade

Sweep Soot O! sweep for your soot.
London Cries for Children, 1806

The sweep, perhaps, some may despise,
And view him with disgustful eyes,
But if he sweeps your chimney clean
He's well employed, though it be mean.
And of the charge be not afraid,
Give him the soot the cost is paid.

A new kind of trader emerged in the
19th century, the manure merchant,
Sweep Soot Ho! 1780
who purchased soot from master sweeps
which was then re-sold to farmers and gardeners.

The price of soot fluctuated. It reached its highest value in 1804 at
18d per bushel, then fell to 5d ten years later. In 1817, it rose again to
9d. Soot was also shipped abroad to the West Indies. On 30th October
1832, Mr Geary of Curtis and Company purchased:

50 Hogsheads of soot amounting to
2000 bushels £58 6s 8d

from Soot Dealer, J. Hughes ((No 18, next door to the White Swan,
Islington turnpike). Mr Geary used the soot on the Canegrove Estate
Sugar Plantation, on the isle of St Vincent, in the Caribbean.

In London (1849) there were approximately 300,000 houses in the
metropolis and the annual use of coal averaged eight tons per household. The London *Post Office Directory* for 1850 lists 33 soot dealers.
The amount of soot from each chimney depended upon the length,
draught and irregular surface of the flue. Kitchen chimneys yielded
most soot because of their length. As each ton of ordinary house coal
produced nearly a quarter of a bushel of soot, the gross quantity of
soot deposited in the chimneys of London each year was 1,000,000
bushels. (N.B. a bushel was a dry measure of 8 gallons.)

The larger houses are swept in some instances once a month, but
generally once in three months, and yield on an average six
bushels of soot per year. A moderate size house, belonging to
the 'middle-class', is usually swept four times a year, and gives
about five bushels of soot per annum; while houses occupied by
the working and poorer classes are seldom swept more than

twice, and sometimes only once, in the twelve month, and yield about two bushels of soot annually.[9]

London was divided into five districts: North, South, East, West and Central. Each district contained a number of areas. The largest quantity of soot was produced in the St Pancras area – District North – where 18 master sweeps, with their 33 journeymen and 4 boys, collected on average 920 bushels of soot each week.

Apart from counties already mentioned, the home counties, Cambridge, Lincolnshire and Norfolk all used soot extensively on meadow lands. Its main function was as a deterrent to pismires (fruit-eating ants) and snails.

At a meeting of the *Hanley and Shelton Chimney Sweeping Association* (17th May 1855) committee members were told that local sweeps took their soot to Sheffield every Saturday evening, where it was stored and sold from 3s to 4s a quarter or 3d per bushel. From 1st January to September 1857, soot gathered in the Sheffield District amounted to 2000 five-bushel bags.

Soot dealers to the south were quick to take advantage of the railways. William Wright, who had worked for his father as a climbing boy, was an established Rag & Soot Merchant in 1865. His trade card informed the public that soot could be sent to any railway station, 'carriage paid in bags. Bags returnable. Price per ton, on application.' William Wright's premises were in Market Street, Alton. It is believed that he had depots in conjunction with other sweeps on the south coast, at Southampton and Portsmouth, where the railway line was completed in 1840.

Completion of St Pancras main-line station in 1866 accelerated the spread of railways to the north, and Lincolnshire became an important distribution centre for London soot. In St Albans City, Soothouse Spring, an industrial estate, was named after the 'Soothouse' used by local sweeps until the Second World War.

Soot Rivals

Scotland

Meanwhile, in Scotland at the beginning of the Victorian era soot was compared with lesser-known fertilisers such as saltpetre. In 1838, Estate Manager Alexander Main carried out field trials[10] on the Earl of Dalhousie's estate. He applied the manures alternately to 18 ridges of grass and proved that grass grew more luxuriantly on the sooted

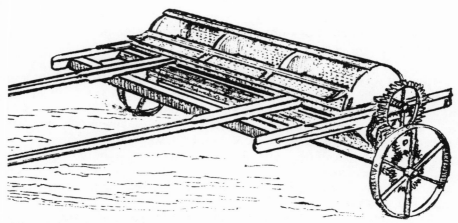

Alexander Main's soot machine, 1839.

ridges. Similar tests with wheat were just as conclusive. Moreover, soot, at 2d per bushel was cheaper than saltpetre.

The following year, when *The Royal Highland Agricultural Society* organised a competition for the invention of farm implements, Alexander Main gained recognition for his soot machine. An illustration of his invention and an explanation of the way it worked[11] were published as a prize essay by the Society. Mr Main's essay contains a reference to sheep:

> Soot does not seem to injure grass in the estimates of sheep. I tried its effect on a small piece of pasture upon which a few sheep were put to graze. The result was curious. There were many ridges in the field beside those dressed with soot, all good grass, but the sheep continued to eat the sooted ridges until they were completely bared. With faces quite blackened, they fed heartily on the soot-dressed pastures.

Sir John Bennet Lawes

In Hertfordshire, three years later, a serious rival to soot emerged; the artificial fertiliser. The man responsible was John Bennet Lawes, squire of Rothamsted Manor. John Lawes developed an interest in fertilisers when he inherited his family's ancient manor and estate in Harpenden. The estate's main wheat crops were Old Red Lammas and Dugdale. Being keen on chemistry John Lawes started to experiment with bone ash. By 1842, aged 26, he was ready to patent his process and set up a factory for making 'Superphosphate.' His first advertisement appeared in the *Gardener's Chronicle* on 1st July 1843:

J B LAWES PATENT MANURE, composed of phosphate of lime, phosphate of ammonia, silicate of potash etc. are now for sale at his factory, Deptford-Creek, London, price 4s.6d. These substances can be had separately.[12]

In 1847, John Lawes had established himself as founder of the great artificial fertiliser industry.

Despite Mr Lawes's success with artificial fertilisers, it appears that in May 1880 he had to resort to the use of soot for wheat on his farm, because of the high price of nitrate of soda. In 1882, John Bennet Lawes was honoured with a Baronetcy.

PUNCH'S FANCY PORTRAITS.—No. 87.

SIR JOHN BENNET LAWES, BART.

THE AGRICULTURAL LAWES, THE NEW WHEEL-BARROW-NET, MOTTO, "LAUS ET HONOR."

Sir John Bennet Lawes, on the conferment of his baronetcy in 1882.

Black smoke

Concern, however, was shown for the effect on health caused by breathing in 'Black smoke'.[13] In London, six eminent scientists gave evidence of their research to a House of Commons Committee. Their accounts paint a grim picture of mid-19th-century London, although it must be pointed out that references were 'to extreme conditions'. Dr Reid spoke of:

> Black particles of soot ... which annoy us at the Houses of Parliament to such an extent that I have been under the necessity of putting up a veil, about 40′ long and 12″ deep, on which, on a single evening, taking the worst kind of weather for the production of soot, we can count occasionally 200,000 visible portions of soot excluded at a single sitting.

Dr Reid explained that individual pieces were counted upon one square inch of cloth.

> ...and on one occasion at the Horse Guards the amount of soot deposited was so great that it formed a complete and continuous

31

film, so that when I walked upon it I saw the impression of my foot.

Mr Booth added that one of the gardeners of the Botanic Gardens in Regent's Park could tell the number of days sheep had been in the park from the blackness of their wool.

Into the Present

As concentrated artificial fertiliser grew in popularity, best soot became scarce. Soot lost status as a valued fertiliser, though its use continued. In the 1920s and 1930s, two Hampshire chimney sweeps, the Doe brothers, regularly dressed the cricket square with soot during the winter months. And in Hertfordshire, *Agricultural Records* (1930)[14] show that 4600 tons of soot were spread on farmland at an average price of 4d per acre. In November 1937 chimney sweeps Pearce & Sons from south east London (see Chapter 10) delivered 200 sacks of soot to Sandy in Bedfordshire.

By 1950, a more scientific approach was favoured. To combat pollution and comply with legislation, people were encouraged to burn 'smokeless' fuel. As the use of gas, electric and oil-burning appliances increased, the quantity of soot diminished. In 1977, Berkhamstead sweep Rex Goodwin rated soot 'a side-product business sold to market gardeners as a fertiliser at 25p a one cwt-size bag. Oil soot was utilised at sewerage farms.'

Chimney sweeps in the 1990s are still asked for soot. At Clacton-on-Sea, Essex, Derek Blake (Guild of Master Sweeps) stores his soot in a reserved area on district allotments, where it is given away as 'goodwill' to local residents.

Notes

[1]*Evidence before Parliament*, 1834.
[2]*Industrial Archaeology In Hertfordshire*, W. Branch Johnson, 1970.
[3]*Reminiscences of a Norwich Sweep*, Alfred Wiseman, 1990s.
[4]One cord of wood (4' × 8' × 4') was the equivalent of one ton of coal.
[5]*A Peep into London for Good Children*, London, 1809.
[6]*Smoke, a study of town air*, Cohen & Ruston, 1925.
[7]*Modern Husbandman*, William Ellis, 1733.
[8]*The Last of the Climbing Boys*, George Elson, 1900.
[9]*London Labour & the London Poor*, Henry Mayhew, 1851.

[10]2cwt (100kg) of saltpetre and 40 bushels (16kg) of soot per Scots acre. Results published by *The Royal Highland Agricultural Society* 1835–1865.

[11]Soot machine: Place soot in cylinder–Close chest–Set machine in motion–Revolutions of upper cylinder cause separation of soot from refuse–Lower cylinder receives soot–Soot discharged through fluted cylinder–Soot evenly distributed on ground, regulated by revolving brush extending length of cylinder–Stones and refuse discharged by opening trapdoor.

[12]*Fertilisers and Manures*, Sir John Russell, 1909.

[13]Scientists; Dr Reid, Dr Ure, Professor Faraday, Professor Brande, Mr Booth, Mr Solly.

[14]*Survey of Agriculture*, H W Gardner, 1962.

3

MASTER SWEEPS' TRADE (18TH & 19TH CENTURIES)

Master Sweeps (18th Century)

...the small coal-man was heard with cadence deep
Till drown'd in shriller of chimney Sweep...
Jonathan Swift (1707)

Advertising

Poor sweeps with no fixed premises or regular contracts for sweeping roamed the streets calling out, competing for trade. These were the 'small masters' employing one or two men and a boy or the 'single-handed sweeps' (see later). Sophie de la Roche, visiting London, recorded in her diary that she was already dressed before 8 in the morning (while the maids slept), when she heard a 'tiny chimney sweep boy, six years old running along barefoot at his master's side, his soot-bag on his back.'[1] The young boy was calling out 'Chimney-sweep! Chimney-sweep!' (see also section on Art, Chapter 5).

'High masters', on the other hand, who held contracts to sweep the homes of the wealthy, could afford to advertise. They used two symbols; the Golden pole and the Sweeps' brush. At first the pole was carried, but it became a permanent fixture later when business premises were established. The golden pole also advertised the sweeps' secondary trade, that of 'nightmen' (see later).

Masters trading solely as chimney sweeps chose to display either a flat circular brush or a brush known as a 'Turk's head', which was short and sturdy. Painted signs and trade cards were also used. Although house numbering was introduced in 1740, wooden signs remained popular in business areas like Cheapside because customers recognised the different trades by their symbols. Signs were hung from posts outside houses or attached to the front wall of business premises by an iron bracket.

Affluent masters or 'governors', as they were known in the trade, used highly distinctive trade cards. The term 'trade-card' is misleading, as they consisted of sheets of paper and were really handbills. The bills – distributed to private homes – advertised the sweep's name, the address of his premises and his range of services. The reverse side was used as an invoice and receipt. They measured 8″ × 6″ and many bore the Royal Coat of Arms and were embellished with illustrated scenes.

An early card of chimney sweeper Robert Edwards, Newtoner's Lane, High Holborn (1757) shows a master sweep with three apprentices. The master dressed in tricorne hat and frock coat is holding a long pole. His two boys are well equipped for work with large sacks, short-handled brushes and scrapers. Their knees are padded and they wear climbing caps. A third boy appears from a chimney pot. In the background, a Turk's head brush and painted sign are shown attached to a pillar outside the sweep's premises. The illustrated scene is enclosed with a scroll. Under the wording is a final message: *Please take care of this Bill to prevent Mistakes.*

Fees and Expenses

Trade expanded considerably during George III's reign. Social conditions improved and people lived longer. Consequently the population doubled, increasing from seven and a half million in 1760 to fourteen million in 1820. More and more houses were built, resulting in an escalation of chimneys.

'Great Houses', as they were called in the trade, had a fixed day for lighting their sitting-room fires. This was generally from September 29th, Michaelmas Day, to the 1st May, May Day. Household accounts (11th November 1772) for Chevening Manor, Kent, home of Lord Stanhope and his wife, Grizel, show that a sum of 18s 4d was paid to Master Sweep William Bowra. Mr Bowra's bill for 'Sweeping 4 chimneys and the Bakehouse flews',[2] (and cleaning clocks) was submitted to estate manager John Bramton while the Stanhope family were living abroad. In preparation for the family's return fourteen months later, the chimneys were checked and John Brampton's letter to his mistress (1st February 1774) reassured her that 'all was well within'. William Bowra had been sent for and 'he put the boy up the chimney who found all safe'.

Similarly, Joseph Barnes would have been helped by an apprentice when he swept the chimneys at 'Hatfield House and offices'[3] in 1776. His bill for one-year from 9th December 1775 to 30th November 1776 came to £2.1s.

In 1785, Jonas Hanway estimated that there were 150 established master sweeps in London and between them they employed 200 journeymen (see later), and 550 climbing boys. Seven years later, at a time when there were 130 boys in his parish (Westminster and St.Mary-le-Bone), David Porter detailed the living expenses of master sweeps as follows:

> A Master sweep who keeps two apprentices pays £8–£10 a year rent; he may have a wife and two children to support, with an average of 2 children this would be 6 persons to be fed, washed and clothed, 4s–6s a week for rent and taxes to be paid out of 6s a day. A master who keeps 3 apprentices, commonly keeps a journeyman, and if 4 apprentices two journeymen. A journeyman's wages are from £3–£6 a year, which is just half the estimated expense of a livery servant [a servant to be paid in a large household].

Earnings of 4 boys per day is 12s or per ann:	£187. 4. 0
	DEBIT
2 Journey-men @ £20 per ann...	£40. 0. 0
1 maid servant @ £20 per ann...	£20. 0. 0
House rent on average...	£25. 0. 0
Taxes (1#3 of rent)...	£8. 6. 8
	£93. 6. 8

TOTAL profit per ann... £93. 17. 4

Chimney Doctors

> A warm room is certainly a desirable retreat in cold weather, but we have carried our notions too far for, by shutting out a friend, we have made an enemy, not less troublesome but more formidable; by preventing a supply of air, we have made a smoky chimney.
> *David Porter, 1792*

By the 18th century, coal fires and smaller fireplaces had become common. Coal was burned on a slightly raised hearth inside the fireplace and smoke made its own way up the flue. Problems arose, however, when smoke 'backfired' and returned to the hearth. The 'smoky chimney' problem continued to intrigue inventors, potters and chimney builders.

Chimney doctors were much in demand and could command a high fee for their services. On 24th October 1735, chimney doctor Mr Taylor received a payment of two guineas (£2 2s) for curing one chimney. The London Assurance Company (see later) paid this large fee.

In June 1795 Bristol surveyor, J. Powell informed Gloucester residents that due to his experiments on 'air and its rarefaction by fire',[5] he could now attend to 'smoaky chimnies'. Mr Powell had evolved a method of dealing with kitchen chimneys by 'Jacks of his peculiar construction', and appliances could be bought from him at the White Hart.

Smoke jacks were not always reliable. Samuel Basleigh, Barrack Master at the Yeomanry Cavalry Barracks, Barnstaple (North Devon), recorded in his 'letter book'[6] that there was a problem in the officers' kitchen chimney. The smoke jack refused to work. It was replaced with a fly jack (driven by weights) and when this proved unsuccessful, all the barrack chimneys were modified

to accommodate a removable stone plug over each fireplace; this was to admit a boy to the flue when the chimney had to be swept.

Any number of High Masters like William Woodward, 1 Marylebone Passage, Wells Street, Oxford Market advertised that they cleaned 'Coppers and Smoak Jacks', and cured 'Smoking Chimneys in Town or Country', and they claimed 'No cure no pay'. Nevertheless, it was Count Rumford's innovative methods for curing smoky fires that brought about a change in the structure of flues (see Appendix for details). However, his specifications for the fireplace still required 'the admission of a climbing boy for the purpose of cleaning it from soot and rubble accumulation.'[7] According to his publication (1796), Count Rumford successfully treated over 500 defective fireplaces in London. The Rumford smoke shelf prevented rain and debris from falling into the fire, and allowed the direction of air in the flue to circulate two ways. Furthermore, the splayed sides and angled back reflected heat forward into the room.

No doubt the services of many London chimney doctors were called upon during the freezing winter (December 1813–February 1814) when:

a frost-fair was held on the ice bound Thames ... and there was more than enough work for chimney-sweepers to do clearing frost-hardened soot from blocked winter flues[8]

37

Chimney Pots

Clay chimney pots became popular from 1760 onwards. Somerset farmer/potter John Yeoman, while visiting London (1774), recorded in his diary that he went to see the potteries, where they 'made tun potts and shugar loafs'.

The main purpose of the pot was to 'minimize the effect of down-draught by reducing the area acted on by the wind'.[9] Conical chimney pots tapered upwards and had a small hole at the top. They were flaunched round the base (encased in a type of cement).

Master builder Robert Clavering had some harsh words to say about chimney pots. He claimed that they were 'mostly of bad construction',[10] being outward sloping and too narrow at the top, and they became clogged with congealed soot. This meant chimneys were swept more often, and the young children who climbed them had to scrape away the soot in the orifice of the pot with a knife (see Chapter 4).

In time, though, the solution was found. 'Tall-boys', up to seven feet high and 'horned cans' with many protuberances were added to existing chimneys to improve the downward draught. Throughout Britain today rooftops still display an astonishing array of pots. *The National Clayware Federation* lists over 500 varieties. Pots range in shape and size from round-bellied pots, to cowl and hood-type pots that were H-shaped, known as 'donkey-legs', and oddities such as the 'lobster backs' (Portsmouth). A 19th-century cure for smoky chimneys was the 'spiral vent'[11] (1845), which was fixed to more than 50 chimneys in Buckingham Palace and Windsor Castle.

Master Sweeps (19th Century)

Advertising

When the Rev. Sydney Smith visited London in 1803, he was astonished to find that trade cards of chimney sweeps proudly advertised 'Little boys for small flues'. Throughout the 19th century masters were sorely divided over the use of newly invented 'machines'. Many, such as J. Andrews & Son, (1820) No 5, Green Harbour Court, Old Bailey, advertised themselves as Mechanical Chimney Sweepers, whereas John Whitney, Leadenhall Street, played safe with: 'Clean cloths for upper apartments, machines or small boys, for register stoves'. The ornate card of James Steers (1820), Bennett's Court, White Street, shows his six apprentices. The wording reads: 'Sweep chimnies in the best manner, with a machine or boys where necessary'. There were many others (see Chapter 9).

Because so many chimney sweeps were needed, the trade became swamped with unscrupulous single-masters. Highly esteemed governors fought back. Jealously guarding their wealthy contracts, they made use of influential 'names':

BRYANT and SPENCER
Chimney Sweeps & Nightmen,
to his Grace the Archbishop of Canterbury

Pride was taken in showing former chimney-sweeping connections:

1816
H. KERNOT (Chimney-Sweeper and Nightman)
late Miller & Kernot, successor to Foster & Smith
at Christopher Court, removed from Wormwood St. to
No 4. NEW RENTS
St.Martin's Le Grand, Nr.Newgate Street.
Orders left with Mr.Reeve, Fruiterers, No 24 New Broad St.
will be faithfully executed.

Illustrated scenes showed the diversity of the trade, and customers were asked: *'PLEASE HANG THIS BILL UP'*. Displayed in a busy kitchen where there were many callers, the bill served as an advertisement and reminder of payment due. Clients were also cautioned against less reputable sweeps who made a practice of 'soliciting custom' in their name.

Trade cards were hand-posted to private houses. In competition with other trades, the sweeps never lost the opportunity to distribute cards whenever crowds gathered. Less fortunate masters ingratiated themselves with the servants of the wealthy. In *Vanity Fair* (1848), William Thackeray relates that 'Mr. Chummy, the chimney-purifier, who had swept the last three families, tried to coax the butler and the boy under him.'

Other types of publicity gradually replaced hanging signs.[12] Peter Hall's advertising expenses (*Hanley & Shelton Chimney Sweeping Association*) for the half-year (January–July 1855) amounted to £11 6s:

Inscription, lamp & gas ...	2	10s
Card plate & 500 cards ...	1	10s
Printing, Staffordsh. Advert ...	2	
ditto ditto Sentinel ...	5	6s
Total	£11	6s

Trade processions were another form of advertising. In Manchester (Saturday 15th September 1877) *The Amalgamated Chimney Sweepers Society* took part in the City's Trades' Procession. Manchester and Salford Chimney Sweeps had formed the society. On 7th August, five weeks before the procession took place, Thomas Green wrote to the organisers informing them that 250 to 300 chimney sweeps would be taking part. He was sorry that the sweeps would be unable to have a band,[13] but their society had just been formed and funds were low. However, Mr Green assured the organisers that the sweeps would make the best turnout they could without one. It appears that they did, as the event was commemorated by an oil painting in which:

> The chimney sweeps, revealing their National background, carried a "mysterious flag" upon which was an unmistakable likeness of Daniel O'Connell.

Fees and Expenses

The common price for sweeping a chimney at the beginning of the 19th century was 6d, although 1s was charged for large kitchen chimneys. In North Wales (1801), the housekeeper's accounts for Erddig – a large country house in Clwyd – show that the sum of 9 shillings was paid for sweeping 12 chimneys.

Henry Mayhew (see later) calculated that the number of chimney sweeps in London (1816) was estimated to be 50 masters, 150 journeymen, and 500 apprentices. Twenty of the high-class (reputable) masters had on average five boys each. All owned horses. Additional carts and barrows would be hired when business was particularly brisk.

NOS. JOURNEYMEN	*£ ANNUAL*
20 @ 40s weekly	780
30 @ 12s ditto	936
100 @ 10s ditto	2,600
BOYS	
Board, lodging, clothing	
500 @ 4s.6d weekly	5,850
RENT	
20 (large traders) 10s	520
30 (others) 7s	516
150 ... 3s.6d	1,365
20 horses 10s	520
General wear & tear	200
	———
	£13,317 (sic.)

Annual payment for sweeping:
Chimneys
624,000 by 500 boys
(averaging 4 daily)
at 10d per chimney ...   26,000
Soot at 5d per chimney ...   13,000

                                                  39,000
less expenses   13,317

Yearly profit   £25,683

Henry Mayhew

Notwithstanding the disrepute in which sweepers have ever been held, there are many class of workers beneath them in intelligence ... the sweepers, from whatever cause it may arise, are known, in many instances, to be shrewd, intelligent and active.

Mayhew, 1851

It is mainly due to Henry Mayhew's contemporary survey of London's working poor that we know so much about London chimney sweeps in the mid-19th century. Henry Mayhew (born 25th November 1812) was a remarkable social reporter. With understanding and skill, he interviewed thousands of Londoners living in and around the East End in Whitechapel, Wapping, and Shadwell. Details of their lives were written as a series of letters in the *Morning Chronicle* (1849–50). Published in book form in 1851, and added to in the 1860s, they became Mayhew's major work, *London Labour and the London Poor*.

Mayhew estimated that there were approximately 823 sweeps working in and around London in 1850. Divided according to their hierarchy within the trade, 106 were high masters, 92 small masters, and the remainder were single-handed sweeps. Large and small masters together employed 400 journeymen and 62 boys. Not all lived in London. The highest proportion lived north of the Thames in Middlesex and the remainder in Surrey. Owing to parliamentary reforms, there was a marked reduction in the number of climbing boys (although the Acts continued to be violated, see Chapter 6).

High Masters

High masters employed from two to ten men and usually two boys. Boys (or girls) were still needed for narrow stove flues or awkward shafts. Trade was regular. When business was brisk extra hands were employed and both master and men worked longer hours.

Prices for sweeping were determined by the rentable value of a house and the type of flue. Lofty chimneys of public and official buildings, and large residences in the wealthier areas were charged at the highest rate. High masters charged 6s–2s 6d (St.George's Hanover Square, Lewisham, and London City). Average charges were:

Lower chimney ...	1s 6d
Kitchen ...	2s
Small flues ...	1s
Lofty flues (with register stoves)	3s 6d

The collected annual income of London master sweeps was estimated to be £100,000. This was calculated by counting the number of dwellings and based on average charges. In total 54,000 houses were owned by the wealthy and their chimneys were swept on average eight times a year. The middle classes owned 90,000 homes and had their flues swept four times a year. Dwellings of the labouring classes numbered about 165,000. Receipts amounted to £85,000. Expenses of master sweeps were calculated as follows:

1200 machines, £2 10s each ...	3,000
3000 sacks, 2s 6d each ...	385
25 horses, £20 each ...	500
25 sets of harness, £2 each ...	50
25 carts, £12 each ...	300
Total	£4,235

In comparison with London, mid-century rates in the Sheffield area varied from 4s a year (house rental up to £15 per annum) to £2 a year (gentlemen's houses four miles out of town). Sweeps with no contracts charged from 2d–12d a flue.

Half-yearly expenses for the *Hanley & Shelton Chimney Sweeping Association* (1856) showed:

	£	s	d
Wages (21 men) ...	1	6	9
Machine rods ...	5	15	0
New brushes (4) ...		6	0
Soot bags (130) ...	9	9	0

	£	s	d
Cash earned:			
Men's earning ...s	30	3	9
Soot sold (399 bags) ...	39	18	0

Single-handed Sweeps

In the poorer suburbs of London 'distress, a desire of change, a vagabond spirit, and a hope to better themselves', all tended to swell the ranks of single-handed masters. 'Leeks' or 'Green-uns' were not classed as masters. They were sweeps who had not served an apprenticeship and were inexperienced. Established sweeps, who prided themselves on having served 7 or 8 years 'duly and truly' treated them with disdain.

'Knullers' and 'queriers' were sweeps working on their own, mostly in Southwark, Chelsea, St Giles, Shoreditch and Whitechapel. 'Knullers' was a name derived from the Saxon word knell (to sound a bell). Queriers obtained trade by calling on householders and making inquiries, often asking only 1d or 2d, or sweeping for soot. In the suburbs they would call out, 'Sweep, sweep', and if asked, 'Are you so and so's man?' would answer 'Yes.' They also called at the houses of both rich and poor openly stating that they had been sent by Mr. .... This practice deprived the established master of his chimneys and soot and ruined his reputation.

One London knuller, his soot-begrimed face accentuated by wrinkles (he was 'not 46'[14] but looked many years older), confessed to doing 'just middling' by 'clearing' 7s a week. Born in Birmingham he had led a varied life. When his widowed mother died in the workhouse he had been sent to a charity school, then apprenticed to a gunsmith. Becoming 'quite as black' as a sweep with all the 'dust and heat, and smoke and stuff', he journeyed to London to better himself. He learned about the chimney-sweeping trade from a fellow lodger in a boarding house in King Street, Drury Lane. The sweep had been too sick to carry on, and before dying had sold him his machine for 17s 6d. He had remained in the trade ever since. He wasn't sure if he was a knuller or a querier, admitting:

> If I'm asked if I'm anybody's man, I don't like to say 'no', and I don't like to say, 'yes', so I says nothing if I can help it ... I lodge with another sweep which is better off nor I am, and pay him 2s 6d a week for a little stair-head place with a bed in it.'

In Manchester, Albert Tomkinson advertised his services as chimney sweep and flue cleaner (No 23, Bamford Road, Heywood), by claiming

'No connection with any other sweep', declaring that he 'does not solicit Orders from door to door, but by shouting "Watercress" in the streets.'

Journeymen

Apprentices who were 'out of their time' (aged 16), and who wished to remain in the chimney-sweeping trade, became journeymen. There were three categories: foreman, under-journeyman, journeyman-sweeper or boy.

Foreman

Unmarried foremen lodged with their masters. They were employed continuously unless discharged for drunkenness or attempting to form 'a connection of their own', (among their master's customers). Less established masters discharged their journeymen during slack periods and took on extra hands when business increased. Of the 400 journeymen employed in the London area, 252 paid board and lodging to their masters. Under 'the old system'[15] this amounted to 8s per week (1s per day for board and 1s for lodging). The remainder either lived with their parents or 'at their own places'.

It was the duty of the foreman or first journeyman to accompany the sweeps, supervise their work and collect payment. Payment for sweeping chimneys was made either in money, part money/part kind, or perquisites. Foremen received weekly wages from 14s to 20s. In addition, they were allowed to keep 'brieze', (cinders from the fireplace) which was sold to the poor at 6d per bushel. Wages (without deduction for board and lodging) were 12s to 18s per week with 'perks', averaging 2s 6d, and 4d a day beer or gin money.

For extinguishing fires, payment was made according to the severity of the fire, the time taken or the degree of risk and personal injury. A foreman was allowed to keep fees from uncommissioned work, and some customers also gave beer money. Other duties included measuring and filling sacks with soot or piling it loose into carts. Additional money was earned from selling soot. There was no set price. Some foremen received 2 shillings for 50 bushels, others less.

Under-journeyman

Part of the duty of the under-journeyman, or the journeyman-sweeper if no boy was employed, was to carry the sweeping machine. He also carried the soot. If called upon to sweep, he was allowed the 'lower-

44

Caricatures of the 5th Division of the United Body of the Journeymen, Chimney Sweepers and Nightmen, 1834. (Acknowledgments, Armley Mills, Leeds)

class' flues. The ashes from the grate were his to sell, and he could keep both brieze and ashes if no foreman was employed.

Wages varied, with masters paying between 2s and 6s per week. Although on a comparatively low wage, unmarried under-journeymen were better off than working men in other self-supporting trades (summer months excepted). Perquisites amounted to 1s–6s extra, enough to pay for clothes and washing.

Lower-class Journeyman

Many journeymen existed on much lower wages. In 1816, London Master Sweep T. Allen, who had been in the trade for 22 years, told a parliamentary committee that some sweeps, at the age of 25, earned only 2 shillings a week. Although they were 'fed and lodged', 2s was not enough to buy clothes and other 'necessaries'. Extra money was obtained by pocketing half the payment for sweeping before handing it to their master. Money was also extorted from apprentices. By gambling with the boys and winning their money, says Mr Allen 'they get half the money from them by force, and the rest by fraud.'

Extinguishing Fires

Assurance Companies

> The engine thund'red through the street,
> Fire-hook, pipe, bucket, all complete;
> And torches glared, and clattering feet
> Along the pavement paced...
> The *Hand-in-Hand* the race begun,
> Then came the *Phoenix* and the *Sun*,
> The *Exchange*, where old insurers run,
> The *Eagle*, where the new.
> J & H Smith, *Theatrum poetarum*, 1812

Assurance companies became established after the Great Fire of London. At first they employed mostly Thames watermen as part-time fire fighters and depended heavily upon the efficiency of local chimney sweeps. The sweeps' climbing boys were inexpensive and remarkably brave (see Chapter 4).

The *Hand-in-Hand* was one of the earliest companies. Founded in 1696 for insuring houses against fire, the company required every

Royal Assurance Badge still on a
building in Holywell Hill, St Albans,
Hertfordshire.

Hand-in-Hand Assurance Company
Badge.

insurer to sign a Deed of Settlement, thereby becoming a partner and
shareholder in profits.[16] In 1777, the *Hand-in-Hand* office was situated
opposite St Sepulchre Church in Angel Court. It kept 30 firemen. They
were provided with clothing annually and wore a silver badge; two
hands joined under a crown. Work clothes consisted of a jerkin with
belted skirt – into which was tucked an axe – a leather cap or helmet
with crest and neck-flap, and breeches and stockings. The ceremonial
uniform (c1810) was dark blue with a 'stand collar, all piped in red'.[17]
Breeches were orange. Black shoes, grey stockings, and a silk top hat
completed the outfit.

Chimney Sweeps

Early in the 19th century when there was countrywide opposition to
chimney sweeping machines (see Chapter 9) assurance companies
were quick to adopt them. To help promote the new machines many
companies subscribed to the *Society for Superseding the Necessity for
Climbing Boys* – SSNCB (1803). Robert Stevens, secretary of the
Hand-in-Hand, was also secretary of the SSNCB. By 1838 Stevens
was able to inform the company's committee members that 12 major
fire offices continued 'exclusively to employ the Agents of the
society', meaning master sweeps who used machines rather than
children.

According to *British Fire Office* books (31st December 1807) chimney fires were extinguished by 'stopping up the throat or breast of the chimney with a wet blanket, or by means of a register or chimney-board' indeed anything that prevented air from passing upward. Sweeps who had taken to using machines tied a coarse cloth over the brush, which was soaked in water, then pushed up the chimney. Inevitably, this caused loss or damage to a machine – a valuable piece of equipment to a sweep. In North Devon, a Bideford chimney sweep named Davis brought a court action against Mr Lock, one of his clients. Davis had sent his son to extinguish a fire in one of Mr Lock's chimneys. The boy succeeded in removing two bushels of burning soot, but in doing so burned part of the machine. The defendant refused to pay the cost of a replacement brush (12s 6d). As a result of the judgement, Davis was paid '1s 6d for sweeping the chimney, and half the sum charged for the brush.'[18]

During the 1830s and 1840s, chimney fires – averaging 94 a year – were the second highest cause of fire in the capital. Poorer citizens were unable to afford premiums. Consequently, just under half the buildings in the capital were uninsured, causing even more reliance upon chimney sweeps.

Mr Nollekens, an esteemed (if somewhat eccentric) sculptor, had decided views on the subject. Mr Nollekens thought that 'many persons'[19] had their chimneys swept too often. He changed his mind, however, after having been 'several times annoyed by the fire-engines and their regular attendants, the mob', and became determined instead to have them cleaned more frequently. So keen was Mr Nollekens that some of his chimneys 'for want of fires', (he was mean with coal) yielded no soot. Nevertheless, Mr Nollekens was still willing to pay for the sweeping, finding consolation in 'fame of a consummation of coal'.

Chimney sweeps were still extinguishing fires late in the 19th century:

> John Hunter, Camden, doe live here,
> Sweeps chimbleys clean, and not too deare;
> And if your chimbley be on fire,
> He'll put it out, if you desire.

By 1882 another sweep from Chipping Campden had taken over the business:

> William Clayton does live here,
> Sweeps chimneys clean, and is not too dear;
> And if your chimney is on fire,
> He'll put it out, if you desire.[20]

George Elson

Despite the example set by assurance companies, climbing boys such as George Elson continued to be sent up chimneys, either to put out flames or to make sure the fire was completely extinguished.

> I have climbed chimnies while still alight, and even though showers of burning soot have repeatedly driven me down again have finally forced my way to the top ... I remember at a gentleman's house in Bedfordshire, going up a chimney and finding burning soot in the bend four days after the fire had occurred.[21]

In other instances George was asked to 'undo the mischief done by thoughtless men-servants', who in attempts to put out fires had resorted to throwing items down the chimney from the top. These included 'small scuttles of coal and wet blankets', which stuck in narrow sections of the flue or lodged in bends.

George once saw a row of thatched cottages set alight by a chimney fire. It happened in a Huntingdon village, and one bed-ridden old lady who had been unable to escape was burned to death. After this tragedy, George and his companions (see Chapter 8) were engaged to sweep every chimney in that village and the adjoining one. 'A rare good turn of work for us', says George.

When working in London, aged 19 (1852) George was sent for one dark night to put out a kitchen fire in Brown's Restaurant, Haymarket. Unable to do anything from the fireplace he decided to dislodge burning soot from the top. He climbed through a trap door, with his machine – three rods and a brush head – then scrambled up the roof. Reaching out he grasped the chimney pot to pull himself up, but it was burnt loose and toppled over. George let go and fell backwards. He managed to save himself from plunging over the parapet into the Haymarket by instinctively thrusting his elbow through the slates. Ignoring his injury George then 'mounted the roof from another side'. After dislodging the blazing soot, he climbed down, thankful for his narrow escape.

If a fire breaks out in your chimney, George's advice is to close all doors and windows to reduce draught; sprinkle salt or sulphur on the fire; then water to create steam. Then get an old blanket steeped in water and fasten over the fireplace – 'all this while the sweep is coming'.

Nightmen

During summer months when the hearth remained unlit, trade became slack. Indeed poorer sweeps had no trade at all. To support their families throughout the year chimney sweeps needed other occupations. Many chose to be 'nightmen' engaged in emptying privies.

Before water-flushing closets were introduced, house privies were emptied at night. (A general sewerage system was not planned for London until 1858. This came about after an exceptionally hot summer and Parliament could no longer tolerate the stench from the Thames.) It was the duty of nightmen to enter the house carrying a large wooden bucket. The bucket was attached to the centre of a pole. Two men were needed to carry the pole on their shoulders, with the bucket hanging between them. Privy soils were carted to 'laystalls' outside the city walls or dumped into the Fleet Ditch (formerly the River of the Wells).

The job was popular with chimney sweeps because it fitted in with their unsociable hours. Night duties could be carried out before chimneys were swept very early in the morning; usually before 5 o'clock in the summer and 6 in winter.

A typical London master sweep who also traded as nightman was John Cole, with premises in Goswell Street. His painted sign (1740) shows a busy street scene, where two sweeps stand on ladders emptying the contents of a wooden barrel into a cart which contains night soil. Two horses share a basket of hay and another is harnessed to the cart. A master sweep stands beside them with a long pole. His three apprentices are shown in the background. (See Appendix for other masters.)

The job might sometimes entail other duties, as an apprentice sweep reveals:

> I have been tied round the middle and let down several privies for the purpose of fetching watches and such things; it is generally made the practice to take the smallest boy to let him through the hole without taking up the seat and to paddle about there till he finds it; they do not take a big boy because it disturbs the seat.[22]

Steam-ship Sweeping

River steam-boats first appeared on the Thames in 1815. Large ocean-going steamers used four separate boilers. Each boiler had three

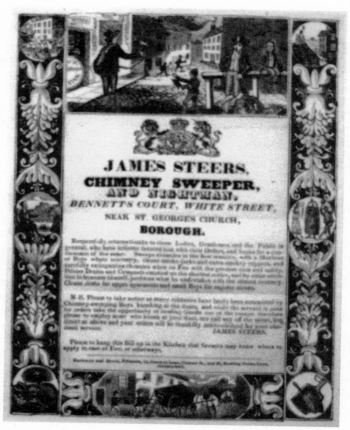

How James Steers, chimney sweeper and nightman, advertised his services. (Reproduced with kind permission of Guildhall Library, Corporation of London)

The trade card of William Woodward.

furnaces with lengthy flues combining into one beneath the funnel. On reaching port, a steam vessel would have burned up to 800 tons of coal, creating an impressive build-up of soot. Soot removal from the flues and funnels of steam vessels was a highly specialised job. In ports abroad stokers and coal-trimmers undertook the task. In London, master sweeps were engaged. In the Port of London in the 1850s, three London masters held profitable contracts:

Mr Allbrook (Chelsea) ... The Chelsea Steamers
Mr Hawsey (Rosemary Lane) ... The Continental
Mr Tuff (East London) ... Irish & Scottish Steamers

They employed a number of adult sweeps who were paid 8d–1s 6d per funnel. The task was accomplished in several stages. To reach the funnel the sweep had to travel a long way through the flues carrying a wick lamp, brush and shovel. He cleaned the funnel first then worked back through each of the flues.

'The moment he steps across the firebridge the sweep sinks to his waist in soot.'[23] ... Above his head is an iron doorway. Clambering up as best he can, he finds himself in a dark passage. It is airy and lofty enough to stand. But the passage is short and soon turns back upon itself. Seven or eight turns, backwards and forwards, like the windings in a maze, till at the last turn a light suddenly breaks upon him, and, looking up he sees the hollow tube of the funnel, black and ragged with soot. Soot is brushed down from the roof and sides of the passage then shovelled before him to the next winding (parts of the passage being already knee deep in soot). The process is repeated, by degrees, until the opening is reached. Whenever the accumulated soot is likely to block up the passage, he wades through and shovels as much as is necessary out of the opening, then returns brushing and shovelling until the flues are clear.

He then climbs down and shovels the soot over the firebridge and into the ashpit of the furnace. The soot is not burned but raked with long iron rakes by 'other persons' and shovelled into sacks. The sacks are fastened to tackle secured to the upper deck, then 'browsed' up out of the engine-room and placed in boats to be taken ashore.

Tron-men of Edinburgh

Reminiscent of the Great Fire of London, a chimney fire was believed to be the cause of one of Edinburgh's worst conflagrations (3rd February 1700). Forty years later after pressure from town sweeps who wanted control over 'rogue sweeps', and public fear of chimney fires, the town council passed their Burgh Act (1741). This in effect created *The Society of Tron-men.*[24]

Twelve chimney-sweeping Tron-men, or 'Custodians of the Flues' as they were affectionately called, were officially appointed to sweep the flues of Edinburgh. They swept from the chimney pot down with long ropes, a besom (bundle of twigs) and lead weight. The system of employing climbing boys was kept from the Old Town of Edinburgh. Outside the gates in the New Town, it was a different matter.

The Custodians were called 'Tron-men' because of their meeting place at the Trone. This was a public weighing beam, which formerly stood in front of Tron Church. Subsequently a small wooden lean-to, adjoining the guard-house at the east end of the town, was erected for their use. This was where they stored equipment and could be contacted by customers.

The 12 men were paid an annual allowance of one guinea. Additional perquisites were gained from the sale of soot. Working in pairs, they took it in turns to watch out for fires at night from the guardhouse. For this service each Tron-man was paid five shillings a year by the Council's collector of watchmoney and cess (taxes). The Tron-men's uniform consisted of a fitted coat, a short apron, knee-length breeches, buckled shoes, and a flat bonnet. The Tron-men enjoyed a monopoly in the town and formed themselves into an exclusive society. Each man paid five pounds initially and the quarterly fees were 3s 6d (18p).

As Edinburgh expanded, new chimney sweepers started businesses in the suburbs. A few were permitted to 'participate in the privileges of the Tron-men', but the allowance of one guinea was limited to the original number. In honour of their status, only the 12 original members were permitted to wear the broad bonnet.

Tron-men assisted in public duties. In 1746 when the standards (flags) belonging to the army of Prince Charles were publicly burned at the Cross, they were carried in procession by 13 Tron-men. Other duties included helping the city hangman.

The reputation of the Tron-men's Society was such that in order to uphold it they had occasion to expel one of their members. On 13th November 1765, Robert Hunter, when sent to assist the hangman at the execution of Captain Ogilvie, disgraced the Society by accepting a fee of five pounds. In addition to losing his position, Hunter was banished to Leith for five years.

The guardhouse was demolished in 1785, and the guard and the Tron-men were given new accommodation in the Old Assembly Rooms. Gradually, however, the chimney sweepers found their

Edinburgh City Tron-men. (Illustration John Kay)

additional duties irksome. When the town was provided with an efficient fire service they sold the Society's property and divided the proceedings. The magistrates subsequently disbanded the union of Tron-men in 1811.

During the time of the Tron-men, the only known private chimney-sweeping business in Edinburgh was run by a sweep named Hamilton. Hamilton died around 1797. He was called Sweep Jack by local residents, and lived in the West Port where he kept a number of men and boys. Hamilton began his business before the Tron-men were established and devoted his entire life to sweeping chimneys.

Notes

[1]Sophie De La Roche, 6th September, 1786. *The Climbing Boys*, Kathleen Strange, 1982.
[2]*Your Most Dutyfull Servant*, Marian Mills, 1992.
[3]*Hatfield Estate Housekeeper's Bills*, 1776.
[4]*Considerations on the Present State of Chimney Sweepers*, David Porter, 1792.
[5]*Gloucester Journal*.
[6]From 1794, it was part of the Barrack Master's duty to make a copy of all correspondence between the barracks and Cavalry Headquarters at Exeter.
[7]*Chimneys and Flues, Domestic and Industrial*, P.L. Marks, 1935.
[8]*Jane Austen*, David Nokes, 1997.
[9]*Chimney Pots & Stacks*, Valentine Fletcher, 1968, 1994.
[10]*Construction & Building of Chimneys*, Robert Clavering, 1779.
[11]*Chimney Pots & Stacks*, Valentine Fletcher, 1968, 1994.
[12]Chimney sweep, Mr Strawson No 72, advertised his trade in bold lettering on a lamp outside his premises (lamp now displayed in Kirkstall Abbey House Museum).
[13]*Manchester Cultural Services Department*.
[14]Henry Mayhew, *London Labour & the London Poor*, 1851.
[15]Climbing boy system, Henry Mayhew.
[16]Conditions: 2s (10p) percent premium; and 10s deposit on brick houses, and double on timber houses. No more than £2000 could be insured in one premium. *Survey of London*, Harrison 1777.
[17]*Occupational Costumes in England*, Phyllis Cunningham & Catherine Lucas, 1967.
[18]*North Devon Journal*, 1st January 1859.
[19]*Nollekens & His Times*, J.T. Smith, 1828.
[20]*Gloucester Notes & Queries*, Vol 11, 1884.
[21]*The Last of the Climbing Boys*, autobiography, George Elson, 1900.
[22]Evidence given by master sweep, to House of Lords Committee, *Roads to Ruin*, E.S. Turner, 1950.
[23]*London Labour & the London Poor*, Henry Mayhew, 1851.
[24]*The City Tron-men*, biographical sketches, John Kay, 1837.

4

APPRENTICES

Introduction

During the 13th century, people of similar occupations and religious beliefs joined together and formed guilds. At first, the children of guild members were taught by their parents. Then an early form of apprenticeship evolved whereby a child was 'bound' to a master craftsman and the guild supervised instruction.

Apprenticeship was firmly established by the 15th century and the apprentice paid a master for his indenture. In 1562 Elizabeth I's *Statute of Artificers* made a seven-year term of apprenticeship compulsory for all industrial workers. (The system remained more or less unchanged until the late 18th century.) Chimney sweeps had no guild but were subject to the same regulations as other trades.

Towards the end of the 16th century, Justices were given power to apprentice the children of the poor. Small undernourished children were perfect for narrow chimney flues and young sweeps often served a longer term of apprenticeship. In 1747, *The London Tradesman* compiled a list of information about the trades. Of the chimney sweepers it stated:

> The proper Business of this black Fraternity is expressed by their Name, and may be seen in their face; it is true they all take Apprentices, and the younger they are the better fit to climb up chimneys; but I would not recommend my friend to breed his Son to this Trade, tho' I know some Masters who live comfortably.[1]

Apprenticeship indentures

An indenture was an agreement made between two parties; the master sweep and his apprentice. Signed in the presence of several appointed witnesses it was binding by law. On 5th July, an agreement[2] was made between Thomas Carter and Master Sweep William Owen from Liver-

Commemorative plaque to Bryan Turberville at St Mary-at-Lambeth Church, who bequeathed one hundred pounds towards the apprenticeship of boys, as long as they were not to be put to chimney-sweepers.

pool. Thomas, a poor boy from the parish of Dean on the outskirts of South West Bolton, agreed to serve his master faithfully, keep his secrets and obey his commands. He had to refrain from unlawful games, cards and dice, and keep away from evil company, alehouses and taverns. Fornication and adultery were forbidden and permission had to be obtained before he could get married.

In return, William Owen agreed to teach Thomas the trade of chimney sweeper and provide for his welfare. The indenture was signed by James Higson, overseer of Middleton, Lancs, and several witnesses. Although William Owen completed the indenture with his mark (a cross) there appeared to be no provision for Thomas Carter's signature.

On 2nd October 1799, William Booth, Overseer of the Poor at Werneth, Chester, arranged for 10-year-old Samuel Gee to be appren-

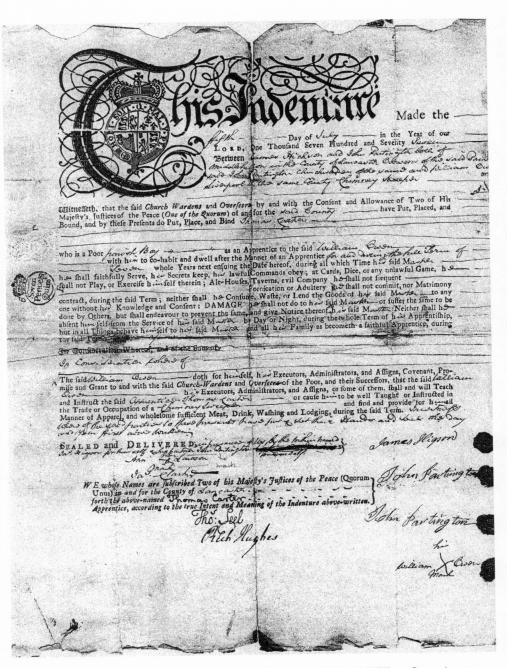

The indenture of 1777 between Thomas Carter (apprentice) and William Owen (master sweep).

58

ticed to Master Sweep Robert Baxter of Manchester. The master sweep agreed to provide 'for climbing, one whole and compleat Suit of Clothing with suitable linen Stockings & Hose and shoes', and pledged 'at least once in every week' to cause his apprentice to be 'Honourably washed and cleansed from Soot and Dirt'. Furthermore, his apprentice should attend church on Sunday but not wear his 'sweeping dress' on that day.

The indenture also stated that an apprentice should not be forced to climb any chimney while it was 'actually on Fire'. Apprentices were to be treated with as much humanity and care as the nature of the employment of chimney sweepers allowed. Both master sweep and apprentice signed the indenture with a cross (See Appendix for other indentures.)

Welfare

Apprentice sweeps lived with their masters. Life was hard and discipline severely enforced. Nevertheless, there was much kindness and often close bonds with the employer's family. The poorer class of sweep lodged in a boarding house. He hired two rooms; one for himself, wife and children, and the other – either an attic or a cellar – for his apprentices, soot and equipment. For bedding, the boys slept on straw or their sootbag. Apprentices with wealthier masters had their own quarters away from the soot and slept on truckle beds. This was a small bed made to run under a larger one (mostly for servants or attendants).

Food

Country sweeps lived off the land during the fruitful season. When work was slack, they earned a wage harvesting or gleaning – gathering leftovers in the cornfields. At other times, food came from the larders of clients. When sweeping the homes of the wealthy – though covered in soot – the boys and their master were welcome to sit in the servants' hall and 'partake at breakfast'.[3] This generally included hot hashed venison, cold roast beef, tea, coffee or ale. Such hospitality was found at Haverholme Priory, the seat of the Earl of Winchelsea, Raunceby Hall and other great houses around Sleaford.

Sometimes breakfast consisted only of ale. It was contained in a large tankard, 'the liquor black as night and mouldy on top with age'. The boys were expected to drink it down quickly on their master's instructions: 'Now, lads, open your shoulders and let it down.'[4] They obeyed in case they did not get anything the next time.

In London, food was mostly bought on the streets. Hot spiced gingerbread was a great favourite, so were oysters at four for 1d. An illustration from Harris's *Cries of London* (1804) shows mischievous chimney sweeps making fun of a gingerbread seller. Another favourite among the apprentices was the saloop-stall (soup), which in time was succeeded by the coffee-stall. On bleak winter mornings the earliest clients were young chimney sweeps, who gathered round the stall until the charcoal under the grate heated the saloop smoking hot.

Mid-day meals consisted of hot eels and a baked potato or hot pea soup, followed by assorted pastries and cakes, or fruit (oranges and nuts). A sandwich was popular for supper, or a meat pudding, or trotter (foot of sheep etc). In his *Praise of Chimney Sweepers*, Charles

Cries of London, 1850. A sweep partaking of his regular fare of a baked potato from a street seller. (Reproduced by kind permission of Guildhall Library, Corporation of London)

Lamb mentions 'a cup of sassafras[5] which a sweep's boy would sniff like a cat sniffing valerian.'

Clothing

In the first half of the 18th century, London climbing boys wore special clothing made from sheepskin. 'The waistcoat was laced on and tucked under the breeches, and though some soot penetrated, it served as a great protection.'[6] The practice was discontinued because the 'dress' cost 7s 6d and needed renewing twice a year. It was also found impracticable: 'When a boy went up a chimney on fire, it was apt to parch and break the leather.' Until the mid-19th century, climbing boys' dress varied according to the status of their masters. Regardless of seasons a shirt and trousers were worn, though it was prudent to remove trousers when descending narrow chimneys as too much soot collected in the pockets.

Feet became hardened when no shoes or stockings were worn. Moreover, walking was preferable to riding a donkey on frosty mornings, as piercing winds caused chilblains or frostbite. When this happened, climbing into a hot chimney was a pleasure. If the mistress of a household was tender-hearted, the sweep's boy was told to beg for shoes. There was not the slightest chance of wearing them, as they would be sold to the rag and snoatcher (bone) man.

A country sweep's only protection against the elements was his soot sack. The sack was large and adaptable. It could be used as a cloak, a head covering, mattress, pillow, or blanket, as well as a screen in front of the open fireplace (while sweeping the chimney). It also served as a weapon or as protection against attack: swung when full, or twisted and knotted when empty. Often used as a handy container for personal goods, it could become a hiding place, either for its owner or any stolen booty – all in addition to its main function, the storage of soot. Considering its many uses it is no surprise that contemporary illustrators always depicted young sweeps with their sacks.

According to an account in the *Wensleydale Advertiser* (1845),[7] several chimney sweeps and their boys lived in Middleham Castle, Yorkshire. It was rumoured that the boys practised various tricks to avoid the 1d toll when crossing the bridge to Leyburn. A group would dash over together before the toll-keeper could catch them, or a journeyman or master sweep would conceal a boy in his soot-sack.

Poor London masters dressed their apprentices in any rags their wives could find. Clothes were picked up second-hand in places such as Rosemary Lane. If their wives could sew, then garments resembling sacks were made. Sometimes a friend who was more skilled, or a poor

The Chimney Sweeper's Boy by Jacopo Amigoni, from *London Street Life*, c. 1739. (Reproduced by kind permission of Guildhall Library, Corporation of London.)

tailor was 'called in' and paid one shilling a day and 'the grub'. When a poor tailor went to work at a customer's house, this was known as 'whipping the cat'. The 'whipped cat's' meals cost about 1s 6d, including beer. The cost of new clothes varied from 3s 6d to 6s 6d (sewing extra). One boy remembered that one Sunday his mistress had bought him a 'werry tidy jacket' for 1s 6d in Petticoat Lane. The jacket had probably been made for a gentleman's son.

Prosperous masters provided their apprentices with trousers, tunic or tight-fitting shirt with sleeves, and a small waistcoat and jacket. A well-dressed apprentice (in the eyes of the more discerning house-holder) signalled a well-run business. Clothes were made from dark hardwearing cloth known as 'chimney-sweeper's cloth'. One apprentice recalled that when he was sweeping the church flues with his master, he noticed that the dark cloth hanging in the church as mourning for Princess Charlotte of Wales (1817) resembled his own clothes. On Sundays, the boys wore either a clean climbing suit or ordinary dress. Shoes and stockings bought secondhand were usually kept at the Sunday school (see later).

When sweeping chimneys a 'climbing cap' was worn. Made of unbleached calico it was drawn over the head and tucked in at the neck. In a good sized chimney it was possible to breathe adequately through the cloth, hear distinctly, and distinguish daylight when nearing the chimney top. It also kept the head warm in winter. However, a climbing cap was not always practical. Breathing became difficult in hot narrow chimneys where there was little draught, and body perspiration became a 'source of anxiety and trouble'.[8]

Clothes became completely black. So did exposed skin, especially when sleeping under soot bags at night. Ingrained soot was difficult to remove. London apprentices used to wash in the river Serpentine, until a sweep boy was accidentally drowned.

Two sketches by satirical artist James Seymour bring out the humour of the apprentices' predicament. In one sketch (1st August 1835), two apprentices in black rags are shown in contrast to their donkey, which they are decorating with colourful garlands:

"Wot a beauty! Missus says theres a great deal in dress."
"To be sure there is Bill, if ve had blue coats with gold buttons,
& red ves-coats and vite trowsers ve should look quite swell."

The second sketch with its ironic twist shows two thin, bow-legged, knock-kneed apprentices with brushes, scrapers, full bags of soot and miserable faces, leaving a well-to-do house. A rotund well-dressed black flunkey stands in the doorway, his face beaming with content-ment. The boys are talking to each other:

Apprentice climbing boy, 1840. (Acknowledgements, Armley Mills, Leeds.)

"Bob, arnt you glad you aint a Black-emoor?"
"I should think so, they're sich ugly warments, Master's daughter wot's come from boarding school, says the sight of em's enough to frighten one into convulsions!!"

Perhaps the final word on apprentice sweeps' appearance should go to a black woman from the West Indies:

A Mrs P arrived at Bristol, from the West Indies and brought with her a female Negro servant, mother of several children left in that country. A few days after their arrival and they had gone into private lodgings, a sweep-boy was sent for by the landlady to sweep the kitchen chimney. This woman, being seated in the kitchen when little *soot* entered, was struck with amazement at the spectacle he presented; and with great vehemence, clapping her hands together, exclaimed, 'Wha dis me see! La, la, dat buckara piccaninny! So help me, nyung Misse,' (addressing herself to the housemaid then present) 'sooner dan see one o'mine piccaninnies tan so, I drown he in de sea.' The progress of the poor child in sweeping the chimney closely engrossed her attention, and when she saw him return from his sooty incarceration, she addressed him with a feeling that did honour to her maternal tenderness, saying, 'child! come yaw, child,' (and without waiting any reply, and putting a sixpence in his hand;) 'who you Mammy? You hab daddy, too? wha dem be, da la you go chimney for?' and moistening her finger at her lips began to rub the child's cheek, to ascertain, what yet appeared doubtful to her, whether he was really a buccaree (white). I saw this woman sometime after in the West Indies; and it was a congratulation to her ever after, that *her* "children were not born to be sweeps."[9]

Orphans (18th Century)

In etchings featuring apprentice chimney sweeps, the London Foundling Hospital is often shown in the background. A popular print published by B. Phillips in *Modern London* (1805) portrays a young sweep by the hospital gates. A metal apprenticeship badge is attached to the front of his cap and he carries a large sack over his shoulder. The boy is well clothed and wears stockings with buckled shoes.

It was during George II's reign that Thomas Coram, a retired Merchant Navy captain (aged over 70 years) followed up a suggestion that abandoned children be cared for in some form of hospital. He managed to involve a number of influential 'names' in the scheme and the hospital received its first 'foundlings'– 19 boys and 11 girls – on 25th March 1741.

When children reached the age of 12, they were apprenticed to different trades and services. In 1770, out of a total number of 1666 children, 963 became apprentices. The following account of apprentices' progress was drawn up in May 1798:

The popular image of an apprentice sweep shown outside the Foundling Hospital. (William Marshall Craig. Reproduced by kind permission of Guildhall Library, Corporation of London.)

Doing well ...	166
Have turned out ill ...	15
In different situations, well apprenticed, no complaint ...	27
Apprenticed to relations ...	23
Not free from blame but requiring judicious management ...	21
Total	252

In 1795 lawyer Sir Thomas Bernard became particularly interested in the climbing boys. He gave up his profession and became treasurer of the Foundling Hospital, remaining in this capacity for 23 years (see Chapter 6). In the 1830s, chimney sweeper Mrs Molloy was engaged to sweep the hospital chimneys. Mrs Molloy professed to sweeping flues with the new machine, but was later found to be to using climbing boys (see Chapter 7). There is no evidence to suggest, however, that foundling children were used in the hospital chimneys. The Foundling Hospital finally closed in 1953. Today the Thomas Coram Foundation Trust is housed on part of the original site at 40 Brunswick Square.

Orphans (19th Century)

At the time of the 1834 Act (banning the apprenticing of boys under the age of 10) local administration was carried out by parish unions. Every union had a workhouse controlled by a Board of Guardians. Parish overseers paid master sweeps £3–£4 to take an orphan apprentice.

Charles Dickens's fictional account of *Oliver Twist* was published in the first year of Queen Victoria's reign (1837). It was sub-titled *The Parish Boy's Progress.*[10] Dickens was familiar with the working conditions of apprentices, as, aged 12 years, he had been removed from school by his mother (when his father was imprisoned for debt), and sent to work in a blacking warehouse. Dickens's portrayal of Mr. Gamfield, a master sweep who is hard up and in need of £5 to pay 'certain arrears of rent', is memorable:

> Mr Gamfield had stopped to read a bill posted on the workhouse gate. It informed the public that Oliver Twist was TO LET for the sum of £5. Mr Gamfield, addressing 'the gentleman in the white waistcoat' who was standing beside it, said:
> "This here boy, Sir, wot the parish wants to 'prentis ... If the parish would like him to learn a right pleasant trade, in a good 'spectable chimbley-sweepin' bisness. I wants a 'prentis, and I am ready to take him."

When Mr Gamfield stated his wish before The Board a short while afterwards, its members were less than enthusiastic. After some discussion, £3 15 was settled upon. However, later that afternoon when Oliver was taken before the Magistrates to have his indenture approved, he appealed so effectively not to be sent away 'with that

67

dreadful man', that the indenture went unsigned, and Oliver was returned to the workhouse.

Payment

> Reader, if thou meetest one of these small gentry in thy early rambles, it is good to give him penny. It is better to give him twopence, if it be starving weather ... the demand on thy humanity will surely rise to a tester (sixpence).
> *Charles Lamb, 1822*

There were no set fees for chimney sweeping. Apprentices were mostly loyal to their masters, often going out unaccompanied to sweep chimneys, yet returning with their earnings. A young sweep in 1792 was paid 9d a chimney and he cleaned about four chimneys a day.[11] In 1817, the average fee, exclusive of soot, was 10d.

Alfred Wiseman from Norwich climbed his first chimney in Trafalgar Street when he was 9 years old (1857). His master, Mr Finch of St Miles, paid him 'A few coppers a week according to the state of his business and his behaviour.'[12] In his employ, Alfred and another boy achieved the distinction of being the first sweeps to climb the chimneys of the Norwich poorhouse. The boys were paid 3d each. When Alfred was 12, he worked for a different master sweep in Hingham. He was paid 6d a week (also food and clothing – no boots or stockings; they were too expensive). He swept up to 21 chimneys before breakfast. Later Alfred's wages were raised to 1s 6d when he went to work for Mr Sainter in Mileham.

Cruelty

The chimney sweeping trade – in common with other trades during the Industrial Revolution – had an abundance of masters who ill-treated their apprentices. Evidence is not difficult to find. Parliamentary reports and court cases were fully documented and misdemeanours and cruelties were read about avidly, just as they are today.

Thomas Allen had been 'articled in a public house in 1795 at the age of three and a half,'[13] and James Dunn from Knightsbridge, recalled being 'bound at 5 years of age.'[14] He was frequently ill treated and was once sent up a chimney, which had been on fire for 48 hours. As a result, he had fallen, and his burns had crippled him for life. He was 10 years old at the time. Dunn claimed that boys were rented out to masters for 6d per day. Masters could have any number of boys, and although 4 or 5 boys were generally thought sufficient, he knew one master who had 24 boys.

Poverty-stricken parents could be accused of cruelty when, driven by family circumstances, they sold or gave away their children to chimney sweeps. The smaller the child the better: different sized heads to fit different sized flues. It was common practice for parents to 'Dispose of them to the best Bidder, as they could not put them apprentice to any other Trade, at so young an age.[15]

On Tuesday 24th August 1809, Bow Street Magistrate Court heard that a Mr Miller had sold his five-year-old son to Master Sweep Henry Doe for the sum of three guineas. Miller, a plumber by trade, had sold the child while his wife was 'out of town'. The case ended happily, however, as the mother, helped by a kind solicitor, managed to get her child returned, and Henry Doe, for having purchased a child 'under age' was fined the sum of £5.

The following cases, selected at random throughout the country, detail instances of extreme cruelty. One of the most publicised cases was that of 10-year-old Valentine Gray, a destitute child from Alverstoke workhouse. There were 122 children at Alverstoke, and Valentine was one of 64 boys. Conditions in the workhouse were reasonable and children were provided with adequate food, clothes and schooling. In 1821, Valentine was apprenticed to a master sweep called Davis from Newport on the Isle of Wight. Shortly after Christmas, both Davis and his wife were brought to court. Their young apprentice had died. When surgeon Dr Bucknell examined Valentine's body, he found the boy filthy, emaciated and bruised. He also had a severe scalp wound. Davis and his wife were convicted of manslaughter and imprisoned for 12 months. The circumstances of Valentine's death were so distressing that the residents of Newport raised a '1d fund' and used the proceeds to erect a monument in Newport churchyard:

VALENTINE GRAY, THE LITTLE SWEEP
INTERRED JANUARY 5th A.D. 1822 ... a testimony
to all innocent children who suffered.

On 7th July 1827, the *Leeds Mercury* reported the death of a sweep in a chimney at Thornton. At about 10 am on Tuesday morning the young boy had been cheerfully employed sweeping a chimney, when his brush became lodged in the flue. Fearful of his master's anger he remained in the chimney. His master, J. Holgate, sent another apprentice up to get him, but the boy climbed out of reach. The enraged Holgate swearing he would 'cut him to pieces', lit a fire in the grate –

69

to no effect. The apprentice was sent up again with a rope, which he tied to the boy's leg. Holgate tugged the rope down a few feet and secured it to the grate. He then climbed up to the boy himself and stayed with him about five minutes. On returning, he declared that he had felt the boy's feet and thought he was dying. The chimney was dismantled around 3 pm but it was too late. The boy had stuck fast in a narrow section of the flue and died. Holgate was tried, found guilty of manslaughter and confined to York Castle. At the next Assizes, Holgate was acquitted. Medical opinion had decided that his apprentice had died of suffocation and not through any wounds or bruising found on his body.

George Cruikshank's portrayal of an incident at Lothbury where two climbing boys lost their lives. (From *The Chimney Sweeper's Friend and Climbing Boys' Album*)

Another fatality through ill treatment occurred on 11th July 1847. Readers of *The Times* learned that Thomas Price, aged seven years, had died of convulsions following a beating, after being taken out of a hot flue. His Master John Gordon had declared that the young devil was 'foxing', when the boy had become half-asphyxiated in the hot flue of Tennants' Chemical Works in Manchester. His master had twice forced Thomas up the flue. Gordon was found guilty of manslaughter and sentenced to transportation for 10 years.

70

Religion and Education

Charity schools at the beginning of the 18th century were mostly associated with the church. In 1733, St Albans Church School, Cheapside, had 75 pupils; 50 boys and 25 girls. The children were taught, clothed, and 'put out in apprentice and service'.[16]

Sunday schools where apprentices were taught after the Sunday service were introduced in 1780 by Robert Raikes, owner/editor of the *Gloucester Journal*. Credit also goes to another Gloucester boy, William Fox, who founded a 'Society for the Establishment and Support of Sunday Schools throughout the Kingdom'. William Fox became a wealthy London merchant. His Society founded six schools in its first year, and nine years later 65,000 pupils had benefited from books supplied by the Society to 1,012 schools.

An anonymous writer, 'Eusebia', wrote in *The Gentleman's Magazine*, 1794:

I know some Master Sweeps dress their boys very decent on Sunday: in particular one whom I employ who takes his to church. He told me he wished he could read himself and then he could instruct his boy, who, he said was a forthright lad and would take anything he was taught.

The writer, (probably from the Sheffield area) had tried in every way he could to encourage a Sunday school for chimney sweeps, suggesting that every ward in the city should maintain one. He reasoned that if every house contributed '1s (5p), this would amount to £10 a year. It would pay 'some elderly man' a small allowance for his trouble, as well as lodging (in one room), half a caldron of coals for firing, two or three benches, and a few cheap books.

Four years later, a lady in the neighbourhood of Kingston upon Thames (believed to be the Countess of Kingston) undertook to supply climbing boys with clothes so that they could attend Sunday school. Each apprentice received:

One jacket and pair of trousers of coarse blue cloth ...	10s 6d
Two shirts ...	7s 0d
One pair of trousers ...	4s 0d
A hat ...	2s 3d
Total	£1 3s 9d

She also sent to each chimney sweeper's house, a weekly allowance of a quarter of a pound of soap, and the following items:

A straw paillasse [mattress]	£1 2s 0d
A pair of blankets ...	17s 0d
A washing tub ...	6s 6d
Total	£2 5s 6d

The idea of teaching apprentice sweeps to read and write appealed to leading Christian philanthropic societies as well as individuals. In August 1798, a Sunday School was started in Brick Lane, Kingston upon Thames, where apprentice sweeps were instructed by a master and mistress appointed by a special committee. Approval came from the Bishop of Durham who reported to the Society for Bettering the Conditions of the Poor in 1799 that the chimney sweepers' boys were 'Improving in their reading ... some beginning to read the New Testament'. They were also 'acquiring habits of cleanliness and attention' and their 'manners and morals' were greatly improved.

On 13th March 1818, a Parliamentary Committee asked William Tooke (see Chapter 6) if he knew, in general, whether master sweepers took care of the educational needs of their apprentices. Mr Tooke replied that although an association had been formed in 1800 with this object in view, little progress had been made and that apprentices had no education whatever; 'out of a total of 750 journeymen and apprentices only about 20 were able to read and most were illiterate'.

Nine years later, W.H. Pyne pointed out that there were more public institutions for the relief of the poor in Great Britain than there were in any other country. In almost every town there was a 'free-school and a charity school'.[17] However, during a Parliamentary Inquiry in the 1850s, Lord Salisbury stated that although there was a great deal of 'professional zeal' at a time when 4,000 children were employed in sweeping chimneys, the results of a survey into the trade showed that, among 482 boys in 170 establishments, only 21 had acquired the rudiments of reading and only two could write.

Chimney Climbing

At the beginning of the 17th century when land was scarce in large towns and cities, architects constructed buildings several storeys high. Fireplaces – already reduced in size for burning coal – became even narrower. Flues, placed within walls to save space, frequently travelled horizontally or zigzagged. This was sometimes necessary to avoid obstacles and so as not upset room decor (see Chapter 9). An average flue measured 9″ × 4″ or 8″ square, and could only be climbed by children.

Historians believe that the art of climbing narrow chimneys was learned from the agile children of Piedmont and Savoy, who came to London as émigrés during the reign of Charles II. Children from the mountainous areas of Northern Italy supplied all Germany and France with climbing sweeps. A once highly esteemed German travel book by Johann George Keysler (1740) records that an old man used regularly to collect children from villages and take them abroad. This exodus of children may have been the inspiration for Robert Browning's narrative poem *The Pied Piper of Hamlyn*, and would explain why much of the 'reported' speech attributed to chimney sweeps in previous centuries was heavily accented, i.e. vot (what), ve (we), etc.

Young children climbed our tortuous flues for more than 200 years. There is no denying their courage and skill.

The Little Sweep's Christmas. A climbing boy from France.

73

Techniques

Large chimneys and stacks were easily climbed. They were often built with stepped sides, iron rungs, metal pegs or protruding bricks, inserted inside the flue to aid the sweeper. Evidence of this could be seen until recently at The Buck's Head, Little Wymondley (Hertford-shire). This small 17th-century inn has a central chimney stack with four flues. Two inglenook fireplaces on the ground floor contain iron rings set at intervals up the interior of the chimney. Basement chimneys in Knightsbridge were fitted with ladders.

Narrow chimneys, however, required considerable skill. Novice sweeps practised on straight flues. They climbed with elbows and legs spread out, feet pressing against the sides of the flue. An older boy or journeyman hoisted the younger boy up the chimney, remaining below him as he climbed. Apprentices learned quickly; often being more afraid of the journeyman than the master.

Reluctant climbers – children with no natural ability or those who were afraid of enclosed dark spaces – were harshly disciplined. A severe beating with a rope or brush on bare skin soon persuaded them. One master sweep[18] calculated that a chimney should be 12″ square for a boy of seven to go up with ease, and when properly taught, flues that were 9″ × 14″ could be climbed effortlessly. Humane masters provided their apprentices with padding for knees and ankles, and waited for their sores to heal, though it was usual to harden the skin by rubbing with brine.

When seven-year-old George Elson climbed his first chimney – a straight one – his master rewarded him with 2d. As George became more experienced, he claimed flues of 14″ square could be 'run up and down'. Young sweeps had their own 'climbing terms'. A large chimney was called 'wide hole'. Small flues 9″ square (which could be upwards of 60 feet in length) were either called 'bare nines' or 'notchy holes'. They had to be climbed 'cape and corner', that is, crosswise; with the face in one angle, the back in the angle behind and an arm in the angle either side. If a flue was unclimbable the only resort was to 'pike it'. That meant sweeping up as far as possible and leaving the remainder untouched. A flue in which a great deal of soot had collected was termed a 'foggy hole'.

When cleaning narrow flues, one arm remained close to the side of the body with the palm of the hand turned outwards, pressing against the side of the flue, while the other arm was extended above the head, holding the scraper. The descent was accomplished by 'scotching' in turn with knees and elbows.

Charles Lamb recalls how, in his childhood (c1780) it gave him

74

a 'mysterious pleasure' to see the young chimney sweeper in action:

> To see a chit no bigger than myself enter, one knew not by what process, into what seemed the fauces Averni [furnaces of hell], to pursue him in imagination, as he went sounding on through so many stifling caverns, horrid shades! – to shudder with the idea that "now, surely, he must be lost for ever!" – to revive at hearing his feeble shout of discovering daylight – and then ... running out of doors, to come just in time to see the sable phenomenon emerge in safety, the brandished weapon of his art victorious like some flag waved over a conquered citadel!

In 1818 kitchen chimneys where stoves had been installed contained flues that were 7", and in some cases, 6" square. Only very young children could sweep these flues. Worthing Vyse (see Chapter 8) describes some of the problems:

> The box of the smoke jack, which contains the oil, is leaky, which is frequently the case, consequently the works of the jack are covered over with a thick coat of oil and soot; but as I have no time to lose, I endeavour to pass by the jack as well as I can, but with all my care, a quantity of the oil and soot wipes off on the back of my shirt, which soon penetrates and sticks fast to my skin: now this, if I only stood in need of it, would form a most excellent strengthening plaster, and as it is, no doubt it prevents me catching cold, as I am exposed alternately to excessive heats, and to a keen and frosty atmosphere.

Hazards

Flues with sharp drawn-in bends or flues that ran parallel and turned back on themselves were death traps to inexperienced climbers. This was because soot accumulated in hidden ledges and crevices. Joseph Glass (see Chapter 9) gave the following description. After passing up through the chimney then descending to the second angle from the fireplace, the boy finds it completely filled with soot, which he dislodges from the sides of the upright part. He tries to get through, and succeeds, after much struggling, as far as his shoulders, but finding that the soot is compressed so hard round him by his exertions that he can recede no further, he tries to move forward: but the sharp angled stone covering of the horizontal flue presses down on his shoulder and prevents him from moving. His face covered by the

75

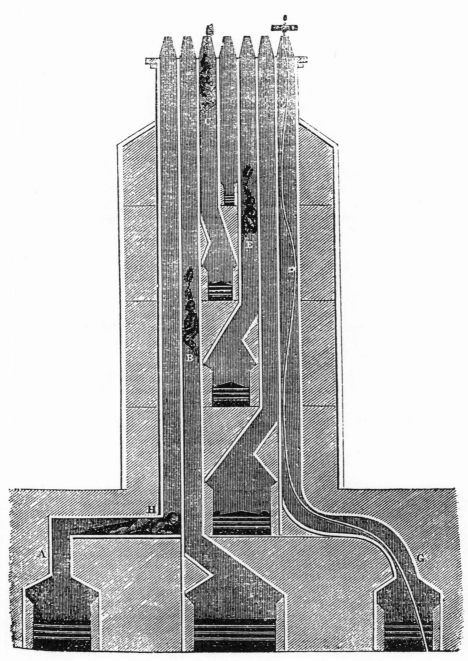

Joseph Glass's illustration of possible positions for climbing boys, c 1814.

climbing cap is forced into the soot and stops him breathing. He struggles, and in a few moments is suffocated.[19] One way of avoiding this predicament was to send two boys up the chimney. While one went to the top, the other cleared away the soot that fell into the slant. Then the first boy could return safely. In most instances this arrangement worked. There were, however, tragic accidents.

On Wednesday 5th March 1817, Master Sweep Edward Gay, No 3 Park Lane, Baker Street, (Mary-le-bone) sent his journeyman and two apprentices to sweep the chimneys at the house of Mr Buck, No 13 Cumberland Street. The two apprentices, Robert Tinson and Thomas Gainham, entered the library chimney. As it was known to be a troublesome one, the smaller boy, Thomas, went up the chimney ahead of Robert. It was a very long shaft. Robert called out to Thomas to come down, and the younger boy descended halfway down the upright. He stopped when he heard Robert groaning beneath him. A large amount of soot had piled up between them. When Thomas reached him, Robert 'moved two or three times', and Thomas tried to speak to him, but Robert 'could not hear'. The frightened boy climbed to the top and called to the journeyman. The journeyman rescued Thomas from the roof then went to find their master. Edward Gay sent for a bricklayer who broke into the chimney. Robert Tinson was found 'suffocated and dead', his head surrounded on all sides by soot.

Chimneys often contained hidden flues exposing the unsuspecting climber to additional danger. The following account concerns the death of George Topham. On Friday 16th February 1855, Master Sweep William Topham sent his young son George up a chimney flue at the Sydney Hotel, Goole. The boy soon came down complaining that the soot got in his mouth. His father made him ascend again but the boy returned. This time his father beat him. He then tied a cloth over George's mouth and forced him up the flue. After some time, when he failed to come down, an alarm was raised. The chimney wall was broken down and George was found suffocated in a different section of flue. A diversion of the original flue had been made in the same room. But no covering had been placed over the flue which descended into the old fireplace.[20] The chimney had been on fire and George, overcome by heat, had fallen down the old flue and suffocated in a pile of accumulated soot behind the fireplace. William Topham was consequently found guilty of manslaughter.

Inexperienced sweeps sometimes stuck fast in perpendicular flues. This was likely to happen when a flue branched off (see Appendix). The flue, instead of being the same width throughout its length, contained wider sections. Problems arose when the climbing boy descended. He unconsciously allowed his knees to rise in the enlarged

77

section of flue, and in that position slid down into the more constricted part and became wedged, remaining for many hours with his knees and back pressed against the sides of the flue. Extraction was painful; another boy had to tie a rope to his ankles and draw his legs down, or pull his arms up from above. If this failed, then a portion of brickwork was removed. Master Sweeper H. Chidlow[21] reported that when he was young he had stuck fast in a flue for seven hours and that his brother had lost his life in a flue at Wolverhampton.

Chimney Pots

Other major hazards were ill-fitting or cracked chimney pots. Soot and other debris collecting inside the pots had to be removed. When pots were wide enough the sweeper passed his body through, waved his brush, and shouted loudly to show he had completed his climb. At other times the inside of the pot was swept clean with an arm and brush, then the side of the pot was rattled in testimony.

In Oxford market (1776) when a young sweep was trying to clear soot from a pot on the back parlour chimney, the pot, with the boy inside, fell down into the back yard. Fortunately, his fall was broken by a heap of rubbish. The boy, at first feared dead, was taken to Middlesex Hospital and he eventually recovered. But a maidservant who was washing in the yard when the pot landed was so terrified that she 'fell into fits and continued ill for some time'.[22]

Another sad case was that of 10-year-old John Pasey. The boy was cleaning a decayed pot in the end flue of a zigzag stack of chimneys at No.60, in the Minories, London, when the pot broke in pieces and the boy fell to the ground breaking his skull.

Although these cases were horrific, a careful study of child labour during the Victorian era shows that fatalities among children in the chimney-sweeping trade were no higher than those recorded for other trades.

Coring and the 'Mysterious Art'

When new chimneys were built, they had to be 'cored', before a fire was lit. Loose rubble such as brick chippings, mortar, cement, or pieces of pargetting, everything that fell down inside the flue, had to be removed. Only climbing children could do the task. George Elson remembered going with his master to St Bernard Monastery, in the Charnwood Forest, to core the new Priory chimneys. George had to climb through all the flues to make sure there was no mortar in the bends. His master met him at each chimney stack to help him out of one chimney and down into the next, in case there was a blockage and George became stuck.

Concerning the 'mysteries' attached to the 'art' of sweeping chimneys, climbing boy Sam Sharp explains:

One day I went with my master to call the streets. In passing through the Strand a person called us in, and said that the chimney in her room up stairs was on fire. We hastened up, and to our surprise found it was the sun which partly shone in at the top ... My master, however, said it was dreadfully on fire, and I was immediately thrust up. I swept the chimney well ... the charge was five shillings: the money was immediately paid, and all parties well pleased.[23]

Sam's second revelation concerned a kitchen chimney. He had swept it on many occasions and each time his master had ordered him to 'pike it'. After some time, the servant complained that it still smoked.

Climbing boy Sam Sharp, c 1830. From *The Climbing Boys' Advocate.*

Sam's master (who had anticipated this) gave Sam the following instructions: 'When I take you there you must go partly up the chimney, and, after being there some time, come down and say there is a large hole in it.' Sam's master would then send another apprentice, Jack, for several large bricks and mortar. Sam next had to sweep the chimney thoroughly and 'stow away' the bricks and mortar, (probably in his soot sack). Five shillings was charged for the job and as the chimney drew well, all parties were satisfied.

Apart from extinguishing chimney fires, scraping, sweeping, coring, and repairs to the flue, a climbing boy was frequently called upon to remove more than soot from chimneys. Pigeons and magpies; swarms of bees, and even cats have been recovered. George Elson confessed that he hated being asked to remove swallow's nests from chimneys. Feeling sorry for the birds, he would leave the eggs or the young birds up on the top bricks, and just bring down the nest.

79

Fun in Flues

There were even occasions of hilarity in climbing. Many a time when in good spirits, I have sung at my work; I and another boy in an empty house have raced each other up and down a pair of chimneys out of fun, and I have dared to ascend when even the chimney-stack has rocked with my weight and movements.

George Elson remembered one particular chimney at Mount Sorrell (four miles from Loughborough), where the house had been pulled down but the chimney remained. He had mischievously climbed it, though it rocked from side to side.

Chatteris, 'the town of treacle chimneys', was the name given by climbing boys to chimneys on the Isle of Ely. Skilful climbers could only attempt the slippery narrow interiors of the chimneys. They were climbed as quickly as possible without stopping, to avoid slipping down with the soot.

Other peculiar chimneys were those contrived with a single shaft for two or three fireplaces. Smoke ascending from a flue that was not being swept caused confusion, particularly when the sweeper returning from the top was unsure which flue he had taken. Descending the wrong flue could sometimes be to their advantage; as a means of escape, for instance, or an unexpected chance to marvel at the cleanliness and wealth of the gentry, either in the dining-room, the parlour, or the upper bed-chambers. Because furnishings were covered or removed when chimney sweeps called, such wonders were rarely seen.

Attitude of Other Children

Other children regarded chimney sweeps their own age with a mixture of fascination and fear. Children working a 16-hour day in the potteries, carrying moulds from the potters to the stoves where temperatures reached over 120°F, no doubt envied the chimney sweeps' comparative freedom and variety of work. Apprentice sweeps might climb more than 20 flues before breakfast but their day ended at around 3 pm. And Monday was usually a slack day, when masters were busy with new contracts.

The young climbers' black appearance was generally scorned, but apprentices from other trades envied the gaily-dressed young sweeps who received alms and special suppers during May Day celebrations (see Chapter 10). And to some children, the climbing boys were heroes. J.C. Hudson (1823) wrote the following account:

I remember well seeing the boy. I never missed getting up at the same time as the servant to witness the horror. In winter I could not help remarking that the atmosphere of the fireplace kitchen, whilst making me shiver, seemed to be a relief to the poor boy just come in from the street. He slipped off his upper garment and drew on his sooty cap all over his face. The mysterious cloth was appended to the mantle-piece by means of two forks, and the boy, with a scraper in his hand, and brush in the other, slipped behind it and disappeared. I used to listen for the sound of his body rubbing against the sides of the chimney, and catch with eagerness every sound of his half-stifled voice, as it answered the gruff call of the Master below, and when I thought him near the top, I used to run out into the Street to see him emerge. At first the rattling of his scraper was heard against the sides of the chimney pot, and then his shrill voice announcing the success of his achievement. Then appeared the brush, and immediately afterwards the little hero himself waving it victoriously and shouting. Resting himself a minute I have seen him take off his cap and take a refreshing draught of cool and wholesome air.[24]

George Elson and his brother were treated with a respect and much kindness after venturing into a village church in the 1840s. One Sunday, while the boys were floating sticks in a stream, two labourers approached them. The men wanted to know why the boys were not at church. After explaining that they wouldn't be let in because of the way they looked, the men good-naturedly supplied them with soap. 'Nothing loth, yet somewhat stricken with the idea', the brothers washed their faces and hands, but having no towel 'produced little better than a smear'. Even so, with bare feet and soot-begrimed clothes they arrived at the morning service. George explains what happened:

> Timidly we entered, to the evident surprise of the whole congregation. We stood up and sat down at the proper moments, and followed the service as best we could, at the close of which we stole quietly away.

That evening they decided to return. Once again their appearance aroused great interest and afterwards quite a crowd watched them go. They were followed by a number of children. Consequentially, the barn where George and his brother were living was shortly afterwards

81

invaded by a deputation of young people bearing in their hands hot tea, milk, bread and butter, and cakes for us to eat and drink. The eagerness with which we accepted these welcome gifts ... was much to their delight.

The children (who were all well dressed) stayed for some time, asking many questions and showing 'much sympathy'. On their departure they bade the brothers 'an affectionate good-night'.

When the brothers arrived in the village early next morning, word of their coming had spread. They were given many chimneys to sweep, including those at the vicarage, where they were provided with shoes and stockings. George fondly remembers that they fared very well indeed and 'ever bore grateful recollections of Ashby Folville'.

It was fashionable among the nannies and nursery maids of the wealthy to teach their carefully brought-up young charges to live in fear of chimney sweeps. During her childhood at Hunstanton Hall, Jamesina Waller (1849) remembers the periodic chimney sweeping and the foolish nurse's threat, 'the black man will get you if you are not good'. She recalls

the half terror of seeing the poor sooty boy standing on a dust sheet on the floor, & mother holding my hand while she led me up to him & obliged me to put a thick piece of bread & butter in to his hand – then to my astonishment at his thanking me & devouring it.[25]

Similarly, Lord Frederic Hamilton, *The Days Before Yesterday*, remembers that in the 1860s 'in common with most other children', he was

Perfectly terrified when the chimney sweep arrived with his attendant coal-black imps, for the usual threat of foolish nurses to their charges, when they proved refractory was, "if you are not good I shall give you to the Sweep, and then you will have to climb up the chimney." When the dust sheets laid on the floor, I used, if possible, to hide until they had left the house...

Lord Hamilton goes on to say that despite all his precautions he sometimes met little sweeps 'in the passages', who could not have been more than eight or nine years old, and were 'inky-black, from head to foot' except for their eyes. When he was older he 'summoned up enough courage' to ask one of them 'whether he had disobeyed his nurse very often in order to be condemned to sweep chimneys'. The 'black urchin' gazed at him, uncomprehending, then with a cheerful grin replied that on the whole he rather enjoyed climbing chimneys.

Notes

[1] *The London Tradesman*, R. Campbell, 1747, 1969.

[2] Indenture, Bolton City Library, Lancashire.

[3] George Elson, *The Last of the Climbing Boys*, 1900.

[4] George Elson, (*Ibid.*)

[5] Small North American tree: the dried bark of its root was used as an aromatic stimulant.

[6] *Sentimental History of Chimney Sweeps*, Jonas Hanway, 1785.

[7] The same paper reported that Charles Kingsley visited Middleham in 1845.

[8] George Elson (*Ibid.*)

[9] Anecdote, J.W. Orderson, Examiner, from *Every-day Book* Vol 1, William Hone, 1825.

[10] Printed in *Bentley's Miscellany*, in instalments (1837–1838).

[11] *Criers & Hawkers of London*, (Chapter 20), Shesgreen, Scolar Press 1990.

[12] *Reminiscences of a Norwich Man, Eastern Evening News*, 16th January 1925.

[13] Evidence, Parliamentary Committee, 1817.

[14] Evidence, David Porter, House of Commons Committee, 1788.

[15] Evidence, James Dunn, House of Commons Journal, 1st May 1788.

[16] *18th Century London*, Sir Walter Besant, 1892.

[17] (*Ibid.*).

[18] *House of Commons Journal*, 1st May 1788.

[19] *Chimney Sweeping Described*, Joseph Glass, 1815.

[20] Minutes of evidence before Parliament, 1817.

[21] *The Climbing Boys Advocate*, 1st July 1856.

[22] *Construction & Building of Chimneys*, Robert Clavering, 1779.

[23] *The Adventures of Sam Sharp*, 1815, Derby Library.

[24] J.C. Hudson, letter to Mistresses of households, in order to promote the idea of sweeping machines.

[25] *Hunstanton Hall, Recollections*, Jamesina Waller, 1910.

5

MASTER SWEEPS' LIFESTYLE (18TH & 19TH CENTURIES)

Depiction in Art

Some idea of the way chimney sweeps lived and spent their leisure time can be gained by studying contemporary paintings and engravings. An impressive oil painting, measuring approximately 3' x 4' entitled *The Curds and Whey Seller* (c1730) can be seen in the Museum of London. It features a blind countrywoman seated beside a brimming tub of curds and whey (the watery part of milk when it separates). Several chimney sweeps are gathered around her. The group is centrally placed beside the Little Conduit, with the buildings of Cheapside and the church of Mary-le-Bow behind them. The boys wear curiously shaped head coverings and carry large sacks. Two are enjoying their curds and whey – a favourite summer-time beverage – while the third hands over money.

During the 1730s–1750s London's most popular engraver was William Hogarth. He was born in the City of London (1697) and later apprenticed to a goldsmith. Although Hogarth studied art at St Martin's Lane Academy, he became more proficient as an engraver. It was his aim to 'compose pictures on canvas', and to treat his subjects 'as a dramatic writer'. Sweeps, young and old feature in many of his engravings. Part of a caption on one of his prints (1724) mentions chimney sweep Jack Hall (See Chapter 8). William Hogarth was an early benefactor and active governor of The Foundling Hospital.[1]

Nineteenth-century illustrations of chimney sweeps – mostly portraying the Cries of London – were reproduced on packs of cards (ace of clubs, and ace of diamonds). The 'SWEEP SOOT, HO!' cry is shown on number 12 in the first series of cigarette cards issued by John Player & Sons. And in the Happy Families card game, 'The Sweep Family' and 'The Soot Family' (Mr, Mrs, Master and Miss) are both characterised by Sir John Tenniel the *Punch* cartoonist.

Artist George Cruikshank frequently included chimney sweeps when illustrating the works of Dickens and Mayhew. 'The Streets, Morning'

84

The Curds and Whey Seller, Cheapside c 1730 (British School, oil on canvas). (Reproduced with permission from the Museum of London)

The *Sweep Soot, Ho!* illustration reproduced on a Player's cigarette card in 1911.

| Mister | Misses | Master | Miss |

The Soot Family.

Sketches by Boz, shows a young apprentice waiting his turn beside a bread and coffee stall.

Apart from coffee, other popular drinks were wine in the taverns, and porter, beer and ale in the pothouse (inn). According to the Hon. Tom Dashall, *Real Life in London* (1821), chimney sweeps were particularly fond of 'Daffy's elixir of life'. This was a drink fashionably named after a celebrated quack doctor whose medicine was reputed to cure all known diseases.

In Mayhew's *London Labour and the London Poor*, a 'sketch taken on the spot' shows the interior of a room where three sweeps are at supper. Their meal consists of potatoes, white bread and ale. They use large curved knives and a fork. The small room is furnished with a wooden table, box seats and an alcove bed with coverings. Circular chimney sweeps' brush heads hang on the wall.

On one occasion, Henry Mayhew was invited into the home of a single-handed master. The man was a 'teetotaller' (one of the few sweeps who did not drink alcohol). His small one-storey dwelling had a low ceiling and the furnishings seemed over-large for the size of the room: 'massive mahogany chairs, table, chest of drawers'. Displayed in two cabinets either side of the fireplace was a large collection of glass and china ornaments. Because of their position, they could easily be seen from the street – viewed through a glass section over the hall doorway.

Caring Masters

High-class masters lived in respectable neighbourhoods with premises large enough at the back to keep their soot. Their boys were washed regularly and generally well cared for. On the 19th March 1800, a number of master sweeps working in Westminster and Holborn met together and formed a Friendly Society to 'promote the general interest and credit of the trade'. (See David Porter, Chapter 8). They pledged to protect and instruct their climbing boys during their apprenticeship, and find them suitable employment when they outgrew their occupation. They would:

> Raise a fund ... to give premiums with them to other traders, when their terms as Chimney Sweepers shall expire, in order to enable them to become useful to themselves and the community.

Money for the fund would come from an admission charge to the Society of 10s 6d, then 1s per month for each of the masters' apprentices. Persons not in the trade could become honorary members on payment of 10 guineas immediately, or 1 guinea (or more) annually. Provided the boys completed their apprenticeship (aged 16) they would be given the sum of £10 and placed with 'some other trade' until reaching the age of 21. Two professions were favoured: 'Sea Service' or 'articled Servant' to a member of the Society.

The Friendly Society was succeeded by the SSNCB (Society for Superseding the Necessity for Climbing Boys) (see Chapter 6). In June 1834 John Bentley, the SSNCB Treasurer, reported that there were '140 boys on the books being paid for by monthly subscriptions by 42 Masters'. One such master was Benjamin Watson who had businesses around Portland Square and Harley Street. Mr Watson was aged 82 years. He had begun as an apprentice in the 1760s, and during 50 years as a Master, he had had 40 apprentices and only one accident: a

Benjamin Watson's trade card. (Reproduced with permission from the Museum of London)

fall from a chimney pot (the boy recovered). There had been no instances of cancer (see later).

Mr Watson was an influential member of the SSNCB. He used both machines and boys (where necessary) and provided for them when they reached the age of 16. They were then given a premium of £10 and positions were found if they wished to leave the trade (see Appendix).

Poor Masters

Chimney sweeps who were unable to afford business premises lived in single rooms in lodging houses. Their boys (if they had any) slept in cellars with the soot. Poor journeymen rarely married. When they did live with a woman, it was in a state of 'concubinage'.[2] The women were invariably lucifer-match or orange girls or the daughters of costermongers (fruit sellers). According to Mayhew, the girls were apt to exchange one partner for another with the same casualness as the men. It was unusual for such couples to have children, unlike Devonshire sweep John Davis who deserted his wife and children in Bideford and ran off with a 'fair but weak damsel'.[3] Davis paid the penalty; a sentence of two months' imprisonment.

Chimney sweeps' clothing in the mid-19th century consisted of jacket, waistcoat and dark corduroy trousers (velveteens), or a waistcoat with long sleeves; as one sweep told Mayhew: 'from 20s slop, to 40s slap', meaning sloppy, poor cut clothes or slap up, posh ones. When working, a short, loose, smock-type blouse made of canvas or strong calico was worn (see also Chapter 10).

With regard to food many single-handed masters and journeymen managed to exist for six days a week on a diet costing as little as 6d:

BREAKFAST –	bread, buffer, coffee …	2d
MAIN MEAL –	chosen from:	
	saveloy, potatoes, cabbage	
	faggot " "	
	fish (fried)	
	pudding (from pudding shop)	
	soup (from eating house) …	2d
TEA –	bread, butter, coffee …	2d
	Total	6d

On Sundays prime fat mutton, oven baked, with 'taturs [potatoes] to bake along with it', or, if the 'old 'oman [wife] was in a good humour'

89

a 'fry of liver', might be cooked. All meals were supplemented with a pint of beer.

Few sweeps could either read or write. Even among the larger masters, apprenticeship indentures were frequently signed with a cross. In many London boroughs, benevolent people such as ladies from the Reverend Cadman's parish in Chelsea attempted to instruct local sweeps. Their efforts, however, were usually thwarted. Other masters, afraid that their men would become more knowledgeable than themselves, always managed to find work for them when they were due to attend class.

Journeyman sweeps, in common with other traders, were 'to a man,'[4] Chartists. They hoped, that in 'the change from one system to another, there might be plenty of noise and riot'. They had little regard for Acts of Parliament. This was because the only Act that related to them threw open their business to anyone 'capable of availing themselves of it' (see Chapter 6).

The following anecdote was recorded in 1846:

A dignified clergyman going to his living to spend the summer, met near his home a comical old chimney-sweeper, with whom he used to chat.
"So John," says the doctor, "whence come you?"
"From your house, Sir," says Mr Soot, "for this morning I swept all your chimnies."
"How many were there?" says the doctor.
"No less than twenty," quoth John.
"Well, and how much a chimney have you?"
"Only a shilling a-piece, Sir."
"Why then," quoth the doctor, "you have earned a great deal of money in a little time."
"Yes, yes," said John, throwing his bag over his shoulder;
"We black coats get our money easy enough."[5]
['we' implying both himself and the clergyman]

Health

Chimney Sweeps' Cancer

Unfortunate sweeps fell victim to a particular form of cancer. Commonly known as 'Chimney-Sweepers' cancer', it was a cancer of the scrotum. The respected surgeon Percivall Pott, of St Bartholomew's Hospital explained that the disease first appeared in the

90

The sweep and the clergyman, from *The Treasury of Wit*.

'inferior parts of the Scrotum', where it produced 'a superficial painful ragged ill-looking sore, with hard and rising edges'. In his *Chirurgical works* (1775), Mr Potts recommended the 'immediate removal of the part affected'. Restricted perspiration and soot, due to lack of hygiene and infrequent washing caused the itchy ulcer, consequently it was also known in the trade as the 'Soot-wart'.

It afflicted adult sweeps, not – as mistakenly alleged – climbing boys, and the specific cause became known only when the value of soot began to depreciate. Mr H. Earle, in a paper on the subject[6] noticed that most cancer cases occurred in men between the ages of 30 and 40 years. He concluded that the small hard swelling, which later formed a cancerous ulcer, was caused by friction of soot with the skin. Sifting soot brought it about. This was a laborious task – which could only be done by an adult – involving separating fragments of mortar and cinders etc. from soot:

In sifting, the man had to stand in a semi-bent position, and with the sieve laden with soot and rubbish swayed backwards and forwards and from side to side. By these movements there was a constant friction between the soot-covered clothes and the scrotum ... the sweat that was induced in the scrotal region added to the irritation caused...

91

Mr Earle's theory was further borne out by 'the remarkable instance of its occurrence on the wrist of a gardener', who was employed every spring to distribute soot in order to destroy slugs.

The Surgical Registrar's notes for Barts shows that 39 patients were under treatment between 1869 and 1888:

Not treated ...	1
Died of operation ...	2
Not traced after operation ...	14
Died of return or advance of disease ...	9
Died of other causes ...	3
Alive during autumn of (1888) ...	10
Total	39[7]

At St Thomas's Hospital, Mr Cline, a surgeon, stated that in the 40 years he had been practising he had seen no more than 20 cases (see Appendix).

Although many chimney sweeps were known to have vomited balls of soot, it is uncertain how many died of cancer. Medical Officers from St George's Hospital (1808), reported that 'six or eight melancholy cases'[8] of cancer in chimney sweepers had occurred since 1802. All proved fatal. The unfortunate patients had let their diseases go too far before seeking help.

John Ashmore aged 35 had been a chimney sweep for 20 years. When he first found a wart on his scrotum, he repeatedly picked it off. After a year, it had ulcerated. He was admitted to Barts (8th August 1808) and discharged after removal of a testicle six weeks later. He told the hospital authorities that his grandfather, father, and one brother had all perished from the effects of the disease. Mr Ashmore was strongly advised to give up his trade but he paid no attention. Fifteen months later he was cured by another operation. He returned again after four months when it was too late to attempt surgery.

Hospital statistics bore no relation to the actual number of cancer cases and deaths among chimney sweeps because – unlike Mr Ashmore – many sweeps were afraid of going into hospital and 'submitting to the knife'. There was also the problem of cleanliness: unwashed patients were refused admittance to hospital.

Cleanliness

A poor chimney sweep, sixteen years old, ragged, barefoot, his legs chapped from the cold, was put in prison for some minor misdemeanour. The bath he was made to take upon entering delighted him; but what caused him most amazement was when he heard he was to put on shoes and stockings. "Am I really to wear this? and this? and this as well?" ... His joy reached its height when he found himself in his cell ... he asked if it could really be true that he was to sleep in a bed. The next day when the governor asked him what he thought of his situation, he cried, "What do I think of it? Well, I'll be damned if ever I work again in my life!" He was as good as his word: later on he was transported.[9]

Prison Report 1837

Chimney sweeps were able to take more care of themselves when public baths and washhouses were introduced. They were first opened in George Street, Euston Square in 1846 and funded by voluntary contributions. In 1847, about 50 sweeps attended each week throughout the year (chimney sweeps' attendance was easily recorded because of their appearance). Most sweeps bathed on a Saturday night, so that they could change into their Sunday clothes.

In summer months, the Euston Square Baths were regularly used by 80 chimney sweeps. They preferred the warm baths, which were more effective in removing soot. Body washing was done in a 'slipper bath', a small cubicle 6' × 7'. The charge for a cold bath with the use of a towel was 1d, a warm bath was 2d (third class). When the baths became self-supporting three others opened: Goulston Street, White-chapel; St Martins (near the National Gallery), and Marylebone (near the Yorkshire Stingo Tavern, New Road).

One master sweep who bathed at Marylebone Baths twice a week (1851) commented that, although many sweeps ate, drank, and slept in soot, washing was 'more common among his class than when he himself was a climbing boy'. The superintendent at Marylebone arranged for chimney sweeps to use baths at particular times. They were courteously allowed one corner of their own, where, one newspaper reported, they could 'comfortably and cheaply' remove the 'honest marks of their calling'. The sweeps' wives did laundering at the baths. Early 20th-century baths, such as the Westminster Baths (1930) off Regent Street, included a 'pram store', where poor women could leave their prams after using them to convey linen.

Crime

London

Expertise in climbing sometimes led to crime. A chimney sweep named Jones who had been imprisoned in Newgate Gaol managed to escape by scaling a wall. Jones remained free for three years. He evaded capture by hiding in a den beneath the large basement cellar of a derelict old house in Clerkenwell. The small den, which was four feet wide by nine feet in depth, had been excavated in rough ground. 'Jones had his food conveyed to him through a small aperture, by a brick or two being left out next the rafters.'[10] Although the police repeatedly searched the house, Jones's hiding place stayed secret – and would have remained so had a fellow rogue not betrayed him.

Edinburgh

Scottish sweep Andrew Ireland became such an expert climber that he was known as 'the climber'. Easy access to houses (legitimate or otherwise) led to a habit of thieving. When 15-year-old Andrew was finally caught, he had been committing petty crimes for three years. Andrew was sentenced to nine months' solitary confinement and imprisoned in the castle high on Carlton Hill. But not for long; the iron grating proved no match for the agile sweep. After climbing through the skylight and down the sheer rock face he was free.

Eight months later (2nd January, 1838) Andrew's mother – pretending that her son was dead – staged a mock funeral. By chance it was witnessed by Officer McWilliams, the lawman who had first caught Andrew. That same day, McWilliams was sent to investigate a break-in at a silversmith's in East Thistle Lane (New Town). When McWilliams and a fellow officer arrived at the premises, they discovered that some newly made silver screws and a brass tinder-box were missing. As soon as it was known that chimney sweep Ronald Kilgour (133 Pleasance, Old Town) and another unknown sweep had recently been employed, the hunt was on. When Andrew was later recaptured, he insisted his name was 'Stewart'. Although Andrew was unrecognisably black with soot, McWilliams was not fooled. His suspicions were confirmed when a body-search revealed the stolen silver. Andrew Ireland completed his sentence in the castle gaol. He was then deported to New South Wales for a further term of 14 years.

North Devon

The theft of a pair of slippers, though well worn, was considered a serious offence in 1857. After sweeping the kitchen chimney in Crackaway Farm, Westdown, Hugh McManus a poor sweep, stole a pair of slippers. The slippers, valued at three shillings, belonged to Mr James Day. Suspecting the sweep, Mr Day mounted his horse and accompanied by Constable Richards, set out after him. They found McManus,

> with the missing slippers on his feet, which being somewhat too small for their comfort ... had improved the accommodation by a long longitudinal opening on the top of the foot.[11]

Mr Day recognised his slippers by 'a particular cut' in the side of one of them. Despite pleading that he would sweep the prosecutor's chimneys 'ever so long for nothing' Hugh McManus was tried and committed to the county gaol for 21 days. Because McManus was bare-footed, a compassionate police officer (Inspector Wood), asked if the prisoner might be sent to Exeter 'by the contractor'.

Cruel Masters

Joseph Rae

Reported instances of crime in the chimney-sweeping trade were relatively few compared with the number of cases of cruelty. Master Sweep Joseph Rae, who ran his business from Roxburgh Place, Edinburgh, fancied himself as a humorist. The sign outside his premises proclaimed:

> Who lives here? Who do you think?
> Joseph Rae who loves to drink
> And if your chimney should chance to fire,
> He'll put it out as you desire,
> The people think it very funny
> He always sweeps for ready money![12]

In 1817, Edinburgh master sweeps, Joseph Rae and Robert Reid (friends and drinking companions) were found guilty of causing the death of Rae's apprentice, John Fraser. Both sweeps were deported to New South Wales; Rae for fourteen years' servitude and Reid for seven.

John Fraser had been orphaned early in life and apprenticed aged nine (1815) to Joseph Rae who lived at Rae's Close, the Cannongate. John led a miserable life with his master. Reports from a neighbour and an older apprentice, Thomas Marwood, testify to the many beatings he received; mostly without cause.

On the morning of his death (3rd June 1817), John had accompanied Alexander Rae, his master's brother, to the chapel in Albany Street. Alexander had been hired to find the cause of a blockage in the chimney on the front corner of the chapel. They arrived about 11 am and John was sent up the flue from the basement. After an hour had passed and he failed to appear on the roof Alexander shouted up the flue. John called down that he was stuck. The householder, thoroughly alarmed, suggested that they should send for Mr Spadin the stone mason. Mr Spadin lived two doors away and came quickly. He estimated John's position in the flue – a bend at ceiling level – and using a ladder climbed up and cut a hole. However, John was higher up and could not be reached.

Then Joseph Rae and Robert Reid arrived. Rae, furious at the time wasted, sent Reid for his young apprentice James Allinson. While they waited, Rae harassed John, threatening to use his gun and 'blow the Chapel (and John) to Hell'. When Reid and his boy returned with some ropes young James was sent up the chimney and instructed to tie a rope to Fraser's foot. Both masters pulled repeatedly on the rope but John was wedged too tightly. A stronger rope was found and knotted round John's ankles. Rae attached a crowbar to the rope to get more leverage and pulled with all his strength. Around 7 pm Robert Reid's wife arrived, and Mr and Mrs Reid and Joseph Rae departed. The problem was left to Alexander Rae, young James and the stone mason.

When James refused to go up again Alexander entered the flue and managed to squeeze himself up. He found that John's arms were above his head and his shirt was round his shoulders. The boy's head was jammed in the chimney bend. Alexander managed to free him. Mr Spadin widened the hole and John's lifeless body was pulled through. It was decided that John Fraser had died as a result of excessive pulling.

In Ireland, Dublin Master Sweep T. Young was convicted for a similar type of cruelty towards his young apprentice. The boy survived but the master sweep was sentenced to be 'whipped twice, at the interval of two months, from the gaol to the Exchange; to be imprisoned two years, and also to be detained in custody until he gave two securities of £25 each, and bound himself in £50.'[13] The master sweep had treated his apprentice like a prisoner and 'used to burn straw and powder under him, to make him go up the chimney quick', then pull him down by a cord tied to his leg.

William Sampson's Petition

On 30th June 1823, Lord Milton presented a petition on behalf of chimney sweep William Sampson to the House of Commons. The petition was read 'in the usual manner' (the petitioner's name, then one or two sentences at the beginning and another at the end) but the matter was not even discussed.

Two weeks later, the sweep's local paper the *Sheffield Iris* took William Sampson's case to heart and printed his petition in full. William Sampson had reported that his parents, though humble, were industrious. But 'hard times, a large family and frequent sickness' had compelled them to apprentice him to a chimney sweeper 'at an unlawful age' (under eight years).

His lodging place was often a shed in the street, a ruinous stable, or any open outhouse. He would leave at 3 or 4 am each day hoping to find enough work, or he 'durst not venture home'. William was inadequately fed and treated brutally, both by his master and 'the different journeymen whom he attended'. (Parts of his petition make uncomfortable reading). His parents had 'frequently remonstrated' with his master but to little effect. On one occasion, William was so severely beaten that his hip was dislocated. Found insensible and nearly dead, he was taken to an infirmary. William eventually recovered, but remained badly deformed.

It was fortunate for William that a Society for the Relief of Climbing Boys had been set up in Sheffield, or he might not have lived to tell his story. The *Sheffield Iris* reported that William Sampson was 29, and that he would have been tall and stout, instead he was 'little more than four feet high'. Mr Sampson was married with three children.

Leisure

Chimney sweeps with their long clay pipes were among the most regular customers in drinking houses. Since the end of Elizabeth I's reign 'common' pipes had been provided in taverns, inns, alehouses, and anyone could indulge in 'tobacco taking'. As the population grew so did the demand for pipes.

The sweeps' unsociable working hours allowed them freedom to devote their afternoons to pleasurable pursuits. They delighted in all forms of gambling and a favourite among the foremen was 'chuck and toss'. Cock fighting was the most popular of all. One cockerel was even named after the trade. In Quennell's *Victorian Low Life* we learn that Lord Hastings, accompanied by the Duke of Hamilton and a number of foreign diplomats, went to a 'subterranean cockpit in Endell Street', where Lord Hastings favourite bird, Old Champion Sweep, won his last battle but 'received his quietus'. In Hogarth's engraving, *The Cock Pit* (1739) a chimney sweeper is among the crowd of onlookers. On his way home from work he carries a full sack of soot, a scraper and long-handled broom.

Participation sports such as donkey derbies and fox hunting were much enjoyed. An extract from *The Month* (5th November 1850) reported a glorious run with the Hampden hounds. The 'faux', being chased from St John's Wood down Grove Road, rested for a while in a drain close to the Ayre Arms, then 'took to the open'. It then returned back through St John's Wood, along Avenue Road, across Barrow Hill towards Regent's Park, and was finally 'pulled down' near its starting place.

> The several gentlemen who had waited on him, afterwards passed the evening merrily together; Mr Chummy [the sweep] being in possession of the Brush [tail of the fox].

Edward Thomas (1853) gives an amusing account of a chimney sweep with donkey and cart racing a party of gentlefolk in a coach. The coach-party was returning from a day at Ascot races:

> Going through the park, we were terribly annoyed by a gentle-man in black, whose whole idea was to race with us; and although beaten several times, always came up again at the first delay ... on he went with his donkey-cart.[14]

Every evening, the Astley and Coburg theatres in London were patronised by 40–50 chimney sweeps. Their attendance in such numbers is explained by a report to the *Morning Herald* (1825), stating that the two theatres were the only theatres that would admit chimney sweeps in their 'working dress'.

Philip Astley's Amphitheatre[15] was situated on the south bank by Westminster Bridge. Established in 1768, Astley's theatre during its heyday outrivalled both Drury Lane Theatre and Covent Garden. On 17th June 1795, *The Prince Chimney Sweeper & The Chimney Sweeper Prince* was performed at Astley's. Described on the billboard as 'a new musical Piece, with Music, Dresses, Decorations, etc, entirely new', it was performed on the Forte Piano by 'The Musical Child from Newcastle Upon Tyne' who was 'only 30 months old'.

Country sweeps also enjoyed the theatre. While visiting Hull with his brother, George Elson remembered being 'highly gratified with seeing a superior theatre as well as performers'. The boys, who were clean and well dressed at the time, enjoyed watching plays. When working for a master in Camden Town, George attended a performance of *Macbeth* at the old Sadlers' Wells theatre. Mr Phelps in the title role was so convincing that – many years later – 'every feature' of his performance remained fresh in George's memory.

Later in the 19th century, there were the attractions of the Victoria Theatre. The audience in the threepenny gallery consisted mainly of young men aged between 12 and 23 years, and among the many costermongers were several 'black-faced sweeps'.[16] The gallery at 'The Vic' was one of the largest in London, holding 1500–2000 people. Often tightly packed at the back, it was usual to see 'piles of boys on each others shoulders'. Highland dances and comic songs were well liked, but the best part of the evening was always when a song was sung and the entire gallery joined in the chorus, such as "Duck-legged Dick" (see Appendix).

Ownership of a donkey reduced the workload of the master sweep and his apprentices and provided much entertainment. The following account of London Pradsellers (sellers of donkeys and horses) was written in 1823: a costermonger who refused to buy a particular donkey from a donkey seller, claimed that it bore no comparison to a horse, was exceedingly sulky, and wouldn't budge:

"I knows better...," cried a chimney sweeper; "for no better aren't no vare to be had; he's long backed and strong legged. Ere, Bill, you get upon him, and give him *rump steaks,* and he'll run like the devil a'ter a parson." Here Bill, a little blear-eyed Chimney-Sweeper, mounted the poor animal, and belaboured him most unmercifully, without producing any other effect than kicking up behind, and most effectively placing poor Bill in the mud, to the great discomfiture of the donkey seller, and the mirth of the spectators. Thus the animal brayed, the bystanders laughed, and the bargain, like poor Bill, was off.[17]

Boxing

Apart from enjoying the spectacle of boxing, many sweeps took an active part. Two chimney sweeps in particular; Henry Pearce and Tom Bale became well-known professional fighters. London prizefighters dominated the sport throughout the 18th and most of the 19th centuries. There were no weight divisions until the mid 19th century and boxers were mostly heavyweight (more than 175lbs). Champion boxers were self-proclaimed. They had no managers, although some were supported by well-born patrons.

Henry Pearce

Henry 'Hen' Pearce became British boxing champion in 1805. Known in the sporting world as 'The Game Chicken' he died undefeated. Henry was born in Keynsham, Bristol, in 1777. Although his father was a collier, the rest of his family were chimney sweeps (first established in 1648, see Chapter 10). Perhaps trying a break from tradition, Henry was first apprenticed to a butcher.

Henry Pearce, 'The Game Chicken', British Boxing Champion, 1805.

After taking up boxing, Henry became well known locally for his skills. He gained experience in boxing booths by travelling around as a country sweep. It was Henry's good fortune that Jem Belcher (reigning British champion) although living in London, had been a Bristol man and knew of Henry's ability. The champion was considering retirement due to an accident. He wanted his title to go to a fellow countryman,[18] so he invited Henry to London. Within two days of arrival, Henry was taken to 'Gentleman' Jackson's rooms in Bond Street to be tried out. Gloves were worn, and the gentlemen present declared 'the rosy-faced "Chicken" from the country a worthy adversary for the Champion'. That same night a secret trial took place.

Around ten o'clock Henry was aroused from bed in lodgings near the Strand by Mr Jackson's messenger, and taken to the Horse and Dolphin, Windmill Street. His new patrons, Edward Hayward Budd – a famous cricketer – and one other gentleman, were not disappointed. Henry defeated boxer Jack Firby in two 'desperate' rounds. The room was ten foot square and the waistcoats of onlookers as well as the walls were splattered with blood.

Henry's next fight took place shortly after midnight on 11th August, at the house of Mr Cullington, where a party of 'swells' put up a purse of 50 guineas (£52.50). Henry's opponent, Joe Berks, was 6ft 2in and weighed over 14 stone. Henry, at 11st 7lbs, was splendidly made. Although under 5ft 9in tall, his chest was ' magnificent – 45in in circumference'. After 15 rounds lasting 20 minutes, Joe was stretched out 'full length upon the floor' with a terrific blow to the forehead.

Having established himself as a fighter (albeit in secret) Henry began serious training: raw eggs to improve the wind and raw bees to make him savage.

Joe Berks had set his heart on being Champion of England. His challenge to Henry took place on Monday 23rd February 1804 on Wimbledon Common. 'Well nigh the whole sporting world of the Metropolis turned out to see the battle.' The big event lasted one hour and twenty minutes. At the end of 24 rounds Chicken sent Joe down with a right to the forehead. When Joe's senses returned he raised his head saying 'Chicken, tha'a licked me.'

Henry Pearce's last fight – the fight confirming him as Champion of England – took place against his old friend Jem Belcher, on 8th December 1805. It was reported in *Sketches of Pugilism* (1812) that 'Pearce displayed great science and courage [pugilists fought with bare-knuckles] .... he was much superior to Belcher' ... 'twice in the fight he could have killed his adversary ... Chicken, elated with the sound of victory', leaped about and threw a somersault.

After defeating Belcher, Henry returned to Bristol and became a publican on Bleckly Hill. While there he distinguished himself by two acts of bravery. The first was the rescue of a young girl from a fire in Denzil Street. On the second occasion, he saved a young woman who was being attacked by three men on Clifton Downs. Henry's personal life was less fortunate. His marriage (date unknown) was a disaster.

His wife, reputedly 'a shameless woman', embittered Henry with her unfaithfulness, and he left Bristol for good.

He began travelling the country towns again, and during this time suffered a 'pulmonary disease'. Although 'remarkably illiterate'[19] Henry was good-natured and generous. His condition worsened after travelling by post-chaise across country from Oxford to Epsom. Despite bleak weather, the Game Chicken was anxious to see Jem's last fight with 'Cribb'. When his friend lost, Henry declared he might teach Cribb how to fight.

Henry's hope was unfulfilled. After returning to London with his friends, he became seriously ill. Mr Neale, of the Coach and Horses, St Martin's Lane, looked after him, and on 9th February 1809, a 'benefit' was arranged. Henry Pearce died of consumption on Sunday 30th April 1809, aged 32 years. He was buried in the burial ground of St James's Church.

Tom Bale

Thomas Bale was still a boy when the British champion died. Though never famous nationally, Tom Bale was well known locally as a professional fighter. Like Henry Pearce, he came from a chimney-sweeping background. Born in Market Harborough, he joined the trade and remained a master sweep all his life. His first fight was won in his home town at the age of 18.

George Elson worked and lodged with Tom Bale when Tom was middle-aged and poor. The master sweep and his wife lived in a two-roomed cottage and were kind to their climbing boys. Tom's wife was impressively tall and a keen boxing supporter. She took an avid interest in her husband's battles and on one occasion kissed him when he sat, exhausted, on his second's knee. Tom was so enraged 'that he went on to win in rare style'.[20]

When George joined the master sweep, Tom was over the age of 50; still a fighter and reigning county champion of Northamptonshire and the surrounding district. He was 5ft 10in tall and squarely built. His massive head and dark piercing eyes gave his face a comic appearance. Although weighing in at 14st he was deceptively agile.

People were of the opinion that Tom had the talent to go further. Instead, he was a 'terror to police constables and bullies alike'. Drink was his downfall. George had replaced his elder brother as Tom's apprentice and both boys remembered Tom with affection, claiming that when sober he was 'kind, generous and honest'. Tom never went to church, but on Sundays he read aloud to his apprentices from the Bible, afterwards explaining and discussing the text.

Most of Tom's trade came from sweeping farmhouse chimneys. He was well liked by the farmers and their wives. In later life when writing about Tom Bale, George surmised that his former master's 'superior natural qualities of courage and endurance were only misplaced'.

Notes

[1] William Hogarth and his wife Jane were some of the first parents to foster a child.
[2] *London Labour & the London Poor*, Henry Mayhew, 1851.
[3] *North Devon Journal*, 7th December, 1854.
[4] Henry Mayhew. *Ibid*
[5] *The Treasury of Wit*, 1846.
[6] H. Earle, *The Lancet*, 26th October 1878.
[7] *The Operative Surgery of Malignant Disease of the Scrotum*, Vol xxv, Henry T. Butlin 1889.
[8] Evidence, Report House of Commons, 1817.
[9] *London Journal of Flora Tristan*, 1842.
[10] *Illustrated London News*, August 17th, 1844.
[11] *North Devon Journal*, 13th August, 1857.
[12] *Edinburgh Evening Dispatch*, 6th June, 1941.
[13] *The Sooty Side*, Ramoneur company, 1914.
[14] *Adventures of a Carpet Bag*, Edward Thomas, 1853.
[15] *Astley's Amphitheatre*, Jacqueline S. Bratton and Jane Traies, Theatre In Focus, pamphlet, 1980.
[16] *Ibid* Henry Mayhew.
[17] *Smithfield and the Prancing Prads*, 1823.
[18] *Fights for the Championship*, F. Henning, 1856, 1902.
[19] *Sketches of Pugilism*, 1812, 1971.
[20] *The Last of the Climbing Boys*, George Elson, 1900.

6

LEGISLATION AND REFORM

PART 1: LEGISLATION (Principal laws affecting the trade)

Sweeping

The earliest chimney-sweeping regulations date from the 16th century. In 1582, the Mayor and Aldermen of the City of Oxford issued a number of Ordinances. To lessen the danger of chimney fire they ordered that:

> All chymneys occupied wth fyre wthin the said Citie frome henceforthe be **swept fower (4) tymes everie yeare** at the charges to the owners thearof.

Despite the implication that it was a professional service there are no records showing who would do the sweeping. Citizens were also told that the penalty for a fire breaking out in 'anye chymney' was 'iij pence'. (3d)

Nearly 50 years later Edinburgh passed its first Burgh Act for the 'Sweipping of Chimneyis'.[1] On 23rd October 1629, citizens were warned that 'The Haill Toun' would be exposed to danger unless chimneys were 'Sweip' and 'mak cleyne'. The penalty was £5. In March 1676 two more Acts were passed. 'Chimneys had to be swept twice yearly' or a £20 fine would be payable. And a further Act, on 28th November 1677, stipulated that chimneys be swept 'once per quarter'.

17th-century Court Leet Records for Southampton show the only evidence (to date) that English chimney sweeps were officially appointed. The first sweep was sworn into office in 1654. His name is unknown but he had to be ready and willing to sweep chimneys at any time, and his payment for every call was 'fourpence apiece'.[2] To 'secure the residence and due attention of so useful a functionary', every householder paid one penny per annum: 'As is used in many other Cytes and townes, called by ye name of a smoake peny.'

In this context the 'smoake' penny was probably a reference to the Hearth Tax or 'hearthpenny' fumage, which had to be paid for every hearth. Taxation on fireplaces was not new to the 17th century. Even in Anglo-Saxon times, 'Smoke Farthings' were paid by all but the poorest in the community. The tax was an important part of the King's revenue and in 1662, except for certain exemptions, two shillings had to be paid for every hearth or stove. The tax was a burden to everyone. On 18th October 1666, Samuel Pepys recorded in his diary: 'One moved that the chimney-money might be taken from the King.'

During the 18th century, rules were introduced in Edinburgh to regulate the City Tron-men. The 1741 Burgh Act stipulated that Tron-men had to live in the city, pay 6d each week 'for the use of the poor' of the Society of Tron-men, and wear: 'one white apron, three or four fathoms of towes and the town badge upon his breast.' Nineteenth-century chimney-sweeping regulations in Glasgow and Edinburgh (1848 Act) required that every sweep had to be licensed and their rates of pay fixed by the local authorities. The Burgh Police Act of 1892 extended these powers to all Scottish municipalities.

Flues

As we have seen, early techniques for sweeping chimneys depended upon the type of soot and (to a lesser extent) the size of the chimney. During the 17th and 18th centuries and towards the end of the 19th, however, the size and length of the chimney flue determined how the task was done.

It was primarily due to legislation that flues were constructed the way they were. When the City was rebuilt following the Great Fire of London, home safety was paramount and great improvement was brought about by the 1667 Act for Rebuilding the City of London. Whereas previously houses were built in a haphazard fashion, to comply with the Act, building construction had to meet specific requirements. Houses were no longer built of wood. 'Timber within the tunell of any chimney' was banned, and businesses involving the use of fire (such as bakeries) were restricted to certain areas.

Regulations that 'all the same houses be re-built within 3 years', specified four types of building. Not counting cellars and garrets, the first and smallest had to be two storeys high and erected in by-lanes; the second, built in streets and lanes, three storeys; the third, erected in the high streets and principal streets, four storeys with balconies. The fourth and largest type 'the mansions of principal citizens and persons of quality', should be built 'at the discretion of the builder', provided they did not exceed four storeys.

Building Acts (1707, 1709) stipulated that all flues had to be pargetted (plastered) from top to bottom. Flues were pargetted by means of a 'traveller' (see Appendix). The method was effective for wood fires, but created extra work for chimney sweeps when coal was burned, (see section on coring, Chapter 4).

In the 19th century, Building of Chimneys Acts 1834, 1840 ordered that all projecting angles in the flue had to be rounded off. Chimneys or flues could be built at angles with each other of 90° or more provided they had doors or openings not less than 6″ square. Flue regulations were introduced to assist the operation of the new chimney-sweeping machines (see Chapter 9).

Ministry of Health Byelaws (1875) ordered that flues should be gathered together 'with as easy bends as possible', and where the bend in a flue exceeded an angle of 135° from the vertical, soot-doors had to be provided. This was to enable the flue to be swept after the change of angle (for 20th-century soot-door regulations, see Appendix).

Chimney Sweeping Acts

Scottish chimney sweeping acts seem to have been introduced as the situation demanded. In England though, any legislation involving chimney sweeps and sweeping was hard won. From 1788, it took nearly a century before the final chimney-sweeping act was passed. The reasons were complex and are fully explained in Chapter 9. For now, it will be helpful to explain a part of English Parliamentary procedure.

Before an Act becomes law, it has to pass successfully through a number of stages. Any citizen can get up a petition listing grievances and offering suggestions for improvement, and the petition can be signed by a large number of people, but the petition can only be presented as a 'bill' for discussion in Parliament by an MP. Before it reaches the bill stage, a Select Committee examines the petition. The bill is 'read' in the Commons and when a majority of members vote to adopt its recommendations (or amendments) then the bill is passed. The bill becomes an Act after a final debate and majority vote in the Lords.

1788 Act

Master Sweep David Porter presented a Petition for the Better Regulation of Chimney Sweepers to Parliament, on 22nd April 1788. The petition was examined by a Select Committee and Mr Robert Burton MP reported its findings to the Commons. After hearing all the evidence a bill was passed stating that:

1. The minimum age for climbing apprentices should be eight years.
2. No master sweep should have more than six apprentices.
3. Stamp duty on indentures – the same as other trades.
4. Masters should be licensed.
5. No apprentice should be hired out.
6. 'Calling the streets' restricted to 7 am–12, winter, 5 am–12, summer.
7. Apprentice badge: The name of master or mistress and their address to be marked or 'put upon a brass plate, to be set or affixed in the front of a leathern cap', to be worn 'when out upon his duty'.
8. No climbing of chimneys 'which shall be actually on fire'.

The bill also required master sweeps to sign a form of indenture whereby they pledged that their apprentices should be properly clothed and fed, thoroughly washed and cleansed of 'soot and dirt at least once a week', and sent to church on the Sabbath.

When the bill was read in the House of Lords several principal clauses were either removed or changed. No approval was given for *the licensing of masters*, and other clauses were amended: 'no person, *not being a householder* ... shall take an apprentice', and 'no apprentice shall hawk or call the streets for employment, *but in company with his master*'. The 1788 Act although inadequate, was hurriedly passed.

1817–1819

Because no provision had been made to enforce the law, the first Chimney Sweeping Act was largely ignored. When Mr Porter asked Sir John Fielding to intervene in the case of a boy who had been hired out and ill-treated, Sir John was unable to help as the law afforded him no authority.

Between 1817 and 1819 the government received a number of petitions calling for the abolition of the climbing boy system (see later section on societies). Shrewsbury MP Henry Grey Bennet presented the petitions to Parliament with support from William Wilberforce. While the subject was being debated in Parliament, children under the lawful age of eight were still climbing chimneys in the Westminster buildings.

Mr Bennet introduced three bills to Parliament. In support of his second bill (9th February 1818), he reported that there had been five fatal accidents to climbing boys in the previous year. Due to this powerful argument, the bill was passed by the Commons. When it reached the Lords, however, it was found that the evidence was not justified, and the bill was delayed pending a report from the Surveyor-general.

The following year, when Mr Bennet tried again, the idea of total abolition was still considered impracticable and many MPs thought that cases of abuse by master sweeps had been exaggerated. Even so, the Commons again passed the bill. When it reached the Lords, though, there were further problems.

Lords' Debate, 1819

The Earl of Lauderdale was the strongest, most outspoken opponent of the bill. He told the House that he would 'resist' legislation 'to his last breath'. Lauderdale was also notorious for his anecdotes. To lighten proceedings during a debate in the Lords it was often the practice to tell stories, but on the occasion of the chimney sweeps' bill the Earl went too far.

Monday 15th March 1819: [*wording from Hansard Report*]
Proceedings had reached the stage where Lord Auckland had just finished commenting on *experiments on the chimnies connected with the House of Commons . . .* and *moved that the bill be now committed,* when Earl Lauderdale stood up and said; [*. . . the supporter of the bill contended, that the chimnies of the metropolis could be nearly all swept by machines. Now, were this the fact, he* (Earl Lauderdale) *would at once withdraw his opposition; but if the report of the Surveyor-general was to be relied on, no such power was to be attributed to the machines. . .*]

Lauderdale then quoted his (now famous) anecdote [*In some parts of Ireland, it had been the practice, instead of employing climbing-boys, to tie a rope round the neck of a goose, and thus drag the bird up the chimney, which was cleaned to the fluttering of its wings. This practice so much interested the feelings of many persons, that, for the sake of protecting the goose, they seem ready to give up all humanity to other animals. A man in a country village having availed himself of the aid of a goose, was accused by his neighbour of inhumanity. In answer to the remonstrances of his accuser, he observed, that he must have his chimney swept. "Yes," replied the humane friend of the goose, "to be sure you must sweep your chimney, but why don't you take two ducks, they will do the job just as well?"*]

Lauderdale continued: [*the zealots for this bill had, in their blind eagerness to relieve a partial suffering as completely forgotten the general interests of society, as the poor Irishman had disregarded the ducks in his anxiety to save the goose. He* (Lauderdale) *certainly should be happy to see the use of climbing boys be totally abolished; but if a machine could be invented to sweep chimneys that invention could not be promoted by this bill. He must therefore, move as an amendment that instead of now, the bill be committed this day six months.*]

The Earl of Harrowby responded: [*he* (Harrowby) *was not able to entertain their Lordships with any jokes, either relative to himself or extracted from Joe Miller, but he believed very little was necessary to be said to induce them to support a measure founded in humanity, and which they had reason to conclude was perfectly practicable ... he thought that unless the bill was passed, the experiment* (with machines) *would never be fairly made.*]

[*Their Lordships divided on the question, that the bill be now committed: Contents, 20; Non-contents, 37. – majority, 17. Lord Lauderdale amendment was then put and carried. The bill was consequently lost.*]

Lauderdale's goose and duck story became legendary. His wording, however, was often misquoted and later accounts omitted the phrase 'instead of employing climbing-boys'. Lord Lauderdale became the villain who killed the bill and consequently condemned thousands of children to a life of misery. George Cruickshank's depiction of 'a noble legislator' was used to illustrate one of James Montgomery's poems (see later). The poem, entitled *The Lay of The Last Chimney Sweeper* shows a young boy on his knees begging the Earl to alter the law, while his master ascends a ladder holding two geese. Later, the Earl's grandson was burned to death in a fire – retribution that did not go unnoticed among campaigners – and in 1832, the Royal Olympic Theatre staged a comic opera, of which the subject of ridicule was Earl Lauderdale.

1834 Act

It was not until 1834, following the 1833 Factory Act and the abolition of the slave trade in Britain, that a second Chimney Sweeping Act was passed.

The 1834 Act raised the age of consent for climbing chimneys to 10 years. No child was to be sent up a chimney flue for the purpose of extinguishing fires and children were allowed a two-month trial period, after which they had to declare before a Magistrate their willingness to be 'bound'. Master sweeps could have four apprentices, but no more

Boy begging 'a noble legislator' to amend the law. From *The Chimney Sweeper's Friend and Climbing Boy's Album.*

than two on trial at any one time. Penalty for 'calling the streets' (plying for trade) was set at 40 shillings (£2).

Perhaps the most meaningful section of the Act was the requirement that a badge identify all apprentices. The apprentice badge was made of brass and curved to fit the top of the head. It measured approximately 7″ × 4″ and was attached to the front of a leather cap. The badge gave little protection from falling soot but served to advertise the Master's name, address, and range of services.

The Commons had agreed to David Porter's recommendation of an apprenticeship badge 46 years before (1788 Bill), and despite the clause being dropped, many high masters adopted the idea. In 1809, a Sheffield Association of Master Sweeps pledged to give their boys 'a cap with a metal plate bearing the master's name'[3] and an illustration in *The World In Miniature*, W.H. Pyne (1827) shows a young sweep wearing a cap badge. An excellent brass apprentice badge can be seen in the Abbeyhouse Museum, Leeds. Inscribed around the curved edge are the words:

JAMES TAYLOR
Chimney Sweeper Flue & Smoak Jack Cleaner
No. 35 King St. Cheltenham

110

The apprentice badge of James Taylor.

1840 Act

Because there were still no regulations for law enforcement, the previous Acts continued to be violated. A third Chimney Sweeping Act was introduced mainly through the intervention of Lord Ashley. When finally passed, the 1840 Act banned the apprenticeship of boys under the age of 16 years, and the climbing of chimneys by those under the age of 21. The fine for entering a flue for the purpose of sweeping or cleaning, or of extinguishing a fire under the lawful age was 'not more than £10 or less than £5'. Although it would appear that the abolition of the climbing boy system had been achieved, there was still a long way to go.

1864 Act

Lord Shaftesbury felt compelled to take up the cause of the climbing boys again in 1864 (Lord Ashley inherited the title Earl of Shaftesbury after his father's death, June 1851). This time there was little resistance. The mood of the public had changed (Charles Kingsley's *Water Babies* had been published the previous year, see Chapter 11) and Shaftesbury's bill was passed. The previous Act was amended and masters were henceforth prohibited from taking boys with them when entering a client's house. *Approval for licensing masters, however, was still not sanctioned.*

Ireland

Meanwhile in Northern Ireland, under the *Licensing and Regulating Carts Act* (1843, 1873) chimney sweeps were required to be licensed. This was necessary when applying for the hire of a cart or when using their own. In common with other users chimney sweeps had to obtain a certificate of registration costing 2s 6d, otherwise a fine of up to 40s (£2) was imposed.

1875 Act

Eleven years after the 1864 Act, Shaftesbury's third attempt – backed by *The Times* and public opinion – was completely successful. The 1875 Chimney Sweeping Bill 'laid upon the chief constable of every district the duty of enforcing the previous Acts of 1840 and 1864'. Finally, it recommended that master sweeps be licensed every year. Certificates would be issued to master sweeps only, and in the case of a partnership one licence fee of 2s 6d was payable per annum.

The recommendation that master sweeps be licensed – proposed more than a century before and successfully carried out in Glasgow and Edinburgh since 1848 – was at last approved. There was no opposition and the bill passed unopposed through both Houses.

PART 2: REFORMERS

Jonas Hanway (1712–1786)

It was due to the support of philanthropist Jonas Hanway and members of The Marine Society that David Porter was able to petition Parliament on behalf of the climbing boys. Jonas was born in Plymouth. When his father – an agent victualler for the navy – was killed in an accident, his mother moved to London. Jonas Hanway's uncle was Major John Hanway. 'Justice' Hanway, as he was known, lived in Oxford Street and was Magistrate for Mary-le-bone.

Aged 17, Jonas was apprenticed to a merchant in Lisbon and after finishing his apprenticeship, he ran his own business for a while. While abroad Hanway was considerably influenced by what he saw (see

112

Appendix). Returning to England in October 1750, Hanway took to wearing 'fur-lined clothes and usually three pairs of stockings'.[4] Physically weakened by the climate abroad he had become very thin and susceptible to chills. To protect himself from English rain Hanway used an umbrella. At that time the 'walking stick with petticoats on',[5] was popular in France but unheard of in England.

Jonas Hanway was a Quaker and tireless campaigner for many worthy causes; he was also a prolific writer. In 1756 Hanway, Fowles Walker and Sir John Fielding founded The Marine Society. This successful venture supplied seamen for the navy and there are implications that former apprentice climbing boys were particularly acceptable (see Chapter 9). Two years later Hanway became Governor of the Foundling Hospital.

In August 1760, *The Public Advertiser* printed an article by 'Ambulator'. The writer, upset by the 'shoeless and stockingless' state of climbing boys, suggested they should be forced to give the names of their masters to magistrates, so that neglectful masters could be punished. Fortunately for the young chimney sweepers, Hanway, who became interested in their welfare, read the article.

His first success was in getting a law passed whereby apprenticeship premiums could be paid in two instalments. This was to help poorer parents who were unable to pay the master sweep's full premium. It also curbed the practice, by parish overseers, of selling children to unscrupulous masters.

Hanway began to collaborate with David Porter in 1770 when they attempted to form a Friendly Society to improve the working conditions of apprentice sweeps. In 1773, Hanway published *The State of Chimney Sweepers' Young Apprentices*. He then formed a committee with city merchants instituting a plan for a proper system of indenture, agreeing to pay (or assist with) the five-shilling stamp that was needed. They suggested that master sweeps should form an Association of Chimney Sweeping, warning them that the society intended appealing to Parliament if the 'evils' of their trade were not remedied. The outcome was disappointing. After six months, only 15 boys had been indentured.

Nevertheless, treatment of apprentices improved for a while. Eventually though, Hanway was forced to admit that 'a legislative regulation' was the only method that could control 'a body of people' who were unaccustomed to moral discipline. He continued to form committees and write letters. Finally, in 1785, 18 of his letters in *The Public Advertiser* were published as a book under one title; *A Sentimental History of Chimney Sweepers*. The publication was a direct appeal to public humanity and it included an open letter to London clergymen. Hanway had discovered that beadles on duty in church habitually refused entry to climbing boys. Among other practical suggestions for reform, such as Sunday schools, Hanway drafted a proposal for a new apprenticeship indenture.

On 5th May 1785 *The Daily Universal Register* (now *The Times*) published an article entitled 'Sweep-Chimnies'. The article drew attention to children of the trade being 'nuisances in the public streets'. It accused them of being 'pickpockets', 'covered with soot', who should be 'prohibited from appearing in their working dress after an early hour in the morning'. The paper reported that:

> Everything that a benevolent heart could dictate to a liberal mind, has been promulgated by Mr Hanway on the sufferings of those unhappy creatures.

Another communication on the subject expressed sincere gratitude to Mr Hanway as well. The writer (unnamed) also wished most heartily that some mechanic would 'invent a patent machine to cleanse chimnies'. This was possibly the first mention of a chimney-sweeping machine.

Jonas Hanway died, unmarried, the following year on 5th September 1786 in Red Lion Square. He was buried in Hanwell Churchyard, Middlesex, and a monument was erected to his memory in Westminster Abbey.

Sir Thomas Bernard (1750–1818)

From Lincoln by birth, Thomas Bernard spent most of his childhood (aged 7–19) in the province of New Jersey where his father was Governor. Thomas gained an MA at Harvard before the family returned to England (1769). Aged 32, after marrying an heiress, Mr Bernard gave up his profession and devoted his time to helping the poor.

Thomas Bernard lived in Bloomsbury, quite close to the Foundling Hospital. In his capacity as treasurer of the hospital, he made friends with Count Rumford (also from Harvard). It was Rumford who personally supervised the provision of food and fuel at the hospital and fitted up the kitchen and fireplaces. (It is more than likely that Rumford personally supervised the chimney cleaning.)

By December 1797, Mr Bernard had become acquainted with David Porter. One Sunday he visited the master sweep at his premises in Welbeck Street and was impressed by the way he treated his appren-

114

tices. The boys, looking clean and well dressed, were seated at the table eating a meal of boiled mutton and rice pudding. Following his visit Mr Bernard published an article about the climbing boys in a report to The Society for Bettering the Conditions of the Poor; a society Mr Bernard had recently founded.

Thomas Bernard attempted to form an Institution for the Protection and Education of 'those infants' (for he considered them little more) 'who are employed as chimney-sweepers'.[6] He was supported in his appeal by the Bishop of Durham who was grieved to find that:

> the chimney-sweeper's boys at Kingston-on-Thames were not only destitute of instruction, but in some degree of clothing, and when unemployed were left to wander about in a state of nature.[7]

Sir Thomas Bernard continued as treasurer of the Foundling Hospital until his death in 1818. Streets in the area are now named after him.

Not far from the site of the Foundling Hospital is the church of St George the Martyr. St George's was built in 1706, and it became known as the Sweeps' Church, after a charity for climbing boys founded by Captain James South in 1843. Captain South bequeathed £1000 to the church on condition that interest from the charity fund be used annually to provide a Christmas meal for 100 apprentice sweeps in the cities of London and Westminster. After attending the church service every boy received 'half-a-pound of roast beef or boiled beef; half a threepenny loaf of bread, half-a-pound of potatoes, half-a-pint of ale or porter, half-a-pound of plum pudding and a new shilling.'[8] Captain South set up his charity as a protest against child labour. After 1875 the Court of Chancery ruled that interest from the fund should be used as prize money for scholars in local schools.

Societies

The first Society for Superseding the Necessity of Climbing Boys (SSNCB) was formed in London on 4th February 1803. The 'Society with the affected name', as Charles Lamb laughingly called it, began with a small group of enlightened masters and their supporters, who wished to improve conditions of children employed by chimney sweepers, and encourage a new method of sweeping.

By 1816, the London society had grown to respectable proportions with the Prince of Wales as patron, The Lord Bishop of Durham, president, The Duke of Bedford and eight other eminent persons as vice presidents. The secretary was Robert Stevens, treasurer, William Tooke, and a committee of 40 members. After a meeting at the Mansion House with the Lord Mayor (12th June 1816) it was decided to aim to legislate for the prohibition of climbing boys. The society recommended that all principal towns and cities should hold meetings and petition Parliament on behalf of the climbing boys. Consequently, many other cities joined the campaign.

Credit must go to Sheffield for being the first society to petition Parliament. Their Society of Master Sweeps formed in 1809 'to popularise the brush', agreed that their boys would be given suitable climbing clothes and wear a cap with metal badge advertising their master's name. They pledged not to send their boys out before 4 am and furthermore there should be 'no more than two boys to every bed'.

In York on 11th June 1817 the Mayor and Dean of York, together with 66 householders, 5 ladies, and a committee of 11 gentlemen, signed a resolution to promote the adoption of machines. A footnote under the signatures reads:

A machine for sweeping chimnies is kept by John Porter, opposite the Globe, Bishophill: who sweeps chimnies upon the usual terms – the other chimney sweepers are informed that machines are made and sold by John Carey, joiner, Walmgate.

Other branches were formed within the counties, namely; Gloucester and Birmingham (1818), and Bristol, Derby and Hitchin (Hertfordshire) (1829). In London the SSNCB claimed that, at the last place in the city – Ironmonger's Hall – no boy had climbed through the company's chimneys since 1830.

In December 1833 William Wood of Bowden who had tried for many years to persuade Manchester sweeps to 'forego the employment of children'[9] finally overcame their obstinacy and persuaded 53 masters to sign an assurance to use machines. The promise was conveniently forgotten, though later they reconsidered. Mr Wood was then elected secretary of the Manchester SSNCB.

After the 1842 Chimney Sweeping Act Mr Wood worked tirelessly, befriending apprentices and taking master sweeps to court for defying the law. At a meeting in Liverpool (June 1856) attended by 50 master sweeps, William Wood was guest of honour and chief speaker. In May 1864, he wrote an informative article for *The Dublin Builder*:

It is now twenty years since the chimney sweepers' Act was passed, notwithstanding which, I find that the inhabitants of your city are in the constant habit of using climbing boys ...

116

When William Wood died in 1868 (aged 86), it was reported that 'six sweeps from five towns carried his coffin'.[10]

A Society for Superseding the Necessity for Climbing Boys was instituted in Ireland in 1835. The committee of 34 met at No 7 Lower Albany Street, where sweeping machines could be obtained. The society moved to a new address six years later and was last heard of in 1843.

Between 1838 and 1840 the Irish public learned about climbing boys through *The Irish Friend*, a monthly magazine. One contributor (JC) recommended a machine invented by Joseph Glass (see Chapter 9). This was also the opinion of Vice-Admiral Robert Oliver from Cheltenham who considered the machine 'superior by far'. The Admiral, writing to Robert Stevens, said he had imported a number of machines into Dublin for the use of 'several noblemen and gentlemen'. He was sorry that there was little progress towards general use of the machine, and offered to donate £5 to 'send a man from London' to demonstrate the machine's efficiency.[11]

The following year, when Queen Victoria agreed to become patroness of The London Society, Robert Stevens reported that 40 new machines had been ordered (see Appendix). Mr Stevens was pleased to say that 'agents for the society (sweeps with machines) had swept 22,713 chimneys, being 520 more chimneys than 1837.' In the same year (1838) Derby SSNCB reported that the demand for machines was so great that they had appointed two agents: John Jepson, 30, St Peter's Street, and Michael Parkins, Court No 2, Bridge Street. Although statistics looked promising and machines had gained precedence in London, elsewhere – throughout most of Britain – climbing boys were still preferred (see Chapter 9).

In 1855, Leicester chimney sweeps were enticed to a feast, at no expense to themselves, where they signed an agreement and received 33 machines. The following year societies began to mushroom: Northampton, Coventry, Nottingham, Liverpool, Newcastle, Gateshead, and all signed pledges. By 1863 SSNBCs had been established throughout Britain.

James Montgomery (1771–1854)

Poet and newspaper proprietor, James Montgomery – probably now remembered solely for his hymn 'Angels from the realms of glory' – was a founder member of the Sheffield SSNCB. During his lifetime he became 'the conscience of the town'[12] and was revered after death as one of Sheffield's most respected citizens.

117

James was born on 4th November at Irvine (Ayreshire). His father was a Moravian minister, but James had no wish to follow; from the age of 10, James preferred to write verse. When he was 18 he left his position in a retail shop at Mirfield (near Rotherham), and set off for London hoping to sell his verse to a publisher. He spent eight months in London, with no success. In 1792, a successful interview for the post of literary assistant on *The Sheffield Register* settled his future. In July 1794, at a time of national unrest, the *Register* changed its name to the Sheffield *Iris*, and the following year Montgomery became its sole proprietor.

Throughout his life, Montgomery interested himself in Christian causes. In connection with the Sheffield SSNCB he probably first heard about the climbing boys through fellow society member, Samuel Roberts, who was appointed Overseer for the Poor in 1804 (see Chapter 9). Montgomery helped the climbing boys' cause through his (mostly) sentimental portrayals of their lives in narrative verse:

Jervis Knill, the Climbing Boy: A Tale of sorrow, founded on Fact

> Who loves the Climbing Boy? – Who cares
> If well or ill I be?
> Is there a living soul that shares
> A thought or wish with me...

Like Hanway before him, Montgomery collected many facts about the chimney sweeps apprentices and published them in book form. His *Chimney-Sweeper's Friend and Climbing-Boys' Album*, (1824), was illustrated by George Cruikshank.

Montgomery prospered both as an editor for over 30 years and as a poet. After his death, the Sunday school teachers and scholars of Sheffield erected a monument to his name. It stood over his grave in the general cemetery, as a tribute to his 'religious disposition' and his 'poetic fame'.

Lord Shaftesbury (1801–1885)

Anthony Ashley-Cooper, born into an aristocratic family, was the eldest son of seven children. From the age of seven, Anthony boarded at Manor House School, Chiswick. Four years later, becoming Lord Ashley,[13] he was sent to Harrow. When he was 14 he was considerably shocked by a pauper funeral and decided from that moment that it was his destiny to help the poor.

The monument to James Montgomery in Sheffield.

After inheriting the title, Anthony's father moved to his Dorset estate at Wimborne St Giles, where Anthony enjoyed country life before going up to Oxford. He left university with a first-class degree and spent some time abroad before becoming MP for Woodstock.

Ashley married Lady Emily (Minny, daughter of Lady Cowper) on 10th June 1830. The first of their nine children, a son, was born the following year. Ashley became increasingly evangelical, and was in demand both as a speaker and chairman of religious societies. Especially fond of children, he was passionately occupied helping the 'Ragged Schools'. During his first year in Parliament Lord Ashley sat on four Select Committees. It was the last – on pauper lunatics and asylums – that renewed his interest in the destitute.

When the Commons were debating the 1842 bill, Ashley told MPs that he had seen 23 climbing boys in Newgate gaol, 'sufficient to prove the bad moral effects of the system'. The Hand-in-Hand Insurance Company supported him in his arguments against climbing boys. Before the bill had passed through the Lords, Ashley wrote in his diary: 'Anxious, very anxious about my sweeps.' Suiting words to

119

action, Lord Ashley and Robert Stevens, Secretary of the Hand-in-Hand, befriended a climbing boy who lived behind Ashley's house in Brook Street. They arranged for the boy to attend the Union School at Norwood Hill. Ashley showed as much concern that the boy be trained in the 'faith' of the 'common Saviour', as he did about his rescue from apprenticeship.

Again in May 1854, Ashley wrote: 'Great anxiety about bill for relief of chimney sweepers ... have suffered actual tortures through solicitude for prevention of these horrid cruelties.' In 1873 Ashley, now Lord Shaftesbury, drew public attention to 'a poor little chimney-sweeper, seven-and-a-half years old, killed in a flue at Washington in the county of Durham.' Two years later Shaftesbury was able to use his influence in the Lords and the final Chimney Sweeping Act was passed.

Notes

[1] *History of Chimney Sweeping*, Scotland, Michael McLenaghan, 1991.
[2] Court Leet Books, 1654, Translation, *A History of Southampton*, Rev L. Silvester Davies, 1883.
[3] *Roads To Ruin*, E.S. Turner, 1950.
[4] *Life of Hanway*, John Pugh, 1787.
[5] *Sheffield in the 18th Century*, Leader. (Although openly mocked, Hanway persisted with the umbrella for nearly 30 years before its general acceptance.)
[6] *The Life of Sir Thomas Bernard*, Rev. James Baker, 1819.
[7] *Child Labour*, Keeling, 1914.
[8] *Brief History of the Church and Parish of St George The Martyr*, R.M. Wilson (1956).
[9] *Climbing Boys' Advocate*, Joseph Glass, 1856.
[10] *The Chimney Sweepers and Their Friends* (1869). *Roads to Ruin*, E.S. Turner, 1950.
[11] Letter, 30th November, 1837.
[12] *Sheffield, its Story and Achievements*, Mary Walton, 1968.
[13] His father had inherited the title Earl of Shaftesbury after the death of his brother.

7

WOMEN IN THE TRADE (18TH & 19TH CENTURIES)

Female Master Sweeps (18th Century)

In London, the most respected woman chimney sweep of the 18th century was Jeane Tempell. In 1740, she was running a thriving chimney sweeping business from large premises in Nutners Street, Holborn. Nutners Street, (now known as Macklin Street off Drury Lane) has a colourful history. 'Nutner' is a corruption of Lewknor's.[1] The City expanded westward in the mid 17th century, and the area around Lewknor's lane lost its wealthy citizens. The poor replaced them and the lane became the 'haunt of Loose women'.[2] The lane was mentioned in John Gay's *Beggar's Opera* (1729), when 'two ladies' were sent for 'from Lewknor's Lane'.

Jeane Tempell's premises, however, were situated at the end of the lane with countryside in front and beyond. She lived in the last house of a terrace of four that were several storeys high. Jeane was the sole proprietor of the business. She had three or more apprentices and was literate and enterprising enough to trade with her own unique sign:

Jeane Tempell, Chimbley-swepers at the Signe of the woman Chimbley Sweper in Nutners Street near the Watch House in Holborn

The trade sign of Jeane Tempell.

121

The sign was attached to the front of her premises and the Turks' head brush above it proclaimed her status as a chimney sweep. The wooden sign was illustrated with a rural landscape of grassland, boulders and trees. The terrace is shown and smoke pours from the chimney of Jeane's house. One of her apprentices is seen emerging from a chimney pot further down the terrace. He points towards the smoke with his long-handled brush. The gesture implies that he extinguishes fires. Jeane is the central figure in the painting. She wears an apron over her long dress. On her head is a wide-brimmed straw hat. A short distance behind her is an apprentice in a peaked cap carrying a bundle of long poles. A large sack is humped over his shoulder. He also points towards the smoking chimney.

Trading a few years after Jeane was Widow Soloman who probably inherited the business from her husband. In 1760 she lived at 12, Cree-Church Lane, Leadenhall Street, not far from Cheapside. Little is known about her except that her grandson John Whitney, who operated as soot dealer and nightman until the late 19th century, succeeded her.

In 1780, Martha Harrison opened a business on the corner of David Street, Oxford Road. She traded under the sign of the Sun and Feathers (it was quite common for traders to use one another's signs). One of Martha's trade bills was made out to Mr Gibbon, an historian, who lived at No 7 Bentinck Street.

Mary Fatt started trading under her own name in 1782. When her father, William Fatt, died she took over his business as Chimney Sweeper to the Admiralty and The Royal Hospital at Chelsea. Her trade card shows that she lived at Lower End, Swallow Street, North Piccadilly. A second card (1783) shows her name as Mary Angell, so she may well have married.

Other Marys, operating towards the end of the 18th century. were Mary Vinson (1787) widow of Richard Vinson, and Mary Wiggett, John Wiggett's widow. Mary Vinson warned her customers that she could 'be heard of at the Sun in Ormond-Street, and at the Swan, near Queen Square', but several 'of the business' went about in her name 'to prejudice' her. She asks 'Be pleased to enquire if they [rogue sweeps] belong to Mary Vinson of Theobald Road.'

Mary Wiggett was commonly known by the name 'Beauty', and her trade card shows an engraving of her by B. Reynolds. From 1792 she followed her late husband's business at the Broom, Price's Court, Queen Street, Southwark. Her card reads:

She makes foul chimneys clean and when on fire puts them out with all possible expedition ... I hope my Worthy Masters and

Mistresses will send home for me when I will forthwith wait upon them by Night or day.

Mrs Bridger

Because of her notoriety far more is known about the 18th-century woman sweep known as 'Mother Brownrigg'. Her real name was Mrs Bridger and she may well have been married several times. Mrs Bridger died on 24th November 1802, 'at a great age'.[3] Throughout her lifetime, she was so well known for her cruelty that she was named after midwife Elizabeth Brownrigg who was hanged in 1767 for brutally mistreating her staff.

Mrs Bridger had business premises in Swallow Street, London, and her apprentices lived with her. Swallow Street (now Regent Street) ran straight and narrow from Oxford Street to St James's Church, Piccadilly. It was described by Victorian journalist, George Sala, as a 'long, devious, dirty thoroughfare ... full of pawnbrokers, dramshops ... and livery stables, which were said to be extensively patronised by professional highway men.'

From the beginning of the 18th century until 1782, one of these stables – Major Henry Foubert's riding and fencing school – was situated in Swallow Street (on the corner). Mrs Bridger's exact address is unknown but she probably lived close by. In a contemporary engraving of the riding school[4] two young chimney sweeps are seen walking past. They are coming from the direction of St George's Church, where Mrs Bridger taught her apprentices to climb. She made them 'mount the perpendicular wall' of the church porch 'at the risk of their lives'.[5]

The boys lived in miserable conditions. Often rising as early as 3 am to sweep chimneys, they were then forced to 'scour the stairs' and do other household chores before eating their meagre meal. Their Mistress drank excessively in her later years, and her legs became badly ulcerated. After her husband's death (ten months before her own), she took to her bed. While sipping gin, she would amuse herself by having an apprentice brought to her. He would be stripped of his clothes, then, sitting up in bed, Mrs Bridger would beat him with a stick, kept by the bedside for that purpose. If in a good humour, her apprentices were 'made to box each other' and the victor awarded with a piece of plum pudding or a halfpenny.

Circumstances worsened when Mrs Bridger's Foreman, William Putney, alias William Williams, was arrested for kidnapping and beating Peter Cavanagh, a child of eight years. Peter had been brought

123

The front wall of St George's, Hanover Square, where Mrs Bridger's boys were taught to climb in the 1780's.

up by his grandmother in Exeter; then she had taken him to live with his father, a London blacksmith, in Sloan Street. It was Peter's task to 'carry out newspapers'[6] in the weekdays and go to school on Sundays. He was unhappy living with his parents and ran away.

Peter had been living on the street for three months when he was found crying by Robert Yates. Robert, aged 12, was one of Mrs Bridger's apprentices. He told his mistress about the boy and when Mrs Bridger saw how small Peter was she decided 'that he would do for her in the winter'. Three weeks later William Putney ordered Peter up the second-floor chimney, to learn his trade. When Peter came down Putney accused him of 'Pickling it' (slang for not sweeping clean) adding: 'If you had done it middling, you should have had a bit of plum pudding: go up and sweep it clean or I will give you a good flogging.' Because Peter could not climb the chimney, he was mercilessly beaten.

The following day he was taken to St George's Church to climb the porch wall but he could not climb fast enough. Putney ordered Robert Yates to follow him and push him up, 'in case he would have fallen on the spikes of the rails which go round the church.'

At William Putney's trial, the court was told that it was usual to

124

make chimney sweepers' boys climb up the sides of the church, and that the practice required the intervention of the officers of the parish. Two neighbours, Mrs Wilson and Mrs Allen, gave evidence of the 'ill usage which the child had been in the constant habit of receiving'. Robert Yates was mercifully 'discharged' from Mrs Bridger's business and William Putney was sentenced to six months' imprisonment. During Putney's trial, there was enough evidence of cruelty against Mrs Bridger to warrant her arrest. However, before she could be brought to court she became seriously ill and remained permanently intoxicated.

Even on her deathbed, Mrs Bridger was capable of deceit. Mrs Bridger's friend and provider was Mrs Voyer, widow of another chimney sweep. In consideration of 'having the house, and some trifling effects, together with the good-will', she looked after Mrs Bridger and paid for all her needs. Two days before her death, Mrs Bridger (who already owed her friend £70) demanded that Mrs Voyer lend her still more money. When Mrs Voyer refused, Mrs Bridger craftily sold all her property to a Mr Woodward for £45. This was done without telling him that 'Mrs Voyer had a prior engagement'. When Mr Woodward returned later to do an inventory, Mrs Bridger mentioned her silver spoons. Mrs Voyer, who was present, contradicted her, saying, 'Surely you forget, you made me pawn them last night, and you burnt the duplicate.' Mrs Bridger was so furious she ordered her friend out of the room, never to return.

Mrs Bridger's funeral attracted much attention. When her remains were interned in St Mary-le-bone burial ground two small sweeps and an old woman followed the coffin from the workhouse. The old woman had been Mrs Bridger's nurse. She was dressed in black mourning clothes, the same clothes previously worn by Mrs Bridger after her husband's death. The three principal mourners were followed by other 'distinguished personages' who cried aloud 'very hideous mock lamentations, with ragged sheets of paper in their hands, as substitutes for weeping handkerchiefs'. More and more curious onlookers joined in the cavalcade as it progressed. All were eager to witness commitment to the earth of so infamous a character as Mrs Bridger.

Female Masters (19th Century)

Out of a total of 5028 chimney sweeps in Britain in 1841, there were 127 female sweeps working in England and 4 in Scotland. It was customary in the 19th century for widows of chimney sweeps to follow

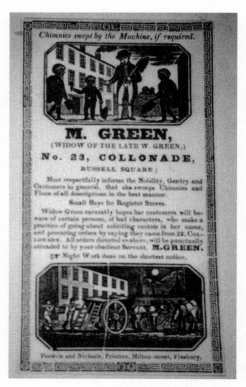

Widow Green's advertisement. (Reproduced with kind permission of Guildhall Library, Corporation of London)

their late husbands' trade, and this probably explains how so many women came to run their own businesses:

1835	Sarah Short, 12, Horse Fair, Bristol.
1835	Harriet Wilkins, 3, Cock and Bottle Lane, Bristol, (also soot dealer).
1844, 1850	Elizabeth Taylor, 35, King Street, Cheltenham (see Chapter 6, apprentice badge).
1864	Mrs M. Banks Church Street, Eccles.

In Hertfordshire, the resourceful Sarah Perrin not only ran a chimney-sweeping business, but kept a lodging house as well. Sarah, born in Hitchin (1811) was listed in the 1851 census as head of the household. Her business premises were in Spicer Street, St Albans. Sarah employed eight chimney sweeps and one boy. The lad, aged seven years, was her nephew, Charles Hyde. She also employed her son, James Perrin, aged 16 years. Both boys were born in Hitchin.

Other chimney sweeps living in the household were: Charles Cassey, 15 years, and Samuel Hawkins, 18 years, both from Hitchin; Matthew Cook, 21 years, from Dunstable; William Wheeler, 21 years, from Balls Pond, Middlesex; William Brown, 23 years, from Deptford, Kent; and Henry Watts, 23 years, from Warwickshire. It is probable that Henry Watts took over Sarah's business in 1878, as he is listed as a master sweep in his own right, in Spicer Street the same year. Together with Sarah and her nine employees, her lodging house accommodated 22 lodgers: 14 males and 8 females. Mostly classed as tramps, they included 3 infants – one aged 7 months – 5 children and an old lady aged 91 years.

There were 44 female 'masters' in London and one of the most successful was Mrs Molloy. Mrs Molloy operated a large business with premises on the Strand and her central address attracted good contracts. Early in the 19th century, when sweeping machines were still 'on trial', Mrs Molloy was contracted by the Commissioner of Stamps and Taxes to sweep the chimneys of Somerset House. She was offered the job after agreeing to use Mr Glass's new chimney-sweeping machine (see Chapter 9).

Although Mrs Molloy kept the contract for many years, members of the London SSNCB suspected that she was using climbing boys. They started to investigate. A small child always accompanied her journeymen when they entered with a machine. 'The little boy was found so handy in sweeping up',[7] (sweeping soot from the hearth) said Mrs Molloy. It was hard to prove otherwise. That is, until 'an active friend' of the society 'leapt in at the window whilst Mrs Molloy was watching the door'.

Mrs Molloy secured another lucrative engagement at the Foundling Hospital. Here, there is little doubt that she used climbing boys. Mrs Molloy had agreed to the hospital contract on condition 'she be allowed to remain' to supervise the work. In 1838, Robert Stevens, the secretary of the society, called at the hospital to ask about Mrs Molloy. The head of one of the departments was sent for, and Mr Stevens asked in how many chimneys did she use her children? The answer was 'in all but one'.

In November the same year, Mrs Molloy was involved in another incident. Three weeks after sweeping a chimney at Abraham's Clothes, Holywell Street (The Strand), the chimney caught fire. When Mrs Molloy arrived, she ordered a child up the heated flue. He stayed quite long enough for her 'to charge an exorbitant fee', then came down claiming the fire was out. The following day the house nearly burned to the ground. The outcome was a heavy claim on the Hand-in-Hand insurance.

127

Accidents and Cruelty

Mrs Bridger was not the only female sweep to cruelly ill-treat her apprentices. When Ann Wilson[8] forced her nine-year-old apprentice John Anderson to climb a hot flue, the heat was so intense that he fainted and died.

Accidental deaths included the unfortunate case of an apprentice called Sharpless. In the summer of 1804, the young boy started sweeping a chimney in Devereux Court. When he reached the upper section of the pot, it crumbled away and the boy fell to the ground. He was taken to St Bartholomew's Hospital but his fractures were so severe that he died. Sharpless was apprenticed to chimney sweep Mrs Whitfield, Little Shire Lane, Temple Bar.

In 1812 charges were made that two 'under age' boys were sold to a chimney sweep named Rose. Charles Barker had sold the boys, William Bellamy and Charles Hinchcliffe to Rose, for the sum of seven shillings each. Barker was charged at Union Hall, Borough, with 'enticing away' the boys and selling them.

Mothers

Unintentional cruelty occurred when mothers sold their children to severe masters. Mary Taylor sold her son to a chimney sweep when he was only six years old. In April 1826, the *Sheffield Iris* reported that 'the unhappy mother', distressed by sores on her son's limbs, had tried to get him released from his apprenticeship. She was refused permission. The magistrate had been informed that sores caused by climbing were inevitable before the skin hardened. Two other women were more fortunate and had their sons returned. *The Climbing Boys' Advocate* (June 1856) published the following letter:

> I Mary Carter, agree to set my son JAMES CARTER to MATTHEW BEGLEY, of Northampton, for the term of 5 years from the date thereof for the sum of 25s per year, and to find him board, lodging, and clothing, for the said term.
> Signed [with a cross].

The agreement was dated 22nd January 1856. Several months later, in reply to a request for her son's wages, Mary received a letter from Matthew Begley:

> Mrs Carter, I received your letter respecting James's wages, and

128

Selling children to the sweep. From *The Climbing Boy's Album*, 1824.

when you was at Northampton you received 7s on account, and he has been here 16 weeks, and I have sent you a 1s worth of stamps, which will make straight up till last Saturday; and I lent him to Mr Hopkins, Chimney Sweep, Bedford, which is a very nice place, and I have had his wages from there, so that is all that is coming to you, so when you want to know anything you can write there.
[unsigned]

When the authorities discovered that Matthew Begley had lent his apprentice to Master Sweep Hopkins, young James was returned to his mother in Leicester.

The case of Mary Davis became legendary. Mrs Davis was the wife of a private in the 2nd Regiment of Foot-Guards. While her husband was away serving under Wellington in the Peninsular War, in order to support herself, her young baby and six-year-old son, Mary went out 'charring and washing'.[9] A neighbour looked after the children. One day, on returning home, she found that the woman had left, taking the boy with her. Every effort to find them proved fruitless. Mary was told that the woman was a native of Leeds, so she set out from London carrying her infant. After walking 106 miles, Mary arrived at the Greyhound Inn, Folkingham. She entered the kitchen to enquire for lodging. Sitting at supper, were a chimney sweep and his boy, who had been cleaning the inn chimneys. As soon as Mary reached the fire-light, the boy rushed to her, exclaiming in frantic tones, 'That's my mother!' In an instant, he was in her arms.

The master sweep explained that he had been on his business in the neighbourhood of Sleaford, where he lived, when he met a ragged woman with a little boy whom she was beating most unmercifully. On inquiry she had told him she was in great distress, that she had a long way to go, that the boy, her son, was very obstinate, and that she did not know how to get him along with her. This led to further conversation that ended in her offering to sell the boy to him as an apprentice for two guineas. The bargain had been struck. The story soon became known in Folkingham, and 'some Christian-hearted individuals' raised a subscription for Mary Davis and her son. A poem written at the time describes:

> ... her son decently clothed
> And restored to his mother, no longer needs creep
> Through lanes, courts, and alleys, a poor little sweep.

Climbing Girls

Until the mid 19th century all working-class children were expected to contribute to the family income, and in many places throughout England young girls as well as boys were employed in sweeping chimneys. Most recorded instances show that the girls generally worked for their parents or close relatives. Master sweeps – both male and female – with family businesses, employed their daughters in the trade when they had insufficient sons, or when the boys grew too large for narrow flues. Girls with their smaller frames could be useful for many years.

In 1819, Benjamin Meggot Forster, a Committee member of the SSNCB, reported that two little girls were employed in sweeping the chimneys of Windsor Castle. Their father was a master sweep by the name of Morgan. Other girls were known to have been employed at Brighton, Headly, (near Barnet, Hertfordshire), Uxbridge, White-chapel, and Witham (Essex). In 1830, a master sweep was charged with maltreating his 11-year-old apprentice. The 'boy' was later discovered to be a young girl who had worked for him since the age of seven.

William Wood from Bowed, Cheshire, remarked; 'some might feel incredulous as to the fact of girls being employed',[10] but he knew of two girls who had been working as climbing sweeps for several years. They lived in Lancashire and he could point out the house where they lived with their father, a master sweep. It is also recorded that a young girl aged six years frequently climbed a seven-inch-square flue.

The use of climbing girls was not confined to Britain. Girls were employed in Nurnberg in 1639. It appears that the practice was stopped only because of opposition from master sweeps who feared for the prospects of their young apprentices. Either the girls were distracting or were better workers... (See Appendix for comparisons with working conditions for girls in other trades.)

Hannah Cullwick

From the diaries of Hannah Cullwick, we make the surprising discovery that chimney sweeping could be an erotic experience. On Friday 16th October 1863, while a maidservant in London, 33-year-old Hannah wrote:

> I lock'd up & waited till half past [ten] till the grate was cool enough & then I took the carpets up & got the tub o'water ready to wash me in – moved the fender & swept ashes up. Stripp'd myself quite naked & put a pair of old boots on tied up my hair & then I got up into the chimney with a brush. There was a lot o'soot & it was soft & warm. Before I swept I pull'd the duster over my eyes, & mouth & I sat on the beam that goes across the middle & crossed my legs along it & I was quite safe & comfortable & out o'sight. I swept lots o'soot down & it come all over me (& I sat ten minutes or more) ... & when I'd swept all round & as far as I could reach I come down ... I was certainly a fright & hideous all over, at least I should o'seem'd so to anybody but Massa...

Hannah wrote her yearly diaries – there were 17 in all – solely for the pleasure of reading them aloud to her lover, Derek Munby. She met Munby, a poet and barrister who she referred to as 'Massa' in 1854, when she was 21 years old. They continued to meet secretly for 17 years. Hannah stopped writing her diaries in 1873 when Munby finally persuaded her to marry him. Hannah had no wish to be 'a Lady', preferring to remain below stairs in the kitchen basement of his chambers in the Temple. The couple lived apart, remaining permanently but secretly married for 36 years until Munby's death.

Family Traders

Ann Russell

When Cheltenham Master Sweep John Russell died in 1843, his wife Ann took over the family business. On 6th January 1844, Ann Russell placed a notice in the *Cheltenham Free Press*. She thanked her husband's clients for their patronage over the past 18 years, and informed them that she had engaged a young man – who had been trading in Bristol for 20 years – to be her foreman. She then 'respectfully' asked for 'a continuance of their support'.

Ann had placed the notice because reports had been circulating about the efficiency of her new foreman. To show he was of good character Ann had a letter printed in the same paper, from Master Sweep and Doctor of Smokey Chimneys, William Bulphin. Writing from 3 Steep Street, Bristol (2nd January 1844), Mr Bulphin confirmed that the foreman was of good character and that he 'knew him as a child and his father before him'.[11] His only fault, according to many in the trade, was that 'he came from Bristol'. (For more information about William Bulphin, see also Chapter 9.)

Ann Russell had not mentioned the name of her foreman, but she had employed James Short and later married him. In 1855 the couple moved from No. 15 Sherborne Street (Ann's late husband's premises) to No 43 in the same street. Their new three-storey home had previously been a beer-house called The Laughing Cat. No more is known about Ann but James Short died in 1869 (see section on Family businesses, Chapter 10).

Marian Dye

The practice of using her own child when sweeping narrow flues led to the accidental death of Mrs Dye's son. Hertford sweep Marian Dye was a formidable size – over six feet tall and she weighed 18 stone. In 1852, one winter morning at around 3 am she set off with her seven-year-old son and their donkey to sweep the chimneys of a mansion known as Goldings.[12] It was the home of Sir Minto Farquhar, MP for Hertford.

On arrival Mrs Dye sent her son up the kitchen flue, then secured the soot-sheet in front of the fireplace. She usually waited outside where she could see the boy emerge from the pot or hear him call from the chimney top. On this occasion, something went wrong. The boy had slipped and lay groaning somewhere in the flue. She heard his cries from the fireplace, but was unable to help him. Because it was

132

too early to wake the household, Marian set off for help. She eventually reached Hertford, delayed and soaked from a fall in the river after attempting a short cut.

Her son was freed by removing brickwork from the chimney. But his tumble into several feet of soot had caused death through suffocation. Sir Minto Farquhar, saddened by the incident joined the campaign for more effective legislation against the use of climbing boys. (See also section on the Dye family, Chapter 10).

Jane Bayes

Jane was born in Holdenby, Nottinghamshire in 1804. She married Richard Bayes from King's Cross, a London sweep who was eight years her senior. Between the years 1830 and 1846, they had four children. In 1845, Jane's husband was working as a master sweep in Northampton. Census returns for 1851 show that both daughters were employed locally (Sarah, 21, as a 'shoe closer' and Mary Ann, 17, as a general servant). Joseph was only 5 years old, but Richard junior, 13, worked as a chimney sweep for his father. Also employed in the business was Journeyman John Stevens, 30, from Clerkenwell.

Five years later 52-year-old Jane Bayes had taken over her husband's Northampton business and was operating as a master sweep in her own right. On 17th May 1856 Jane (and four other master sweeps) signed a public chimney sweepers declaration saying she would abide by the 1842 Act prohibiting climbing of chimneys by children under the age of 21 (see Chapter 9). Jane was still operating her business in 1858 from Silver Street, Northampton.

Sweeping Machines

When concern was growing about the use of children in the sweeping of chimneys, inventors – unknown to the public – quietly began registering patents for chimney-sweeping machines (see Chapter 9). It was not until the Society for the Encouragement of Arts, Manufactures and Commerce took an active interest that machines for sweeping began to appear.

Mrs Bates

Not commonly known was the fact that public enthusiasm (in some quarters) for a better way of sweeping chimneys was generated through the incentive of a lady, Mrs Bates. On 4th November 1802,

Mrs Bates, signing herself 'a Friend to Progress in Social Life', sent a letter to *The St James's Chronicle*:

> In this age of ... improvement, I rejoice when scientific specula-tion can be brought into useful practice ... As men we are inter-ested in whatever concerns humanity, and my proposal being to rescue a class of Citizens from a state of wretched degradation. I hope some will condescend to take it into consideration. Whilst machines and engines are daily invented ... can no contrivance be imagined to sweep our chimnies? Must a number of children be dwarfed and disfigured ... who, if rescued ... might contri-bute to the strength of our Navy, the culture of our fields ... but my design is not to excite useless compassion ... but to set on foot some invention.
>
> The two public patrons [Jonas Hanway and Mrs Montagu, see later] are removed by death; but if a few generous persons would unite and propose a premium for the best-constructed machine to do the work, I doubt it would be speedily accom-plished.

Response to the letter was swift. The following week (Monday 15th November), Charles Baldwin wrote a one-and-half-page editorial comment. He applauded the many 'benevolent Correspondents' who sent their contributions 'to set on foot a subscription for a premium, to the inventor of a machine ...' and offered *The St James's Chronicle* as a medium of Communication'. This resulted in a proposal from Mrs Bates that 'persons interested in offering a premium' should meet on 'February 4th 1803 at the London Coffee House to form an organi-sation and donate money'.[13]

Who was Mrs Bates? Her Christian name is unknown, but she was connected with the 'politically powerful family of Stanhope'. She was married to Eli Bates, a Minister in the Moravian church. When her husband died she gained control of her vast fortune and, although not of the Church, became a 'munificient benefactor ... of the Brethren'.

Mrs Bates's knowledge of chimney sweeps was probably gained through her acquaintance with James Montgomery. The poet's father was a Moravian minister. James Montgomery mentions Mrs Bates in his *Chimney-Sweeper's Friend and Climbing-Boys' Album* (1824), and doubtless, he held her in high esteem. Yet when asked to write a 'memoir of her'[14] after her death, he refused. His reason is thought to have been 'some religious notions entertained by her'.

Although not honoured as a champion of apprentice chimney

sweeps, an inscription on Mrs Bates's tomb testifies: 'She had the merit to obtain for her husband and children, twelve appointments in Church and State.'[15]

Elizabeth Bell

Spinster Elizabeth Bell is the only woman who is known to have invented a chimney sweeping machine. She registered a patent for her invention in 1803. Elizabeth, who lived in Hampstead, Middlesex, described her machine (Patent No 2702) as: 'An Artificial method of Sweeping ... in such a way as to lessen the danger and inconvenience from fire and smoke.' Her method of sweeping chimneys depended upon 'a frame with cross bars' being fitted at the top of the chimney. This would support 'pulleys or rollers leading or conducting a metallic chain or rope from the bottom of the chimney to the top'.

Elizabeth had developed two kinds of apparatus: the first consisted of a wooden prism 'of a convenient length' with levers fixed to the sides, 'each moving severally on its own joint'. The levers would be 'fitted with brushes or brooms of hair or wire'.

The second, and in her opinion preferable method, was 'an elastic sweeper' which was 'eggshaped' and made of wood or leather 'covered with brushes of hair, wire or scrapers'. Her somewhat involved description concludes: 'the apparatus at the bottom of the fireplace consists of a frame of wood so made to cover the opening...' Miss Bell also explains how to 'construct chimnies from blocks or masses of brick or pottery' (A method not dissimilar to present-day chimney construction).

In 1807, Elizabeth Bell submitted 'Improvements' to her sweeping machine (Patent No 3019), suggesting that the frame at the top of the chimney should be made of iron and composed of 'two semicircles', which could be adjusted to fit different sized chimney pots.

I have constructed a small circular brush, with a perforation to permit the chain to pass thro' it; in order to ascend before any of the Sweeping brushes, for the purpose of cleaning the pot...

Elizabeth had adapted her eggshaped elastic sweeper to a square or parallelogram, and improved her cylinder brush by dividing it longitudinally into several pieces 'by means of iron or leather hinges'. As to her wooden frame for the fireplace:

I made it in 2, 3 or more divisions which are attached to each

135

other by means of leather or flexible hinges folded in the manner of bellows.

Unfortunately nothing further was heard of her invention.

Elizabeth Montagu

Ah! drop a tear, for Montagu's no more,
To spread for craving sweeps the May-day store.
The Chimney Sweeps Friend, JAMES MONTGOMERY, 1823

Mrs Montagu became famous during her lifetime and remained so for almost a century afterwards, achieving recognition in high society as well as low. References to her life, her writings and her benevolence towards the London chimney sweeps are found in nearly all works by contemporary writers (see Dickens and Mayhew, Chapter 10). Montagu Square, London, is named after her.

Elizabeth Robinson was born in York, 2nd October 1720. Both her parents were rich and well connected. On 5th August 1742, she married a quiet bespectacled mathematician many years her senior. Her husband, Edward Montagu, was the wealthy owner of coalmines at Denton, Northumberland and MP for Huntingdon.

In 1744, Elizabeth gave birth to her only child, a son, but he died the following September aged 14 months, (see Chapter 10). From 1750 onwards, Mrs Montagu reigned supreme as London's most celebrated hostess. She became known as 'the Blue-Stocking of Bloomsbury'[16] (ladies at her parties wore blue stockings to distinguish them from rival societies). She was described as a most entertaining creature, fat, handsome and witty. But above all, she was intelligent and well liked.

When Edward Montagu died (12th May 1775) he left his wife the Denton Collieries and £7000 a year. The following year Elizabeth turned her attention to house building. Her most ambitious project was a new town house on the north-west corner of Portman Square. The sumptuous mansion, known as Montagu House, was completed on Easter Day 1782 (see Appendix). From that time on, every year on May Day, Elizabeth Montagu entertained the chimney sweeps of London on the lawn in front of Montagu House. The climbing boys were given a shilling each, and a grand feast consisting of 'roast beef and plum pudding'[17] with beer, and dancing afterwards. It was an event eagerly looked forward to.

In 1793, Mrs Hannah More paid a visit to London from New York. In a letter home to her sister she wrote: 'I was invited to dine in

The chimney sweeps at Mrs Montagu's house, Portman Square on May Day, during the 1790's. Water-colour, by T. Hosmer Shepherd.

Portman-Square with the chimney-sweepers on Mayday. A feast I should have liked much had I been well enough.' London Society did not share her opinion. That a lady of such high esteem, moreover, a lady who in June 1791 entertained the King and Queen at Montagu House and shortly afterwards accommodated as many as 700 guests for breakfast in her 'feather-room', could show the same regard for 'little Sooties', to them seemed inconceivable. Consequently, Mrs Montagu's (undisclosed) reason for holding this annual event gave rise to much rumour and a fable that persisted (see Chapter 10). Elizabeth Montagu is also known to have shown compassion towards her colliery workers at Denton. 'Kind-hearted Lady, may thy soul in heaven a blessing reap, Whose bounty at that season flows, to cheer the little sweep.'[18]

Elizabeth Montagu was well acquainted with Master Sweep David Porter. On 2nd April 1800, though a frail old lady of 80, she attended the first meeting of the chimney sweepers' Friendly Society at Mr Porter's house. Mrs Montagu was elected vice-patroness of the society, but died later the same year.

Her brother's son, Matthew, who lived with her and became her heir, continued Mrs Montagu's May Day Feast for several years. He took the name Montagu, and was responsible for publishing her letters and writings. Her best known work was an *Essay on the Writings and*

Genius of Shakespeare (1769) but London sweeps would have remembered her best for her kind-hearted benevolence.

Notes

[1]Lewknor's, After Sir Lewis Lewknor, poet and Master of Ceremonies to James I.
[2]*St Giles of the The Lepers*, Walk 11, Edward C. W. Grey, Longmans, 1905.
[3]*Kirby's Wonderful Museum*, Vol 1, 1803.
[4]*Ibid*
[5]*Gentleman's Magazine*, 1802.
[6]*St James Chronicle*, October, 1802.
[7]*Society for Superseding the Necessity for Climbing Boys*, 1838.
[8]*Ibid*, 1829.
[9]*Chimney Sweepers and Their Friends*, S.W. Partridge & Co, London, 1804.
[10]*Climbing Boys' Advocate*, 1st August, 1856.
[11]Information supplied by Cheltenham Museum.
[12]*The Boy Who Died in a Chimney*, Cyril Heath, *Hertfordshire Countryside*, 1983.
[13]Pamphlet, *England's Climbing Boys*, Professor G.L. Phillips, San Diego State College, 1949.
[14]*Memoirs of James Montgomery*, J. Holland & J. Everett, 1855.
[15]*England in the Age of Hogarth*, Derek Jarrett, 1974.
[16]*Mrs Montagu, Queen of the Blues*, John Busse, 1928.
[17]*The Times*, 1799.
[18]Verse, William Lisle Bowles, 1824.

8

PERSONALITIES

John Cottington

John Cottington was born in Cheapside, London, around 1604. Known as 'Mull'd Sack',[1] he became a highwayman, a debonair adventurer, and the most notorious chimney-sweeping rogue of the 17th century.

John was the youngest of 19 children. His father, a haberdasher of small wares, was reputed at one time to have been quite wealthy, but he was too fond of drink. After his death, the impoverished family had to be looked after by the parish of St Mary-le-bow. In 1612 the overseer of the poor apprenticed John, aged eight, to a chimney sweep. When he was 13, John ran away from his master and started his own chimney-sweeping business.

He became successful and soon had enough money to frequent the local taverns. It was at the Devil Tavern (now part of Childe's Bank, Fleet Street) that he earned the name 'Mull'd Sack'. Sack – a Rhenish wine sold by apothecaries in their shops – was named after the sacks or borrachies in which it was contained. It was usually drunk in a warm or mulled state sweetened with sugar. John became partial to sack and drank nothing else. One evening after drinking too much in the Devil Tavern, he fell in love and agreed to matrimony. The ceremony took place at the Fleet Prison. However, when the time came 'to be bedded', John discovered his partner was the well-known hermaphrodite, Aniseed-Water Robin.

Life then took a different course for Mulled Sack. Although continuing to trade as a chimney sweep he became increasingly attracted to a life of crime. Women were his undoing. His first conquests were five women barbers. They were known throughout the City as the five celebrated shavers of Drury Lane. Mulled Sack wasted money on these 'furies' until their true characters were revealed.

> Did you ever hear the like,
> Or ever hear the fame
> Of five women barbers
> That lived in Drury Lane?...
>
> *Contemporary ballad*

139

After this unpromising start, Mulled Sack's fortunes took an upward turn. His chimney-sweeping clients were mostly wealthy traders, and 'his gentle air and mien, though a chimney sweeper, made a rich Merchant's wife in March Lane enamoured with him.' Their liaison did not last long, however; indeed he only managed to 'get above £120 by her' before she became ill and died. Biographers hint that Mulled Sack was the father of her last child.

Having lost his benefactress, Mulled Sack became an accomplished robber and 'soon rose to top man in that profession'. He dressed genteelly and 'carried himself with good deportment towards the ladies', combining charm and ruthlessness to great effect.

Known for his royalist sympathies he stole a valuable gold and diamond watch from Lady Fairfax (wife of a General in Cromwell's Parliament). Mulled Sack, with some of his cronies, waited until she attended a lecture at St Martin's Church (Ludgate) and removed a pin from her coach wheel 'which was going upwards through the gate'. The wheel fell off. Gallantly offering his arm, Mulled Sack pushed aside her gentleman usher and led her through the gate and into the church. While doing so he cut the watch chain that hung from her waist.

Mulled Sack practised many other ploys to rob unsuspecting citizens, and emboldened by his successes, he took to the road. The highwayman era was at its height. London had no highway planning authority and the amount of wheeled traffic steadily increased. Mulled Sack was favoured with good luck. In company with a Captain Horne, the two robbed Oliver Cromwell on Hounslow Heath. Pursuit was swift. Captain Horne was captured but Mulled Sack escaped. Still professing royalist sympathies, he could not resist the challenge of robbing a pay waggon carrying £4,000 for Cromwell's troops on its way to Oxford. It was well guarded so he decided to take five or six accomplices. At twilight, when the waggon passed Wheatley, at the foot of Shotover Hill, Mulled Sack and his companions ambushed the troopers, furiously attacking them with pistols and swords. The soldiers, thinking they were outnumbered, fled. Several passengers who had travelled with the waggon for safety were left abandoned and terrified. Mulled Sack, ever the gentleman, reassured them by declaring that he was only 'after the Commonwealth's money, which those great thieves of Westminster had fleeced out of the public'.

In time, Mulled Sack became the wealthiest highwayman of his age. He dressed with the extravagance of a merchant, earning the reputation that he 'constantly wore a watchmaker's and jeweller's shop in his pocket, and could at any time command a thousand pounds'.

Eventually, however, he was brought to trial. His spies told him that the General Receiver's Office at Reading was to send £6,000 up to London by an ammunition wain (waggon) under escort. The money reached its destination but not via the convoy. Mulled Sack was suspected and sent to Reading prison. During his trial at Abingdon Assizes, he is thought to have bribed the jury. Despite Judge Jermyn having done all he could to convict him (there being very good circumstantial proof that he had been seen in the town that very night) he was acquitted.

Shortly after, Mulled Sack committed a more serious crime. He had fallen in love with the wife of John Bridges. After an affair lasting four years, he killed Mr Bridges and escaped abroad. Despite Mulled Sack's reputed loyalty to the King, he nevertheless robbed Charles of silver plate valued at £1,500 during the King's exile at Cologne. Mulled Sack later returned to England and promised to supply Cromwell with secret papers stolen from the King (hoping possibly to secure a pardon). It transpired that Cromwell did not receive the papers. Mulled Sack was arrested and sent to Newgate gaol.

In April 1659, John Cottington, aged 55, was sentenced to death for the murder of John Bridges, and hanged at Smithfield Rounds.

Mulled Sack's Portrait

Mulled Sack was immortalised in an exceptional full-length portrait. Engraved during the early years of his life (some sources say 1630), James Caulfield's *Printsellers Chronicle* (1814), describes MULLD:-SAKE as 'a fantastic and humorous Chimney-Sweeper, Highwayman and Murderer'.

Represented as a 'chimney-sweep-cum-courtier,' he is clean-shaven except for a thin drooping moustache and narrow sideburns. His hair is short (although it may have been tied back). A flat cap, worn rakishly to the left and decorated with five feathers, is more in keeping with mid-16th-century Tudor headwear. The width of his ornate lace collar shows he was a royalist. The scarf around his right arm and the right shoe with a 'shoe rose' show off the courtly fashion.

On his left leg, Mulled Sack wears a high boot with turned down top and scarf. The spur on his boot and sword hung on the left side, show him as a man of action. His long cloak is tucked up revealing knee-length breeches and nether stocks (stockings). In his left hand he carries a long pole with an upturned horn on the end. The horn could be representative of the chimney-sweeping trade or indicate his status as a felon (the King's messenger blew three blasts on a horn to proclaim an outlaw).

The fascination of Mulled Sack's portrait lies in the details depicting

MULLED SACK

P.N.C

I walke the Strand, and Westminster; and scorne
to march i'th, Cittie, though I beare the Horne.
My Feather, and my yellow Band accord
to proue me Courtier: My Boote Spurr, and; Sword

My smokinge Pipe, Scarfe, Garter Rose on shoe,
showe my braue minde t'affect what Gallants doe.
I singe, dance, drinke, and merrily passe the day,
and like a Chimney Sweepe all care away

Mulled Sack. (Sketch by P N Cullingford, after an etching attributed to Elstrack, prior to 1630) his trade. He carries the tools of a chimney sweep. A large soot-sack hangs down his back and two poles are carried over his right shoulder. Tightly bound on the end of one is a small holly bush. His coat is ripped and the fingers of his right hand grip a long clay pipe.

In the foreground of the illustration, Mulled Sack strides arrogantly along a cobbled road. In the background is a street with several shops and houses. The shops are open-fronted and chimneys are much in evidence. Smoke billows from two of the chimneys and also from Mulled Sack's pipe. Emerging from a dual chimney top are the head and torso of a young boy. He triumphantly brandishes a scraper. The boy, dressed in a loose-fitting shirt with a hood, represents John in his youth.

Under the portrait are eight lines of verse. The rhyme – written in early 17th century script – sums up Mulled Sack's appearance and attitude to life:

> I walke the Strand and Westminster, and scorne
> To march i' the cittie though I beare the horne,
> My feather and my yellow band accord
> To prove me courtier; my boote, spurr and sword,
> My smokinge pipe, scarfe, garter rose on shoe,
> Showe my brave minde t'affect what gallants doe.
> I singe, dance, drink, and merrily passe the day,
> And like a chimney sweepe all care away.

Jack Hall

Although not as famous as John Cottington, John (Jack) Hall also achieved notoriety as a highwayman. Jack was born in 1675. His parents lived at Bishop's Head Court off Gray's Inn Lane. The family were very poor and young Jack was sold to a chimney sweep for the sum of one guinea (105p).

According to Captain Alexander Smith's *Lives of the Highwaymen* (1719), Jack took to stealing and became 'as dextrous in picking a pocket as ever he was in sweeping a chimney'. Unlike Mulled Sack, Jack was frequently caught. When only seven years old, he was convicted at the Old Bailey for stealing a pair of shoes and sentenced to a whipping at the cart's tail. Undeterred, his life of crime (in and out of chimney sweeping) continued for the next 18 years.

When Jack was 25 he was caught breaking into the house of Jonathan Bretail and sentenced to transportation to the American colonies. On this occasion, luck was with him and he escaped from the convict ship. From then on he took to highway robbery; stealing portmanteaus from coaches. In 1702 he was arrested and sent to Bridewell for two years. In prison, he suffered the disfigurement of cheek branding (possibly with F for felon, or T for thief). When released, his misdemeanours could only be carried out at night, so he embarked on 'faggot and storm'; breaking into houses and gagging the occupants.

One evening after midnight, Jack and two fellow villains broke into Clare's bakery in Hackney. They surprised the journeymen and apprentice who were baking bread, and threw them into the kneading-trough.[2] Jack guarded them with a rusty single-edged sword while the others went upstairs. Mr Clare and his wife were in bed, with their six-year-old granddaughter in a truckle bed beside them. When Mr Clare refused to hand over his money, Jack was called. The elderly gentleman was so alarmed at Jack's appearance and threat to his granddaughter: ('D...n me,' said Jack, 'if I won't bake the child in a pie and eat it,') that he pulled a small leather-bound chest from under the bed. The gang departed with 78 guineas in gold (£81 18s).

Eventually, after two other imprisonments and acquittals, Jack Hall was arrested with his companions for a burglary at the house of Captain Guyon, near Stepney. All three were convicted and hanged at Tyburn on December 7th 1707. As with Mulled Sack, the legend of Jack Hall lived on. A contemporary tract, *Memoirs of The Right Villainous Jack Hall* (1717), describes in grisly detail the conditions of Jack's sojourn in Newgate gaol. On a more cheerful note, there were a number of Jack Hall ballads. Ballads were printed on one side of sheets of paper known as 'broadsides' and sold in the streets. The supposedly 'true confessions' of past criminals were very popular.

The Ballad of Jack Hall

My name is Jack Hall, chimney sweep, chimney sweep.
My name is Jack Hall, and I'll rob both great and small.

Chorus:
My neck shall pay for all when I die, when I die.
[continued in Appendix]

In addition to ballads, rogues that caught the public fancy were satirised in theatrical productions, and became the subject of etchings sold in the streets. An early print by William Hogarth, *A Just View of the British Stage* (1724) shows up the hypocrisy of the theatre. In his print, Hogarth makes fun of the 'high art' of producing pantomimes

144

about a thief's life. In the centre of the print, depicting a crowd scene in Newgate gaol, the tragic actor Barton Booth is shown holding a little puppet figure of Jack Hall. The sweep with his brush is wearing the frilled collar of a clown. He is being dangled from the actor's hand over one of the holes of a three-seater privy. Words under the print describe the scene.

'This print Represents the Rehearsing a new Farce that will Include ye two famous Entertainments Dr Faustus & Harlequin Shepherd to wth will be added Scaramouch Jack Hall the Chimney-Sweeper's Escape from Newgate through ye Privy, with ye Comical Humours of Ben Johnson's Ghost. Concluding with the Hay-Dance Performed in ye air ... Bricks, Rubbish &c, will be real, but the Excrement upon Jack Hall will be made of chew'd gingerbread to prevent offence.'

In her biography of Hogarth (1997), Jenny Uglow explains that Hogarth chose this scene because Jack Hall became famous for escaping from Newgate gaol into the sewers by squeezing through the privies.

Although Jack evaded transportation to America, his notoriety was celebrated in the colonies. His name was changed from Jack to 'Sam,' and there were numerous variations of his ballad. One particular version was favoured by The Adventure Campfire Club, Berkeley, California (see Appendix).

David Porter

David Porter was born in 1747. He became the wealthiest and most influential master sweep of his era.

It was my lot to be born a Chimney Sweeper; I swept chimnies nine years, and laboured under the disadvantages common to a chimney sweeping boy.[3]

David Porter, 1792

According to Samuel Smiles, 'in his early boyhood Porter was kidnapped for a sweep'.[4] How this fanciful notion came about remains a mystery. David learned the chimney sweeping trade from his father, Stephen Porter.

Mr Porter senior had served an apprenticeship with a London sweep

145

living in wretched conditions. When old enough he travelled around as a country sweep. In 1762, he settled in Boongate, Peterborough with his wife Mary and their two sons. Stephen Porter died of chimney sweeps' cancer four years later, aged 38. He was buried in St John's Churchyard on 12th July 1766.[5]

At the time of their father's death, both boys were self-supporting. John (the elder) had become a blacksmith, and David a chimney sweeper. For two years after his father's death, David tried something else for a living, then returned to sweeping chimneys. In his first year as a travelling sweep, he experienced some of the discomforts of the trade. During slack summer months, he managed to save money by working on Lincolnshire farms as a harvester.

David, who had never attended school, possessed enough 'extraordinary energy of body and mind'[6] to become proficient in literacy skills. Later in life, he confessed 'he wrote at the expense of his pillow, mostly before 6 am, and published at the expense of his pocket, giving away what he wrote with thanks to all who did him the favour of wanting to read.'

On 26th April 1770, David Porter married Edith Glithero, (daughter of Elizabeth and John Glithero, a stone mason from Wansford). The young couple moved to London where David quickly established himself as a master sweep. By 1774, David's business had prospered to such an extent that he was able to move to the affluent West End. There he bought premises; a house and soot-yard in the parish of St Mary-le-bone, at No 9 Little Welbeck Street.

Edith gave birth to two children; Mary Elizabeth (baptised 7th April 1771), and Stephen (13th September 1772). After moving to Welbeck Street, three more children were born. Two sons died in infancy. A second daughter, Prudence (baptised 12th July 1779), lived to be old enough to nurse one of her father's apprentices, who was ill with 'a Putrid Fever'. The boy recovered, but Prudence caught the same fever and died. (An illegitimate son was born in 1801, see later.)

During the 1770s, David Porter and philanthropist Jonas Hanway became firm friends. Their collaboration with other London master sweeps in 1780 resulted in the forming of a Friendly Society to promote the interests of chimney sweepers. The first meeting of the society took place at The Swan, Chandos Street, Covent Garden. David Porter drew up articles, a subscription was raised and Jonas Hanway appointed treasurer. Despite such a promising start, subsequent meetings became so infrequent and disorganised that Mr Porter felt obliged to return subscriptions and disband the society.

David's business continued to flourish. By 1783, he claimed to have run away with 'the bulk of the business' of the fashionable West End.

146

His impressively scrolled trade card, topped by a Royal Coat of Arms, advertised the patronage of the King's daughter, HRH Princess Amelia. Furthermore, the master sweep professed to rectifying and making operable 'smoakey chimnies and Coppers', thought incurable by 'Eminent professors', claiming 'No cure no pay'.

The illustrated card shows Mr Porter with four apprentices and a well-dressed client. The small boys have sacks over their shoulders and carry an assortment of short-handled brushes and scrapers. They are adequately clothed and all wear shoes. One lad holds a long striped pole, which appears to be flaming at the top (this could be a linkboy's torch for lighting the way during early winter mornings). Additional wording on the card refers to the brass cap badges worn by the boys showing David Porter's name. The master sweep also ran a lucrative soot business.

When the 1788 Chimney Sweeping Act was passed David Porter considered the Bill to be so 'mangled as to destroy its effect'. He objected to the restrictions on 'calling the streets' because it meant that journeymen who had completed their apprenticeship would have difficulty finding employment, and the bill did nothing to help their cause.

In 1792, still deeply critical of the Chimney Sweeping Act, David Porter published his *Considerations on the Present State of Chimney Sweepers*. He pointed out that boys continued to be hired out, and were still inadequately clothed. Among his list of 30 proposals, he advocated that: master sweeps should 'set aside one uniform for one year for Sunday', and apprentices should be sent to a central Sunday school. Funds could be raised through public subscription and officials appointed to supervise each apprentice. Furthermore, boys who had reached the age of 16 and did not want to continue in the trade should be apprenticed to another trade.

In 1795, still retaining his yard at No 9, Mr Porter moved with his family to No 7 Little Welbeck Street, where, five years later, several London master sweeps met and formed the new Friendly Society. Among the officers who attended were William Wilberforce, the Bishop of Durham, and Elizabeth Montagu. David Porter drew up articles of agreement and he was appointed treasurer.

The society's aims were to protect and instruct chimney sweeps' apprentices, and enforce the 1788 Chimney Sweeping Regulations. To this end, Mr Porter was asked to revise and republish his *Considerations*. Unfortunately the Friendly Society, attracting only high-class masters, soon foundered.

Although continuing to take an active interest in the welfare of chimney sweeps, David Porter diversified his interests in 1803, and became a builder and property developer. In March 1805, the

Mary-le-bone Vestry (Town Council) elected him onto their committee, where he served as a vestryman for 14 years.

Proving to be an astute businessman, he eventually gave up chimney sweeping. When pastureland on the estate of Henry William Portman in Mary-le-bone was offered for rural development, Mr Porter bought many of the ground leases. In 1811, he moved from Welbeck Street to No 15, Park Place. The prestigious corner-house in Upper Baker Street (now 29 Park Road) where he had a coach-house and stables, was close to Regent's Park, and well suited his wealth and status.

He built houses and sub-let to tenants so rapidly that by 1812, the greater part of the Portman Estate[7] had been leased to him. Apart from his *Considerations* Mr Porter's most lasting venture was the building of Montagu Square. The squares (some sources couple it with its neighbour, Bryanston Square) of high class housing were built on land formerly known as Apple Village; a small hamlet of cottages with a large pond. (During his days as a master sweep, Mr. Porter's apprentices had swept the chimneys of Apple village.) The Georgian terraced squares, built in the 'Brighton fashion',[8] were reputed to be 'the best examples of well constructed town residences' of their day.

In 1810, during the building of the squares, David Porter roped off an area in Montagu Square and, following the example of the Honourable Mrs Montagu, lavishly entertained his workmen and their families to a substantial feast. The occasion was George III's Jubilee. Observers noted there was much 'conviviality and harmony around the festive board'. The squares were completed in 1813.

Five years later, David Porter was called to give evidence before a House of Lords committee. The committee were considering a bill for The Better Regulation of Chimney Sweepers and their apprentices. Perversely (or so it appeared), Mr Porter argued with convincing eloquence against the bill. He was unwavering in his conviction that a chimney could only be cleaned adequately by a climbing boy. In his own writings (*Considerations* etc.) David Porter admitted that the task was arduous, and that there was a degree of misery which should be alleviated. He explained to the committee that boys should be properly trained, and that when living in Welbeck Street he had a chimney purposely built, in which to train his apprentices.

Mr Porter's reputation as a reformer was slightly tarnished when further evidence to the committee revealed that a young climbing boy had suffocated in a flue in Cumberland Street, the flue having been built by Mr Porter. The fatality was one of five deaths occurring in 1817. In defence of his horizontal flues, Mr Porter was of the opinion that no flue was too dangerous for a boy of eight. It was a question of technique; 'the boy should have had another to take the soot as he

148

Montagu Square, built by David Porter, as it is today.

travelled on, and then the Accident would not have happened.' The bill was rejected.

David Porter died on 31st May 1819, aged 72 years. Present day residents of Marlebone will be familiar with place names associated with him: Porters Street, David Mews, Portman Mansions (built by him) Montagu Square etc. (see Appendix).

Worthing Vyse

Whilst still a young journeyman, Worthing Vyse wrote a short account of his life as a climbing boy. Abandoned as a baby in the summer of 1817, he had been found under a tree near Worthing, on the Sussex coast. His rescuer was a travelling tinker named Vyse.

For the first five years of his life, strolling gypsies looked after Worthing. When the gypsies eventually took lodgings in Essex Street, Whitechapel, Worthing was too young to find work. After begging on the streets, he 'engaged' himself to a chimney sweeper. It happened to be May Day, and to the destitute seven-year-old, the apprentice climbing-boys 'appeared happier, merrier, and better off than any boy

149

Worthing Vyse was found under a tree by a travelling tinker, c 1817.

besides'.[9] His new master 'pretended to bind' him as an apprentice. Worthing was still working for the same master sweep 10 years later when he wrote of the 'privileges, and preservations' of the trade:

My master is a Chimney Sweeper and Nightman; you may see this on all his cards and bills. A Nightman is a person who undertakes to clean out vaults that contain privy soil. By an Act of Parliament, this must be done in the middle of the night, consequently I have been called upon at midnight to strip and pass through a narrow aperture, and stand up above my knees in privy soil for the purpose of filling the bucket. In Winter it is extremely cold, and when I first enter it, it makes me shudder and shake as though I have an ague. The men on some occasions have supplied me with gin, as they said to keep out the cold, but this only made me worse, for that and the offensive odour of the place made me sick. I had therefore no alternative but to fill the buckets as fast as I could, to insure a speedy liberation from a place as disgusting as can well be imagined. As soon as my task is performed I am drawn through the aperture to breathe a purer air.

150

One of the party procures a mop and pail of cold water, when I am immediately dealt with the same as a coach wheel under the hands of a groom; after which, my shirt and other sable habiliments are restored to their proper places, and it is then found that Worthing Vyse has just done time enough to begin his morning's work of chimney sweeping.

Worthing was particularly grateful for Sunday schools. He well remembered the Sunday morning when he and three other climbing boys were in their living quarters in the master's cellar, when they overheard three gentlemen inquiring how many climbing boys their master had: 'We burst open the trap door that leads into the cellar from the street, and all four of us made our appearance.' Within the week they were given clothes, and on the following Sunday morning, 'a wash-tub with hot water, soap, flannels, and towels'. When they were taken upstairs and dressed in their new clothes, they scarcely recognised each other. To Worthing it was a memorable day, for apart from being thoroughly washed for the first time in four years, it was his first experience of wearing stockings. Later, at the Sunday school, they found themselves in the company of 50 or so other apprentices. Within three months, Worthing had learned to read. He was then allowed to go one evening a week to learn writing.

George Elson

Chimney sweeping is a needful and honest calling, but the sweeps do not sufficiently estimate the character it should bear.

Master Sweep, George Elson

In the year 1900, George Elson published his autobiography. Memories of his boyhood are recalled in such detail that they add a new perspective to the story of apprentice climbing boys. George was born in Northampton on 19th May 1833. His father, a hawker of haberdashery, died of drink while George was still young. Because the family were destitute his mother, elder brother Charlie and other brothers and sisters were sent to the workhouse.

Later, the family was transferred to the Lutterworth Union in Leicester (the parish of George's grandfather). For a while George travelled around the country with his grandfather, also a hawker. Then, hearing from Charlie that their mother had remarried, the boys went to live with her in Leicester. Their stepfather was a potter and dealer in earthenware. Life was hard with a new baby to support and there was little

151

money, so George and Charlie ran away. George was seven at the time and Charlie ten.

George's career as a country chimney sweep began when the brothers were befriended by a master sweep outside Long Bennington, (eight miles from Newark). George remained with his first master for seven months. During this time, he accompanied his master's son, journeying up to ten miles outside Newark to sweep chimneys. They left at 3 or 4 am without breakfast and when poorer householders were unable to give them food, they went hungry until the evening.

> In this way we would often sleep out for the best part of the week, returning to Newark on Saturday – a time I would long for, as it meant rest, clean clothes, and the luxury of hot meals.

After leaving his first master, George and Charlie, who had been working for a master sweep in Lincoln, decided to set up their own business. They got a blacksmith to make up a steel scraper; bought a brush at the grocers, and a coarse cloth, needles, and thread, at the drapers. There seemed to be no problem finding chimneys to sweep and business went well. George did the climbing and Charlie 'attended at the fireplace'.

> With thirteen shillings in my pocket, I felt quite rich, though my clothes did not give that appearance. A ragged shirt, trousers, black with soot, were augmented by a swallow-tailed coat, many sizes too large. The tails of the coat flapped about my legs but an inch above my bare feet, and the brass livery buttons with which it was adorned shone out gaily from the sombre background. With my climbing-cap on my head, and some implements under my arm, I must have cut a comical figure.

From time to time, the brothers based their business in Loughborough, returning to their mother each evening. Despite being happy at home and 'alternately coaxed and threatened' by both parents to leave their trade, the boys chose to continue.

They were treated with kindness and hospitality at the Monastery of St Bernard in Charnwood Forest (Leicester), and George returned several times during his climbing boy days. At first, the monastery was little more than a four-roomed cottage, with a tiny chapel and belfry. After sweeping the chimneys the boys helped the monks cultivate their garden, where they 'sowed the soot'.[10] In 1841, the small community consisted of six English Cistercian monks and their Prior, Bernard Palmer.

Two years later, while working for two poor master sweeps in Leicester, George revisited the monastery (see Appendix). He was astonished to see a group of 'massive buildings'. His master had been engaged to 'core' the new chimneys. This, of course, was George's job. Fortunately they were free of masonry and did not take too long. He and his master then 'enjoyed a plenty of the good monk's soup and roast beef'. It happened to be a public holiday and George and his master joined other sweeps in a 'picnic party':

Mount St Bernard Abbey, Abbey Church and guest house.

A gratuitous supply of the Monastery ale served to make the whole party very merry. At dusk we . . .drove homewards, singing by the way the *Friar of Orders Grey* and the *Monks are Jolly good Fellows*.

George's happy episode with the monks was followed by two sudden deaths. George's master (the senior partner) 'pined away' after the death of his wife Bessy. George had loved hearing Bessy sing and, saddened by her death left soon after. (George's younger brother replaced him, working for the remaining partner.)

George recalls that in bad weather, a 'haven's rest' was the village blacksmith's shop. Here shelter was never denied, and mounting the forge in front of the blazing fire, he would discuss the gossip of the day with the brawny wielder of the hammer:

153

There many a hundred times have I warmed my cold bare feet and dried my wet clothes, and partaken of a scant meal, in thankful return for which I have sung to both Blacksmith and his plough-boy visitors.

An enjoyable period was spent with a respectable master and mistress in Bedfordshire. His employers, who were a 'credit to the trade', lived in a large well-furnished house with comfortable premises for their apprentices. Favoured with the patronage of the gentry, they possessed a first-rate business. It was a treat to sweep the chimneys of the large halls that surrounded Bedford because of the 'perks' (small donations of suitable cash).

A favourite place was that of one lady who provided a sumptuous breakfast for whoever swept her kitchen chimney. Furthermore, when the sweeper went to the front window of a room 'where sat the venerable Mistress', and made a bow, they were rewarded with a shilling. Not, George hastens to add, that they ever wanted for anything; their master kept them well fed and even provided a horse and cart so that they could drive to work. He was also a local preacher (though, it must be noted, none of his apprentices went to church, through lack of suitable clothes).

When working for his Bedford master, George slipped while cleaning a kitchen chimney. The large flue, 5′ × 3′ in a house close to Woburn Abbey, was a type disliked by George. He reached the top without mishap, but coming down lost his hold and was unable to break his fall except by outspread hands and feet. On reaching the fireplace, he found the toes of his right foot torn open to the bone and bleeding. The mistress of the house sent for the doctor who bandaged George's toes and advised him to get some rest and treatment in Bedford. 'I did so, but found it a painful task to walk 18 miles.' George's toes healed in time but left a black ring marking his injuries.

Although George mentions in his autobiography that he avidly read everything his 'slender purse' could afford, he never went to school. At first, his reading material was restricted to newspapers, the *London Journal*, and other cheap miscellany. At a later stage in his boyhood, when employed by Tom Bale in Northampton, he learned to appreciate the Bible. George's account of himself, Tom Bale, and their moke (donkey), is particularly memorable. The donkey – which George grew to love – had been purchased to carry soot to a farmer who used it all the year round. When 'not otherwise burdened' George rode him.

A quaintly grotesque pair we must have looked. Tom, burly and

154

stately even in his soot-begrimed clothing, strode boldly along, the while I, in ragged shirt and knickerbockers, with bare legs as black as the top hat which I gravely wore, sat perched on the back of the donkey, who vainly endeavoured to keep pace with Tom's rapid stride. The top hat I wore was a gift from one of our patrons, as was the one Tom wore. I cannot recall if it was a fashionable shape, even had it been, I am afraid the fact would have been somewhat disguised, as, having been concertinered once or twice, some of the beautiful curves it originally possessed had been distorted.

Tom had paid 2s 6d for the donkey. When in a good mood it galloped at a fair pace for a good hundred yards, 'to show he could do so'. Although the donkey never bit anyone it possessed a powerful kick, and had an 'awkward knack' of stopping in the middle of the road when it saw a cart or waggon approaching. Tom, however, had perfected a simple cure for the donkey's kicking habits. The large man would 'mount him and hold up one of the moke's forelegs with his right foot, leaving him but three to stand on'. The discomforted donkey neither cared for his master's 14 stones nor liked being laughed at, and soon learned its lesson.

George's education was completed by observing and appreciating 'all that was beautiful in art', not only in the great houses of their clients, but also in humble cottages. George and Charlie acquired a large collection of books. They were mostly on travel and biography and had to be carried around strapped to their backs.

On their own again, they travelled north. As it was summer and warm, the two lads sat by the roadside and examined each other's library. They attracted much attention. Passers-by were amazed that two chimney-sweeping boys could own so many books. The situation became embarrassing, and when it was suggested that the books might have been stolen the brothers quickly sought refuge in Sherwood Forest. They decided to sell their books. A small newsagent offered far more than they expected and George and his brother journeyed on to York, Harrogate and Rippon. In Rippon, they greatly enjoyed the races.

Despite the Chimney Sweeping Act (1840) banning the apprenticing of boys under the age of 16 years, George makes no mention of ever being apprenticed or of having signed an indenture.

In 1851, aged 18 years, George journeyed to London with Charlie and found employment with a master sweep in Camden Town. Although his brother persuaded him to return to the country for a time the 'stirring life and business' of London attracted George back to the capital. He found work with a high master sweep in Windmill Street, Haymarket. His master's customers were the gentry and trades-people near Leicester Square, Piccadilly and Oxford Street. George was taught to 'work the machines', and paid a man's wages. During his first eight months in London, George enjoyed drinking and smoking with other young journeymen in the taverns. Then, wanting to better himself he moved away to a quieter part of the Metropolis.

George Elson, like David Porter (50 years before), proved that a poor background was no hindrance to self-education. Living comfortably with a good master and mistress, George began to improve his 'personal attainments'. For the next ten years, he read avidly. Starting with the *History of England* (Hume and Smallet); he read *Uncle Tom's Cabin*, Fox's *Book of Martyrs*, Cowper, Burns, and Elizabeth Cook. He attended lectures on history and science and paid visits to Westminster Abbey, the Tower and The National Gallery. Later he witnessed the lying-in-state of the Duke of Wellington at the Chelsea Hospital. His favourite (weekly) newspaper was the *News of the World*.

Aged 21, he became patriotic, closely following reports of the Indian Mutiny, the Crimean and Sardinian Wars. After joining the Congregational church, he remained sober for two years. Then, meeting up with his brother who was working for a master in High Holborn, they 'went on a binge'. George gave up drinking. He signed a 'pledge' on 27th January 1857, aged 24 and remained teetotal for the rest of his life.

After studying physiology and dietetics, George was asked to 'speak on the platform' and serve on committees. To his dismay, he found he was no good at public speaking. He considered his personal life to be 'most successful', with his choice of wife 'well made'. Although George's wife is never mentioned by name, she bore him two healthy children. He now had his own business as a master sweep. Managing to get good connections, he did well for ten years, even supporting his mother who was dependent upon him until she died in 1863.

For a while George had to give up his chimney-sweeping business because of ill health and a near-fatal act of bravery. The cause and nature of George's illness is unknown, but he managed to keep it under control through his own efforts. After trying different treatments he went to Margate and bathed in the sea every morning. This remedy dramatically improved his health, and he continued to swim daily in the Serpentine. Gradually though, feeling 'unfit for the work', George sold his business to another sweep for £60 and settled with his family in Teddington village close to the Thames and Bushey Park. This decision was taken after involvement in a serious incident.

Late in the afternoon, Tuesday 26th April 1866, George was about to sweep the kitchen chimney of a gentleman's house, and had just 'unstrapped the machine' and fastened his cloth, when a distraught housemaid rushed into the kitchen. She had disturbed thieves in the house. George immediately gave chase. Following through the gardens, he managed to catch up with them. Unfortunately, they turned out to be three violent criminals wanted by the police. They turned on George one with a 'terrible weapon' – and beat him so savagely he almost died.

Their trial took place in the Old Bailey during the first week in June. With 48 convictions between them, they were sentenced to 15–21 years' imprisonment. George's appearance in court caused quite a stir. He was so 'slightly built' that it seemed incredible that the 'little fellow' should attempt to capture the men in the dock. For his bravery, George received one sovereign from the Commissioner of Police, and £10 from the Judge who sympathised with George's suffering. Donations were given by kind friends and well wishers, namely: the Right Hon. the Earl of Airlie, Lord Macaulay, Sir James South, Mr Thorneycroft, and the eminent painter, Mr Holman Hunt RA.

Now that he lived near the Thames, George swam every day. He also attended lectures and 1d readings of The Mutual Instruction Society, and read in their extensive library. Meanwhile he had restarted his chimney-sweeping business and taken on another sweep. George was appointed Secretary of The Mutual Society and held the position for three years, with a nominal salary of £5 per annum. With justifiable pride he points out the irony of his situation: for long years he had been 'an outcast of society ... and now while yet a chimney-sweep, thought worthy of a post of trust'.

George finally gave up chimney sweeping, again feeling unfit, he confessed: 'I was beginning to feel ashamed of it.' In 30 years he had climbed 'thousands of chimneys of every kind; ... thirty before break-fast, 50 in one day ... clambered up and onto the steepest and highest of house-tops for the purpose of sweeping out cowls, pots and wind-guards'. Then 'over an area of half London' he had 'swept with the machine, also the ball and line, all sorts of chimneys and flues'.

The Elson family took their first trip on the new railway to Glouce-ster, then to Hereford, where George opened a haberdashery and agency for maps and charts. While travelling through Worcester about his business, he visited a swimming bath. The proprietor was adver-tising for a swimming master for his Turkish baths. George applied and got the job. As he observed himself, this was a job contrast 'with a vengeance'. Instead of doctoring chimneys with soot-bag and brush, he was 'installed' in a hotter than tropical atmosphere doctoring men.

157

After three years, George took a position as shampooer at Leamington Turkish baths. George's wife assisted him with the massaging and they became prosperous enough to afford servants.

George Elson's first publication (of 20 minutes reading) was entitled *A Shampooer's View of the Turkish Bath*. It was well received. In 1900, aged 67, he published his autobiography: *The Last of the Climbing Boys*.

Notes

[1] Mulled Sack: earliest recorded biography, *Lives of Highwaymen*, Captain Alexander Smith, 1719, also *Biographical History of England*, Rev. J. Grainger.
[2] *Half-Hours with the Highwaymen*, Vol 1, Charles George Harper, 1908.
[3] *Considerations On The Present State of Chimney Sweepers*, David Porter, 1792.
[4] *Self-Help*, Samuel Smiles, 1859.
[5] *A Short Life of David Porter of St Marylebone, 1747–1819*, Sonia Addis-Smith, 1993 (descendant of David Charles Porter).
[6] *Report to The Society For Improving the Condition of The Poor*, Sir Thomas Bernard, 1798.
[7] *The Red Book of Leases*, Portman Estate office: 330 leases, referring to over 700 properties, recorded by Sonia Addis-Smith, 1978.
[8] *Marlebone Squares*, G. Mackenzie, History of Marylebone, Smith, 1833.
[9] *The Adventures of Worthing Vyse, a climbing boy*, autobiography c. 1830.
[10] Mr Ambrose Lisle Phillips gave the monks 227 acres of forest.

9

THE MACHINE CONTROVERSEY

PART 1: CHIMNEY SWEEPING MACHINES

Now that we are familiar with the fitted rods and circular brush-heads used by present-day sweeps, and remembering how sweeps in the 16th century solved the problem of sweeping long flues by tying poles together, it is hard to imagine how such a simple device could take so long to invent. The truth is appliances were available towards the end of the 18th century but they were unwelcome, and machines for sweeping chimneys were not in general use until 1875. The reasons for this were far from simple.

Patents (18th Century)

Procedure for Patents

For any inventor it was a sensible precaution to register or patent their hitherto untried machine. Official registration was proof of ownership should there be any imitations. Before 1852, though, the formalities of registration were so daunting that a large number of the population was automatically precluded. Registration was tedious and costly and patentees needed to be literate and moderately well off.

In 1850, Dickens published a satirical short story about the system in his new weekly periodical *Household Words*. In *The Poor Man's Tale of a Patent*, Dickens portrays, with telling insight, what happens when 'Old Tom' (aged 56) who works in a shop in Birmingham and is married with six children, decides to patent his own invention. Tom had to follow a set procedure: patentees first prepared a written specification describing the invention and the way it worked, then visited seven different offices: the Chancery Office, Home Office (three times), Law Officer's chambers, Patent Bill Office, Signet Office, Lord Privy Seal's Office, and the Great Seal Patent Office.[1] The Sovereign's signature was required twice, and at each stage fees had to be paid (totalling

159

£100). This procedure had to be endured so that law officers could examine and assess the patent, deal with any objection, check and recheck. [Tom eventually managed the procedure, and his (unspecified) invention was a great success.]

In 1852, after much agitation by reformers, the Patent Law Amendment Act was passed. From then onwards registration was simplified. One office, the Patent Office at 25 Southampton Buildings, Chancery Lane, was made responsible for all stages of granting patents for inventions.

Patents

On 28th May 1789, John Elin became the first person to register a patent for a chimney-sweeping machine. Mr Elin, Gentleman, Pimlico, Hanover Square, described his invention (patent No 1682) as an 'elastic brush' that would 'last for years and serve every chimney in the House'.

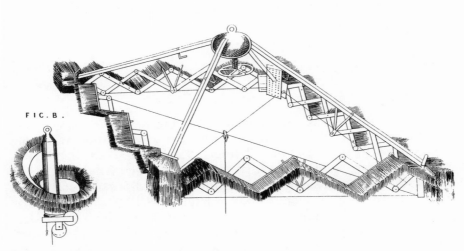

First chimney sweeping machine, 1789, designed by John Elin.

His machine consisted of brushes attached around four frames. The apparatus forming either a square or rectangular shape could extend to 18″ and contract to 3″. The brush was drawn up the chimney by a 'horse-hair line constantly suspended in the chimney, over a pulley fixed at the top', and it was contracted by 'drawing down the under cross lines'. Mr Elin's specifications included diagrams of his machine and the way it worked in flues. Also indicated was a smaller brush for circular flues, where bristles 'worked upon leather', were capable of 'bending with the spring into a spiral form'.

Another 18th-century invention was that of Daniel Davis from St Giles-in-the-Fields. Registered on 4th July 1796 the main structure of his patent (No 2124) consisted of a frame on two feet, that stood in the fireplace. The frame acted as a support for a brushing machine. Fixed to the frame was a box containing a wheel with teeth for raising a rack. The rack held a large brush which could be made of 'stout elastic hair, wire, or sponge'. It was worked up the flue by a handle attached to an axis extending the length of the frame.

Machine Competition

RSA

The Society of Arts, Manufactures, and Commerce was founded in 1754. (Granted Royal status in 1908, it is now known as The Royal Society of Arts, RSA.) In 1796, the Society of Arts launched a national competition. The first prize – a gold medal or 40 guineas (£42) – would be awarded to anyone who could invent: 'The most simple, cheap, and proper apparatus, superior to any hitherto known or in use for cleansing chimneys from soot.'[2]

A condition of the prize stipulated that 'the apparatus, with certificates of its having been used with proper effect' had to be produced before the third Tuesday in February 1797.

The result was disappointing. There were many submissions but no prize awarded. The offer was repeated the following year, then intermittently for several years, with no claimant. No awards were offered in 1802. Instead, a Society for Abolishing the Common Method of Sweeping Chimneys donated several premiums of £200 and under, for the invention of 'mechanical apparatus'.[3]

Interest in the competition was revived in 1803. This was due to public response to Mrs Bates's letter in the *St James's Chronicle*, and the founding of the London SSNCB. At the time, William Tooke, who was vice-president of The Society of Arts also became treasurer of the SSNCB, uniting the two societies in a common cause. Two years passed. Finally in 1805, The Society of Arts awarded the gold medal to George Smart, a member of their own society. In the succeeding years both gold and silver medals were awarded (see later) until the practice ended in 1809.

161

George Smart

Mr George Smart, Ordnance Wharf, Westminster Bridge, was a carpenter by trade. During the early years of the competition he saw 'so many superfluous things brought forward'[4] that on his way home one evening (1803), he thought up an invention himself.

The idea came to him when he remembered the way children inserted string through tobacco pipes, to make a rod. Too excited to sleep, he and his foreman stayed up all night making a machine. By morning, they had swept all the chimneys in the house before the servants were up. The following Thursday, Mr Smart put himself forward 'as a candidate for the prize'. Despite a certificate from John Trotter, Soho Square (2nd May 1803) testifying to the successful sweeping of his hall and parlour chimneys, and signed certificates from four other householders, Mr Smart's first submission failed.

In 1805, the society received additional certificates from Mr Smart and the enclosed letter:

> Sir, It is nearly two years since I sent to the Society of Arts a machine for cleaning chimnies ... I had since tried many other plans, such as joining small round raftons together with tubes, and the fastenings like that of a bayonet; but none have succeeded as well as the hollow tubes, with a cord through ... One great improvement I have made in the brush, which now opens and shuts upon the principle of an umbrella, and shall send a machine if the Society request it...

Mr Smart's certificates, signed by a number of respectable householders, showed that he had swept 378 flues with his machine. He employed 'six men and horses daily' and would continue to do so until his machine was 'generally adopted by the Master Sweeper'. The Society was finally convinced and awarded George Smart the gold medal.

On 21st December 1807, Mr Smart wrote to the society again informing them that his machine was succeeding far beyond expectations:

> His Royal Highness the Prince of Wales, has directed that the chimnies at Carlton-house, also those at the Pavilion, shall for the future be cleansed by machine. I have also had orders to send to different parts of the Kingdom my machines ready-made...

The society awarded George Smart a second gold medal, this time for successfully sweeping more chimneys than any other competitor.

162

Mr Smart's machine became known as the 'Scandiscope'. It consisted of jointed rods of ash or cane that fitted together like a fishing rod, a new joint being added until it reached the chimney pot. Each hollowed rod was equal in length and numbered. Through them ran a long cord. The brush-head, made of small whalebone sticks, fastened into a round ball of wood which extended to a diameter of two feet. It was thrust up the flue where it remained furled. On reaching the pot, it was opened by means of the cord then hauled back down. To contain loosened soot a green baize curtain was hung in front of the hearth and the machine was worked through a hole in the centre.

George Smart gave up carpentry to devote time to perfecting his invention. The cost of his machine in 1807 – with an extension of rods up to 60 feet – was £4 14s 6d. The price included a box and extra brush. Ten years later he was making rods that varied in length. The average size was four feet; price per rod, 2s 6d. For a tall chimney (68 feet), 17 rods were needed. The brush-head cost 10 shillings.

Rods lasted well if looked after. One master sweep told Henry Mayhew that apart from 'occasional renewal of the ferules' he had been using the same rods for nine years. A well-made head was either 'injured or worn down' in about two years.

In 1826, just before May Day, a cartoon of Mr Smart's Scandiscope was distributed as a handbill. The cartoon showed chimney sweeps dancing in their May Day finery (see Chapter 10) and the rhyme:

> Some wooden tubes, a brush, and rope,
> Are all you need employ;
> Pray order, maids, the Scandiscope,
> And not the climbing boy.[5]

It is interesting to note that on 17th June, 1800 a Mr George Smart, timber merchant, of Camden Town, St Pancras, registered a patent (No 2415) for a 'new method of combining masts, yards, and bowsprits *hollow* so as to give them lightness & strength'. He suggested that his invention could be 'applied to other useful purposes'. Perhaps this was the same George Smart, and he later adapted his innovative idea for shipwrights to suit the purpose of chimney sweeps.

Joseph Davis

In 1803, The Society of Arts had also received a submission from Joseph Davis, No. 14, Crescent, Kingsland Road. Certificates testifying that Mr Davis's machine had swept chimneys in the Military

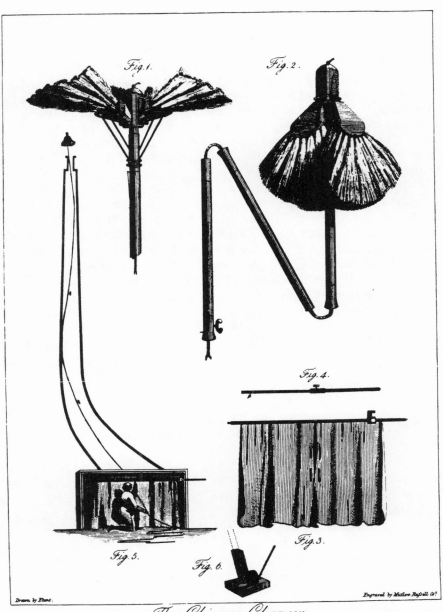

Fig. 1.

Fig. 2.

Fig. 4.

Fig. 3.

Fig. 5.

Fig. 6.

Drawn by Blunt.

Engraved by Midlow Russell Co.

The Chimney Cleanser,
Invented, & brought into Practice by Mr. Geo. Smart,
of Ordnance Wharf, Westminster Bridge.

George Smart's chimney sweeping machine, 1805.

𝕿𝖍𝖊 𝖑𝖆𝖘𝖙 𝕮𝖍𝖎𝖒𝖓𝖊𝖞 𝕾𝖜𝖊𝖊𝖕𝖊𝖗.

Cartoon of the sweeping machine, the Scandiscope.

Hospital, Westminster and the Jennerian Society, Salisbury Square, accompanied his chimney-sweeping apparatus. Three years later (18th March 1806), Mr Davis sent the following letter:

> Sir, The brush part of the model of my machine for cleansing chimnies, which I sent you on the 3rd May 1803, not having any hair in it, I am now enabled to forward you one in a more perfect state...

Mr Davis's machine, comprising four brushes fixed to four arms attached to a central rod, had an additional ball-like brush on top, which swept the pot. The brushes were 6″ long and 5″ wide. This time The Society of Arts was impressed. They judged the machine to be 'next in merit' to that of Mr Smart and awarded Joseph Davis the silver medal.

Patents (19th Century)

Meanwhile other inventions were being patented. On 11th April 1803, Daniel Paulin Davis, surveyor, Bloomsbury Square, registered an

165

'improved machine'. His patent (No 2697) was for a method of sweeping by chain or rope with 'brush or brushes suspended ... going up on the one side and down on the other'.

Some machines deserve mention for originality. James Hume's invention (patent No. 3399, 28th February 1811) consisted of a cylindrical box which rotated on an axis. The brush was supported and enclosed in the box except for the bottom where it protruded. The apparatus, which looked like a traditional-style lawn mower, was pushed up the chimney flue by a wooden handle. Soot collected inside the box. Mr Hume lived in Percy Street, Middlesex.

The appliance of William Fenner, carpenter (patent No. 5358, 6th May 1826) Bushell Rents, Wapping, will interest present-day 'flueologists'. His invention consisted of a spiral pipe which when placed inside the upper section of the chimney flue 'increased draft' and gave 'a better direction to the smoke'. The spiral pipe was made of copper with fitted joints. Mr Fenner's method of cleaning involved gently tapping the outside of the chimney with a hammer. The taps were made where the brickwork was purposefully thinner and bolts had been inserted through the chimney. The bolts knocked the pipe joints and shook down the soot.

Other machine inventors included Jonathan Snow, No. 6, Baker's Court, Halfmoon Alley, Bishopsgate, this machine was similar to Mr Smart's except that it had two brush-heads; and Thomas Mumford, a timber merchant. Mr Mumford's machine had rods with joints. Both inventors gave evidence before a Commons committee in 1817. After their statements, a member of the committee, Joseph Birch, described his own method of sweeping by using an 18-pound ball. At first, the ball was placed in a canvas bag, but Mr Birch found that it clogged with soot and was difficult to get down the chimney. He solved the problem by contriving a wire bag, though he thought that it might be better to have 'balls constructed for the purpose, with holes through them, so that a rope might be passed through the ball and fastened with a knot'. (See Appendix for patents registered before 1852.)

Joseph Glass (1791–1867)

Monetary incentives also came from private citizens. For instance, a Mrs Denyer bequeathed a legacy of £200 with the proviso that the money be given to the inventor of a machine for sweeping chimneys that had been 'approved by Parliament'.[6]

When Joseph Glass introduced his machine in 1828, it won the approval of both Parliament and the SSNCB. The machine was generally considered superior to that of Mr Smart. Made of solid cane with

166

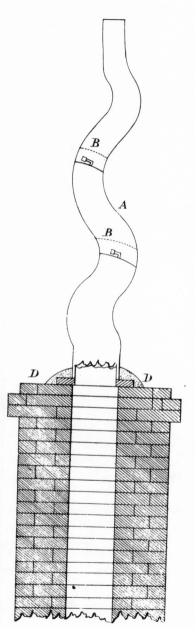

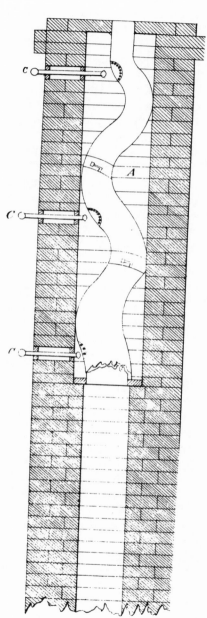

The spiral pipe invention of William Fenner, 1826.

167

brass screw joints which when put together formed one connecting rod, it had the advantage of both strength and pliability. Furthermore, a wheel fixed to the top of the brush-head enabled it to be pushed easily up the flue.

Mr Glass claimed that his machine 'when properly applied' would effectively sweep angular and crooked flues. Lighter materials had been used and no supplementary sweeping methods were necessary (i.e. ball and brush from the top). Whereas formerly 'the mysterious cloth was appended to the mantelpiece by means of two forks',[7] Mr Glass's chimney cloth was fixed within the fireplace by means of a sliding rod and screw. It was also provided with a sleeve in the centre through which the machine could be worked. A similar, smaller cloth could be inserted in soot-doors. (Later 'bump sheets'[8] were used. The principle was similar except that they were tucked into the grate to catch the soot. The bundle could then be carried away.)

An advertisement in the London SSNCB 22nd Report shows that machines, manufactured by Mr Glass, could be bought from his address, No 2, Moor Lane, Fore-Street (Cripplegate). Prices, including chimney cloth:

	cane		ash or crab
	£ s		£ s
40 feet ...	3 10	40 feet ...	2 5
50 feet ...	4 0	50 feet ...	2 11
60 feet ...	4 10	60 feet ...	2 17
70 feet ...	5 0	70 feet ...	3 3
80 feet ...	5 10	80 feet ...	3 8

For a machine part-cane part-ash, the price was proportionate. Cane rods, being more pliable, could be used further up the flue on reaching a bend. Mr Glass's name was stamped on the screw joints of his rods as a precaution against 'spurious' machines.

Joseph Glass was a builder who had spent many years constructing chimneys in various parts of the kingdom. He professed to having superintended 'the sweeping of nearly 30,000 chimneys in the metropolis' and wrote several articles about the trade. His drawing of seven flue arrangements in a single stack (*Mechanics Magazine* 1834) graphically illustrates how they were swept by climbing boys (see Chapter 4).

Mr Glass took up the trade himself. In 1847 a signed debit note for two shillings for sweeping two vestry chimneys in St Swithin's Church, was made out to Joseph Glass, Chimney Sweeper.

Master sweep and apprentice with Joseph Glass's machine, 1850. (Reproduced by kind permission of Guildhall Library, Corporation of London.)

PART 2: MACHINES vs CLIMBING BOYS

For Machines

Apart from master sweeps and reformers supporting the Society for Superseding the Necessity for Climbing Boys, machines were favoured by many other citizens. Mr Bevans, an architect familiar with London buildings, had no doubt that three quarters of the chimneys in the metropolis could be 'as cleanly and as cheaply swept by mechanical means'[9] as by climbing boys. He was sure that 'easy substitutes could be found' for the remainder, although difficulties might be encountered when sweeping horizontal flues because of the quantity of soot.

Samuel Roberts was one of the north of England's most hard-working campaigners. His publication, *A Cry From The Chimneys*, (dedicated to William Tooke, 1817) likened the arduous tasks of climbing boys to those of African slaves: 'Slavery, excepting only the middle passage, has not a feature comparably horrid'. At a public meeting in Sheffield (1838), he supported his case by introducing a deformed boy. Climbing at too early an age had caused the boy's twisted limbs, while his bones were soft.

By the 1830s major insurance companies either engaged masters who used machines, or donated funds so that machines could be bought. In 1838, Robert Stevens reported that machines had successfully swept 22,193 London chimneys. Most of them were as part of large contracts: Bank of England, 170 chimneys; East India House, 220; St Thomas's Hospital, 329.

In Northampton, Matthias Begley, John Merrick, Jane Bayes, Matthias Begley junior and Francis Begley advertised that they used machines. The five master sweeps signed a public Chimney Sweepers Declaration promising that they would not allow any child to 'ascend or descend a chimney, or enter a flue' for the purpose of sweeping, cleaning or coring. They respectfully invited 'the assistance and co-operation of the public', and hoped that 'the Builders of new premises' would construct chimneys in accordance with the Chimney Sweeping Acts. Furthermore, they trusted that other chimneys would be 'altered as to admit of the machines being properly used'.

Other masters needed persuading. At Stockton-on-Tees where a committee was formed to promote the use of sweeping machines, enough subscription money was collected to present a machine to a local sweep. At the time, the master sweep was considering taking on two new apprentices as climbing boys. The committee found out later that the master sweep's wife had taken the machine and used it herself with great expertise. 'One morning before breakfast she swept with it 11 chimneys and that without an assistant'.[10]

Against Machines

William Wilkins . . .	Cock & Bottle Lane, Castle Street
William Head . . .	Gloucester Lane
Thomas Hill . . .	Berkeley Place
Thomas Moore . . .	Ellbroad Street
Robert Taylor . . .	Redcliff Hill

On 28th June 1817 the above-named Bristol master sweeps formed an alliance and launched an appeal of a different nature. They published an impressive booklet entitled *The Master Chimney-Sweepers of Bristol*. It was well documented with facts, personal histories, and illustrations, and was issued as a sincere appeal to the public against what the sweeps called 'Erroneous Application to their Practice and Character'. The Bristol sweeps were upset by 'Facts' in a pamphlet about the 'State of children employed as climbing boys' printed by the Bristol Machine Company and distributed in York.

The Bristol masters, with 'honesty of intention', stated that they had no quarrel with machines, but contended that only boys could sweep some chimneys. They did not agree that machines swept cleaner, nor did they think that 'greater risk of life and limb was attached to the sweeping of chimneys by boys'.

If machines were used they questioned how pots and baffle holes were to be swept, unless from outside, incurring danger and expense. They pointed out that where pipes had been introduced from adjoining fireplaces, great quantities of soot accumulated on the ledges (ledges formed by constriction of the original flue). It happened too, that 'massive beams came in contact with the soot', with serious consequences.

Horizontal flues running 'variously 20 to 30 feet', (known as flats) could be swept by boys alone. The same applied to the London Bell-pot, with its baffler-holes underneath; the Armed-pot, the Fly, and the Dutch-head. The Dutch-head – common in Bristol – emitted smoke in various directions.

In their booklet, the Bristol masters showed compassion and appreciation of the tasks carried out by their climbing boys. They pointed out that:

It must be evident that the only chimneys in which machines can be used, are those which climbing-boys may sweep with the greatest facility. It might be worthwhile to imagine, how boys are to be trained and reconciled to the rough work, by depriving them of that which is smooth?

North Devon master sweeps had been fortunate in enlisting the aid of Mr F.M. Ommaney, MP for Barnstaple. During a Common's debate (1819), he spoke heartily in support of climbing boys. Waving the Master Sweeps' Petition, he shouted; 'machinery was inadequate to the task'. What was to become of 'the poor boys from poorhouses', must they be deprived of their substance? He firmly believed that: 'The climbing boys were generally possessed of good animal spirits and were gay, cheerful and contented.'[11]

This was also the opinion of W.H. Pyne (*World in Miniature*, 1827) who stated:

the condition of the apprentice to this seemingly loathsome occupation is much less disagreeable than is generally supposed ... there are no people more remarkable for good order in their families, than the industrious master chimney-sweepers.

It is certainly true that many youths survived their apprenticeship remarkably unscathed. When young, Master Sweep William Bulphin served a seven-year apprenticeship. During this time, he climbed through 70 of the 100 chimneys of the Bristol Exchange. He also swept every chimney in King's Weston House, the residence of Lord de Clifford. Because the main chimneystack was situated in the middle of the building, and every flue ran round the central grand staircase the flues were particularly difficult to sweep. Despite the smallness of the flues – measuring 9″ × 11″ for the most part – William had never stuck once or been in danger of suffocation.

When Master Sweep Bulphin became Foreman of Bristol Fire Office Engines (1828), he used four of Mr Glass's machines and swept 30 chimneys a week (1500 a year). He also used a rope, ball and brush from the top. Even so, he discovered that chimney pots were a problem. Mr Bulphin could not clean 20 out of 100 'as effectively as it ought to be done, and would be done with a climbing boy'.[12] He defied all the machines in the world that had been invented to clean one of them.

Giving evidence to a Parliamentary Committee in 1834, another reputable master sweep Benjamin Watson said he swept only half his flues with machines. This was because 'hardly a kitchen chimney in Portland Street Place' could be done 'without a boy'. The flues had a run of very long shafts and the same applied to Grafton Street chimneys.

Mr Watson used Mr Smart's machine, although 'a boy was still preferable'. Sometimes he went up so far with a machine, then finished the job from the roof with a ball and brush. Machine heads came undone and had to be retrieved with a grappling iron. 'I have been many times with a machine to a place and been frequently asked not to bring it again.' Mr Watson had been recalled to sweep the chimneys of the Wyndham Club House, St James's Square. (Before the building became a clubhouse it was owned by Lord Glastonbury and Mr Watson held the chimney-sweeping contract.) For the past year, 'Mr Glass's people' had swept the chimneys. The club owners were dissatisfied; the chimney caught fire '2 or 3 times'.

The committee asked Mr Watson if he had been to Sir Charles Flint's in Bolton Street. 'Yes', he replied, 'they were annoyed very much with smoke'. When his climbing boys had gone up the 9 × 4 inch flues with candles, they found them full of 'cracks and holes'. The boys 'made good' three parlours, two drawing rooms, and two bedrooms. Mr Watson finished his evidence by saying; 'our business lies so much at the mercy of servants' (see later).

Summing Up

At the time of Henry Mayhew's study of London sweeps in the mid-19th century, one factor was clear: more chimneys were being swept by machine than by climbing boys. However, this applied to the capital alone. Elsewhere in the country, the position was reversed. Continuing resistance to sweeping machines seemed to stem from three main anxieties: expense, efficiency, and fear of change.

Expense

Wealthy masters could easily adapt to machines. In fact, machines increased their status in society. Nevertheless, for the majority of sweeps the purchase of a machine caused a change in lifestyle. The master himself had to 'work' the machine; men were employed instead of boys, and higher wages paid. Machines were expensive and had to be maintained. The cost depended upon the number of 'joints' or rods and added to the expense was the loss of income from parish overseers, since small boys were no longer necessary. To a poor sweep, a machine was a valued item. A Birmingham chimney sweep was sentenced to two months' imprisonment for illegally pawning one.

In 1838, the London SSNCB recommended the services of five masters who they considered were the 'only persons in London' who could be trusted to work the machines 'effectually' (see Appendix). The masters punctually attended to orders by the twopenny post, and charged exactly the same prices 'as those paid to the common chimney sweeper'.

Soot-doors constituted another expense, this time to householders. Master Peter Hall reported that the chimneys of the Earl of Hardwicke's home could be fitted with soot-doors priced 8s to 10s a chimney. In 1838, eight doors were fitted at the Penitentiary and thirteen at the Bank of England; the average cost was 9s 6d per chimney.

Many of the gentry, particularly owners of castles, were opposed to soot-doors. Unsightly iron doors spoiled their room decor. Mr John Hawker from Baker Street, writing to *The Times* (25th March 1875), explained that the principal flues in his country house ran horizontally, turned corners, and then ascended to the roof. He had overcome the difficulty of deciding where to install soot-doors by 'hitting the wall' and listening for the hollow sound, which revealed 'the passing of the flues'.

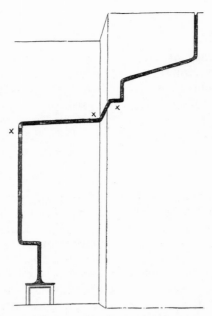

Panshanger's illustration of a flue with three soot doors, 1842.

Efficiency

The efficiency of machines, depended, it seemed, on who was working the machine. Antipathy by some masters towards the machine was based solely on fear: fear that it would deprive them of perquisites, because no householder gave pennies or pies to a machine; or a greater fear that the 'art and mystery' of their trade would be gone forever.

It was easy to claim that machines were hard to operate, and easier still to create a mess. Sweeps were known to have intentionally knocked pots from the roof and jammed brush-heads in flues. Moreover, apprentices were sometimes caught deliberately placing soot in the flue. A Lord's Committee found that a drawing of the stillroom flue in a London house had been distorted to discredit the machine.

A more understandable worry was that the use of machines would 'open up' the trade. Any leek or unskilled worker could learn to operate a machine. This did happen. In 1855 the Hanley & Shelton Chimney Sweeping Association appointed Peter Hall to recruit workers from outside the ranks of practising sweeps who could be trained to work the machines. During the first six months of 1856 this undertaking cost the Association £5 7s 6d in rail fares.

174

In horizontal flues, the accumulation of soot caused problems, and so did 'woolly' soot and 'peat' soot which had to be prized free with a scraper. George Elson sums up the dilemma:

> To do the masters justice they did their best. Where the soot was light and easy to come off, say in London and large centres the improved machines were effective. Not so in the provinces ... whalebone here was no match against a steel scraper in the hands of a well-trained boy. Housekeepers noticed the difference and openly declared for the boys' return.

It was generally agreed that machines could not sweep horizontal flues. Countless masters, who were formerly climbing boys, testified to sweeping winding flues. One master told of a flue in Goldsmith's Hall[13] that took him six hours to clean.

With regard to extinguishing chimney fires, allegations that boys were forced up chimneys 'like a bundle of wet rags' were denied by Bristol masters. They asked if anyone could name a single boy. They, however, could name 'an avowed supporter of the machine', who after a chimney fire had insisted that a boy ascend his chimney to make sure the machine had done the job. This sort of incident was not uncommon.

Masters claimed that boys who learned their trade correctly and stayed alert need never be burnt in chimney fires. One master recalled that as a climbing boy he 'rejoiced'[14] when such a job came to his master because it meant 6d for himself, or even 1s. 'We pin the Bosom of the shirt over, secure it in every way ... We wet the brush and when one boy is tired we send up another.'

Then there was the problem of coring. Every year the building of chimneys increased. Added to this were the alterations in existing flues to accommodate soot-doors. No machine could remove builders' rubble or repair a defective flue.

In 1810, George Frederic Eckstein proposed a plan to supersede climbing boys in the coring of chimneys. He had attended a meeting in the Lords and heard that one of the parliamentary chimneys 'had occupied three weeks in the coring'. Eckstein's idea was to 'leave out or lightly place two or three bricks at each angle of the stack'. Rubble could then be removed and the bricks replaced before plastering. Later though, Eckstein, in his *Practical Treatise on Chimneys* (1852) – after failing with a kitchen chimney on Uxbridge Moors – admitted to 'the application of the old fashioned brush, in the shape of a human being'.

Other plans included one whereby 'one or two children'[15] were apprenticed to 'intelligent bricklayers' in different parts of London. It was suggested they learn the trade and then be taken to the 'chimney requiring attention'. The plan failed when the dimensions of flues were found to be 12 or 14 inches. The scheme was impracticable since even the smallest child barely had room to raise his arms let alone apply mortar.

Fear of Change

The London Society for Superseding the Necessity for Climbing Boys had been in existence 35 years when Secretary Robert Stevens commented that 'the main cause of the Society's feebleness was due to servants'.[16] He surmised that the reason why so few people were prepared to abandon the old system of climbing boys was due to 'the fraud' practised 'by servants upon their employers'; an opinion previously voiced by Master Sweep Benjamin Watson.

George Smart could also testify to a servant's attitude. Mr Smart had paid his first visit with a machine to Mr Burke's house in Token-house Yard. Mr Burke was a friend, but his housekeeper kept Mr Smart waiting outside for over an hour on a cold morning before she came down. In quite a rage, 'she swore she wished the machine and the inventor at the devil'. Mr Smart (who was not known to the house-keeper) swept all the chimneys then asked what objection she had to the machine. She replied:

A very serious one, that if there was a thing by which a servant could get any emolument, some d–d invention was sure to take it away from them, for that she received the perquisites.[17]

Other housekeepers feared that the machine would ruin their carpets 'Which case is worse?' wrote Mr James Dennington (*Climbing Boys' Advocate* 1st October 1856) 'the sweep, or the housekeeper who employs him? ... Would that the penalty could attach to the house-keeper.' During House of Commons' debates, it was shown that elderly ladies were among the worst offenders.

Lord Shaftesbury also reported resistance to change. During a Lords' debate (1864), he explained that one lady had been most indig-nant when she could not have her chimneys swept in the afternoon because the sweeps were at school. 'A chimney sweep indeed, wanting education! What next?'[18]

By 1869, the satirical magazine *Punch* had allied itself with machines: 'Fine ladies ... and devout ladies who send missionaries to the Chinese had better know what is done in their own homes...' The magazine commented that women took next to no part in the emanci-

A DREADFUL SHOCK TO THE NERVES.

"PLEASE, MEM, LET'S COME UNDER YOUR RUMBERELLER !"

Cartoon from Punch, 1860s.

pation of climbing boys, and that a man was induced to allow boys to ascend flues only because his wife 'nagged and scolded at him'.

There were nevertheless, many unsung heroines. Two Quaker-ladies in particular were notable for their concern for climbing boys.

Ann Alexander

Ann Tuke was born in York (16th May 1767). A serious child, who took an early interest in religion, she subsequently joined her brother Henry on ministerial visits to Scotland and Ireland. In 1796 Ann married William Alexander, a printer and bookseller, and went to live in Needham Market, Suffolk. She continued to work for the ministry while caring for her husband and two sons. Between 1803 and 1805 she visited America attending meetings of the Society of Friends. The family moved to York in 1808 to take over her mother's school. They remained in York until the death of one of her sons (1804).

Ann Alexander wrote *Facts Relative to the State of Children who are Employed by Chimney Sweepers, as Climbing Boys*, in 1816. In the

177

introduction she confessed to feeling sorry for the climbing boys and hoped that wherever the Society of Friends had any influence they would do all in their power to assist them. Her 46-page booklet was published by William and reprinted the following year.

Ann's husband and son continued to campaign for abolishing the climbing boy system. They printed monthly editions of the *Climbing Boys Album*, for which they were paid £10 6s by the London SSNCB.

Until William's death in 1841, Ann travelled extensively working for the Quaker ministry. Then she moved into a small house in Ipswich to be near her son and his family. She died aged 82, on 19th September 1849.

Ann Fairbank

It was due to Ann Fairbank, a Quaker minister, that Samuel Roberts first became aware of the conditions of Sheffield's climbing boys. Ann was born in Sheffield in 1761. She became a minister when she was 30, serving the Quaker community in most of the eastern counties from 1791 to 1823. She met Mr Roberts in 1806 and three years later the Sheffield SSNCB was formed. When James Montgomery wrote about an Easter Monday banquet for the climbing boys, he mentioned a young climbing-girl whom he placed 'close at a Quaker-lady's side'. This was the poet's tribute to Ann Fairbank, who died unmarried in 1849.

(See Appendix for London gentlewomen who made donations towards the purchase of machines.)

Upholding the Law

Perhaps the greatest challenge to campaigners was attempting to uphold the law on such a divided issue, particularly as matters were made worse by conflicting opinions between the law-enforcers themselves. The success rate in bringing convictions against offenders varied around the country. In Hull 20 master sweeps were taken to court between the years 1836 and 1852. The Sheffield SSNCB owed its success to lawyer Mr Aitchison who was paid one guinea for every case brought before the justices. Being taken to court, though, did not necessarily result in a conviction.

William Wood, however, was particularly victorious. In 1856, he secured a conviction against pawnbroker William Newton, who was fined £5 for specifically requesting a climbing boy. Master Sweep James Boot had obliged by sending his young brother Thomas twice up Newton's chimney. Before the case was heard, Newton had attempted to bribe the master sweep not to appear in court by offering him a machine.

A Manchester screw and bolt manufacturer from Hood Street was also fined £5 for employing two boys to sweep the flues of his boiler (Sunday 19th February 1856). The boys were working in the factory at the time, having been previously dismissed from employment with a master sweep. They received threepence halfpenny each for working in the flues from 7 am until 12.30 pm.

The worst offenders operated in the Midlands. Peter Hall, while agent for two societies, managed to secure 400 convictions against chimney sweeps. Birmingham SSNCB spent £500 over five years trying to suppress the use of climbing boys. Nevertheless, despite their efforts 26 boys were still being employed in 1862.

In the same year, Shaftesbury received a letter from a chimney sweep living near Hemel Hempstead (Hertfordshire). The sweep declared he was the only chimney sweep in the county using machines. He complained that he had taken a sweep to court for using boys, 'having secured a police-constable as witness to the offence' but the magistrate dismissed the case and ordered him (the correspondent) to pay 12s costs. The sweep strongly implied that other magistrates 'abused the Act'.[19]

This accusation was not unfounded. Letters to the secretaries of the various SSNCBs were full of complaints of the difficulty in securing convictions, because 'the magistrates themselves sweep their own chimneys by boys, and thus throw every obstacle in the way'.[20]

Machines finally superseded climbing boys in 1875 when the last Chimney Sweeping Act was passed.

Ramoneur Machine

The French name for chimney sweep is 'ramoneur', and the name became popular in England during the 19th century. In 1841, The Patent Ramoneur Association of Cambridge and Huntingdon claimed that they afforded 'the only effectual legal mode of Sweeping Chimneys'. During the association's first year, they estimated that their profits would amount to £6,765. Estimates were based on an average of two sweepings a year and sale of two bushels of soot per chimney annually, to be collected from 31,240 houses averaging two chimneys per house.

Receipts	£
187,440 sweepings, average charge of 6d ...	4,686
187,440 Bushels of Soot @ 8d ...	6,248
	10,934

"IF YOU WANT A THING DONE, DO IT YOURSELF." NEVER DISTURB THE
MAIDS IN THE MORNING, BUT JUMP OUT OF BED THE MOMENT YOU HEAR THE
SWEEP, AND LET HIM IN; IT ISN'T MUCH TROUBLE, AND SAVES A WORLD OF
GRUMBLING."

Cartoon from *Punch, 1865*.

Expenses amounting to £6,765, included:

	(£)
Rent and taxes for 5 establishments ...	200
(Warehouses for soot, stables etc)	
Salaries of 10 clerks, average £60 ...	600
Maintenance etc of 5 horses, £60 ...	200
Wages of £50 labourers @ 15s per week ...	1950
Extra wages for 5 Superintendents @ 6s ...	78
Wear & tear of machines etc 20s per week ...	276

180

The Patent Ramoneur Company was established in London in 1848. It became the capital's most prestigious 'mechanical' chimney-sweeping company. By 1851 four stations were operating: Little Harcourt Street, Bryanston Square; Charles Place, Euston Square; New Road, Sloane Street; and William Street, Portland-town. The company swept chimneys with their own machine, which 'surmounted with a double revolving ball'[21] was capable of turning a right-angle. Fifteen men were employed, each with his own machine. They charged the usual rates and received a weekly wage of 14 shillings and a suit of clothes annually. The suit comprised jacket, waistcoat and trousers of dark corduroy, and when sweeping, a 'frock' or blouse and cap. Wages were comparable to those of journeymen because no benefits were allowed.

Station managers were working chimney sweeps. They received the same pay as other sweeps in the association, but their premises were rent-free. Saving in rent amounted to £50 per year. Accommodation consisted of two comfortably furnished upstairs rooms, with a cellar just below ground level. Business was conducted in the cellar that was boarded off into compartments for soot.

In 1914 the company, renamed The Ramoneur Company Ltd, operated from 19 Buckingham Street, Strand. Listed in their promotion booklet, *The Sooty Side* (1914) are eight London branches. Testimonials to their success show that the company had swept the chimneys of the Foundling Hospital since 1851, a total of 63 years. Other contracts included the Royal Geographic Society and the Royal Pharmaceutical Society chimneys, which they had swept for 62 years.

Householders who paid an annual contract fee of one guinea and upwards were offered a discount. The fee varied according to the size of the house and work involved. The usual charge for sweeping a house of 18–20 rooms on six floors, such as Cornwall Gardens or St George's Square, would amount to £3 15s a year. The discount worked out at a saving of 25%.

	£	s	d
Kitchen chimney, 8 times @ 2s 6d ...	1	0	0
3 basement: pantry, Servants' Hall Housekeeper's rooms, twice @ 1s 6d ...		9	0
2 dining rooms, 2 drawing rooms twice a year @ 1s 6d ...		12	0
6 other rooms once a year @ 1s ...		6	0
	2	7	0

181

Modern Machines

The image of the chimney sweep changed dramatically after the First World War. Affluent 'chimney cleaners' were dressed in short white coats and flat-topped caps, and they used motorised vans, although single-handed sweeps preferred the bicycle – balancing their bundle of rods across the handlebars – and some took to using motorcycles with handy side-cars. Photographs taken by the *Northampton Independent* (1st October 1937) show five members of Hygienic Chimney Cleaners Ltd with their three vans. Their trade is advertised by a painting on each side of the van. It shows the image of a friendly white-coated sweep.

The Northampton sweeps had to travel further in search of customers, but when a member of the team arrived, madam was assured that no precautions (laying down of paper or covering of surfaces)

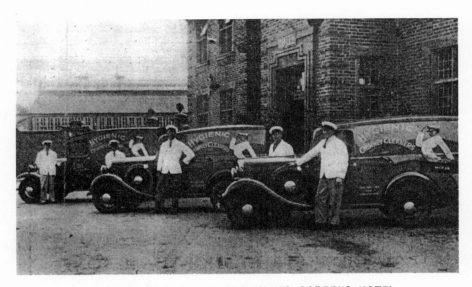

HYGIENIC SERVICE AT FRANKLIN'S GARDENS HOTEL

Northampton's Hygienic Chimney Cleaners, 1937.

were necessary, and sweeping began. An appropriately sized brush-head was fitted to the first rod and it was placed on the grate. Then the fireplace was screened by a black rubber covering under which the

182

sweep inserted his hands. Rods were screwed into place and the brush slowly pushed up the flue. A spiral action was used. Soot was brushed down and caught in a bag – a papier-maché container – attached inside the screen.[22]

The technique was so perfected that in Leicester (September 1937) at an exclusive club, stewards were able to lay the tables for lunch while the sweep cleaned the dining-room chimney, and the meal was served soon after. One month later, the local paper reported that, while a chimney was being swept 'an invalid child' was 'allowed by doctors to be in his cot throughout the cleaning operation'.

Although the trade went through a period of decline, due to a change in fuels and the Clean Air Act, a reduced number of chimney sweeps remained active. In 1954, the total number of chimney sweeps listed in the *London Trade Directory* was 471. As to the cost of machines: in 1958, Leicester sweeps E. Ellmore & Son, advertised:

Ten 3 foot tradesman's rods, fitted heavy brass universal joints and good quality brush ... 39 shillings; postage and package 3s 6d extra. Extra rods 3s 6d. Soot cloths to seal to fireplace with tape, 12s 6d each, postage paid. All goods direct from the makers, All Saints Works, 146 High Cross Street. Makers for over a century.

Notes

[1] *A Patent Office Centenary*, H. Harding, 1952.
[2] *History of the RSA*, Sir Henry Truemans Wood, 1913.
[3] *The Ramoneur Company*, publication, 1914.
[4] George Smart, Evidence to Lords Committee, 1818.
[5] *The Every-Day Book*, Hone, 1826.
[6] *Chimney Sweeping Described*, Joseph Glass, 1815.
[7] Account of boyhood, J.C. Hudson, 1823.
[8] *Hanley & Shelton Chimney Sweeping Association*, 1855.
[9] *Parliamentary Papers*, 17th May, 1817.
[10] Committee formed to promote machines, 4th August, 1817.
[11] *Roads To Ruin*, E.S. Turner, 1950.
[12] Evidence to Chimney Sweepers Regulation Bill, 16th June, 1834.
[13] *The Chimney Sweepers Report*, Commons Committee, 23rd June, 1817.
[14] Evidence to the Lords Committee, 1818.
[15] Evidence before the Commons, 1840.
[16] Report, London SSNCB.
[17] *London Labour and The London Poor*, Henry Mayhew, 1851.
[18] *Lord Shaftesbury*, J. Wesley Bready, 1933.

[19] *Child Labour*, Frederick Keeling, 1914.

[20] *Tit for Tat*, a Lady from New Orleans, 1855. (See chapter 11.)

[21] *London Labour and The London Poor*, Henry Mayhew, 1851.

[22] Present day sweeps use a vacuum cleaner to sweep up the soot in the grate. *Warning*: rogue sweeps use it up the chimney!

10

FABLE AND TRADITION

Superstition

Chimneys and chimney sweeps have long been associated with super-stition. In the 17th century, it was common practice to place 'building sacrifices' in the chimney to keep evil spirits away. In North Yorkshire the jamb post – at the side of the fireplace – was known as the 'witch post'. It was often covered in designs, and to protect the hearth 'sprigs of rowan'[1] were tied to the top.

Other devices for appeasing witches can be seen in the Pennine hamlet of Feizor (near Settle) where, on the chimney stack of an old cottage, a nine-inch shelf of slate projects from the chimney. Such projections were known as 'witch's seats'.[2] Chimneys with witch's seats can also be seen in Guernsey.

In Tring, Hertfordshire (1751), a chimney sweep named Colley was hanged for the murder of a witch. The supposed witch was Ruth Osborne, a destitute old woman who lived with her husband in the workhouse. Ruth was accused of bewitching Mr Butterfield, a local publican. On the day appointed for her 'ducking' (a local punishment) a large crowd collected outside the workhouse. The governor tried to protect the elderly couple, but the mob became incensed. They threatened to kill him and burn down the town. Ruth and her husband were stripped of their clothes and dragged two miles to a stream. In the approved manner, 'their big toes and thumbs were tied together' and they were repeatedly ducked in the water. Then Ruth, half drowned, was beaten to death. Her body was tied to her husband – who was still alive – and 'the two were put to bed together'.[3]

Colley acted as ringleader throughout. He also collected money from onlookers for providing them with such good entertainment. Four months later, when Colley was hanged for murder the villagers were dissatisfied. They watched only from a distance. 'It was a hard case,' they grumbled, 'to hang a man for destroying an old wicked witch who had done so much mischief by her witchcraft'.[4]

Tales of superstition did not end there. A large black dog was said to haunt the crossroads where Colley's body had hung from the gibbet

185

in chains. Tring's village schoolmaster reported seeing 'an immense black dog ... gaunt and shabby with long ears and a tail, eyes like balls of fire and large long teeth'.[5] The schoolmaster and companion noted that 'it opened its mouth and seemed to grin at us; in a few minutes it seemed to sink into the earth'.

Good Fortune

By tradition, though, chimney sweeps have always been taken as talismans of good fortune. Early evidence of this is found in Abigail Hill's account of a walk she took one October day in London (c1698). Abigail (cousin of Sarah, Duchess of Marlborough) while walking near the Cross-Keys, Camden, saw a group of tradespeople, among whom was a chimney sweep.

> To him Abigail bowed and said, 'Good morning, master chimney sweep' and crossed her thumbs; for as everybody knew, a chimney sweep to whom you bowed and said 'good morning', brought you luck.[6]

Customs varied according to where one lived. In some parts of the country to tap a sweep's shoulder or touch his clothing, or even walk in his shadow was thought lucky. One tradition, though, remains paramount: the presence of a chimney sweep at a wedding. If a chimney sweep kisses the bride on the cheek then good fortune is sure to follow.

No one knows why chimney sweeps are supposed to bring luck to a wedding. The tradition is thought to originate from the 18th century, when it is rumoured that an unknown chimney sweep grabbed the reins of a panicking horse saving the rider from a fatal accident. The sweep then disappeared into the crowd before he could be thanked. The grateful rider, being none other than the king himself, afterwards declared that all chimney sweeps should be treated with honour. The 'luck' of the monarch then became the sweeps' talisman.

It is more likely, though, that the association between weddings, luck, and chimney sweeps evolved from a much earlier time. In Imperial Rome (around the first century AD) weddings took place in the bridegroom's home. After the ceremony, the bride's husband presented her with a lighted torch and a vessel of water (symbolising fire and water; essentials for maintaining a Roman home). The bride lit a fire on the hearth, then tossed the torch to the guests who 'scrambled for it as a lucky memento'.[7]

186

Nineteenth-century sweeps adopted the fashion of the day and wore a waistcoat, tailed frock coat and a top hat. This custom has survived, though present day sweeps, when attending a wedding, usually dress in a boiler suit – blue or white – and uphold tradition by wearing a top hat.

WHEN MR. SAM DARK, MASTER SWEEP OF HAMMERSMITH, WAS MARRIED TO MISS DOROTHEA WHITE LAST SATERDAY THE GUARD OF HONOUR WAS COMPOSED OF MEMBERS OF THE SABLE FRATERNITY, WHOSE BRUSHES MADE A TASTEFUL ARCH UNDER WHICH THE HAPPY PAIR LEFT THE CHURCH.

A *Punch* cartoon showing chimney sweeps forming the guard of honour at the wedding of their master sweep, 1912. (Acknowledgements, Ken Bryant, chimney sweep)

Arabs called the top hat 'the father of the chimney'. Top hats were worn throughout the 19th century. The fashion originated in France during the Revolution (1790s) and spread. By the 1780s in England the three-cornered hat had gradually been replaced by a round hat. As the flat crown grew taller, the rim shrank. *The Times* (1799) reported: 'The hatter has of late years perpetually diminished

187

the little brim he allows us'. Top hats were first made of beaver then black silk was used. They varied in height and slightly in crown and brim shape. Top hats were popular with all classes. Poorer tradesmen and boys either acquired them (cast-offs given by employers) or bought them second-hand. The top hat also became known as the chimney-pot hat. According to the *Western Gazette* (25th July 1907), the name was acquired because top hats were always worn by German chimney sweeps (in Germany today the custom still prevails). Lincolnshire sweep Billy Baker from Burgh village still wore his top hat in 1914, when he was aged 83.

Traditional children's games often featured chimney sweeps and a wedding was a popular theme. One such game took the form of a shadow play. A theatre was made by cutting a large square in a thick piece of cardboard and the hole covered by muslin. Behind this, cutout characters were passed in front of a lighted candle and the following rhyme was sung.

The Sweep's Wedding

Once upon a time
If there's truth in my rhyme,
In love a poor sweep got entangled,
With a beauty hard by
Bewitching and sly
Who artfully often him dangled.

Then fixed on the day
The sweet first of May
That they all in dress suits might appear.
In the midst of the scene
Was Jack in the green
So alter'd were all you'd not know'em,
Mokes braying, drums playing,
Horns blowing, fiddles going,
Wait a short while and I'll show em ...

In Victorian times, chimney sweeps were paid for their services. Even today, attendance at weddings can be profitable. Any bride hiring Kevin Giddings from East Grinstead will receive double luck. Mr Giddings has trained his black cat, 'Milborrow' to accompany him. The cat sits on his master's shoulders. [Author's report: Milborrow enjoys the occasion.]

188

Kevin Giddings and his cat Milborrow, who continue the tradition of attending weddings to bring the couple good luck.

Celebrations

May Day

Celebrations, such as the Sweeps' May Day Festival can be traced back to Roman times when the Feast of Flora commemorated the coming of spring.

In the 15th century King Henry, his Queen Katherine and their courtiers 'on pleasure bente, rode a-maying from Greenwich to Shooter's Hill where an effective Robin Hood pageant delighted their hearts.'[8] And in the 16th century:

> Young men and maides, olde men and wives, ran gadding over night to the woods ... and in the morning they return bringing with them birch and branches of trees, to deck their assemblies withall.
>
> (*Phillip Stubbs, 1583*)

From James II's reign (1685–1689) the May holiday was held towards the end of the first fortnight in May (London's fashionable district, Mayfair, took its name from this time). After the mid-18th century, May Day was celebrated at the beginning of the month.[9]

Returning from the Masquerade, early 18th century. (Acknowledgements, Armley Mills, Leeds.)

The first of May became known as Chimney-Sweeps' day, when the sweeps took the principal roles of 'My Lord and My Lady' with a Maid Marian and 'Jack-in-the-green,' a green man, as Robin. The 'Jack' of the 18th century wore 'flowers in his beaver, and carried one of the footmen's long canes wreathed with flowers', which he 'wisked about in the dance'.[10] Dancers accompanied him with their faces disguised by soot. (This is the origin of Morris dancers: Moorish, black like Moors. The dancers were also called 'sweeps' and this may have prompted chimney sweeps to take on the role themselves.)

Milkmaids also celebrated the first of May. They collected alms

190

parading through the town with a decorated bower. A May Day poem (1769) sets the scene. It was written in four parts; *The Milkmaids Garland*, and *The Chimney Sweepers Garland* being parts II and III respectively:

> ... The scenes indeed, which now we show,
> Are somewhat simple somewhat low;
> But such as all must love.
>
> For being poor is not the thing,
> A Lord, a Minister, or King;
>
> The highest earthly station,
> May be, if rightly understood,
> As Chimney-Sweepers, bad or good;
> and bless or curse the nation.
>
> ......
>
> Now mind they trip a frolic round,
> Their brushes twang, their shovels sound,
> And deftly moves their feet;
> With powder'd cheeks they laugh and grin,
> For care, they do not care a pin,
> But all their joys compleat...
>
> *The Chimney Sweepers Garland*

The poem is illustrated with copperplate etchings. Chimney sweeps are shown with a central character dressed in a frock coat. Balanced on his head is a tall bower. Young sweeps accompany him carrying brushes and shovels. Most of them wear wigs and three-cornered hats although one has a crown and another the steeple hat of a medieval queen. The queen holds a deep bag for collecting alms.

The sweeps' and the milkmaids' trades eventually combined. Then the sweeps took over completely, and a milkmaid played the role of the queen and the boys wore 'ribbons and silver paper'.[11] Catherine Middleton writing about May Day in London (1809) noted that one of the chimney sweepers, decorated in gold leaf and coloured ribbons, rode upon an ass, while several of his companions as fine as himself beat time and danced with their shovels and brushes.

The Chimney Sweeps' May Day Parade became one of London's best known pageants. Festivities lasted for four days. The bower became a large cone of holly and ivy framed upon hoops. The green man walked inside, unseen, giving the cone the appearance of a

191

The Chimney Sweepers' Dance, May Day 1826. (Acknowledgements, Armley Mills, Leeds.)

'moving hillock of greenery'. In 1826, a clown was added. He walked on his hands before the Jack-in-the-green and performed numerous tricks.

A mercenary element also crept in and the masters shared 'a certain proportion of their apprentices profits.'[12] In the 1850s 'My Lady, who acted as Columbine, received 2s per day; My Lord, usually one of the journeymen, 3s, Jack-in-the-green [often an acquaintance, not a sweep], 3s, the clown 3s, the drummer 4s, and the boys 1s to 1s 6d.'[13] Proceeds for the first three days often amounted to £4 per day. Money collected on the fourth day was put towards a celebration supper.

May Day celebrations were not confined to London. In Lancashire, when children first saw the Field Woodrush (*Luzula Campestris*) which they had named the 'Chimney Sweeper', they repeated this rhyme:

> Chimney-sweeper, all in black,
> Go to the brook and wash your back;
> Wash it clean or wash it none;
> Chimney-sweeper, have you done?

In Tring, Hertfordshire, it was the custom to hold Jack-in-the-green

A chimney sweeper in traditional May Day garb.

craft fairs. In Leicester, companies of sweeps 'adorned with aprons and head-gear of coloured calico and flowers, brush and pan in hand, and headed by a Jack-in-the-green, paraded the streets and danced in a ring for coppers'.[14] Local sweeps in Hampshire celebrated on an open space near the church at St Mary Bourne the Summerhaugh. They decorated a green bower and danced around their Jack-in-the-green 'clattering their brushes and shovels against each other'.[15]

The inhabitants of Evesham eagerly looked forward to May Day, when the streets became crowded waiting for the sweeps to come. Most of them lived in Bewdley. They arrived dressed in fantastic attire carrying various instruments of their craft, accompanied by a gaily-dressed vehicle 'in which was seated the Queen of the May and the little Boy Sweep'[16] (see later section on Montagu). The company was made up of masters, journeymen and juveniles (1856).

Birmingham sweeps, who lived mostly around Pinfold Street, dressed up as Morris Men and danced through the streets. They also took part in a Sweeps' Parade and marched with painted faces. In Portsmouth, local sweeps held their festival in the stone mason's yard on the front corner of Surrey Street (1863). And in Congleton, Cheshire, sweeps danced with 'Chimney Sweeps' bells', (purpose-made leather strappings with bells attached). A similar belt, with three bells attached, was used to drive away evil spirits. The belt was known as St Peter's Chains, and it was customary for a priest to dance around the town ringing the bells. When this happened local chimney sweeps were allowed a day off. An

193

official 'Chimney Looker' was employed, and it was his job to inform any sweep – who might happen to be in a chimney at the time, and had not heard the bells – that he could stop working.

The Cheltenham Chimney Sweeps

When hawthorn buds are creaming white,
And the red foolscap all stuck with may,
Then lasses walk with eyes alight,
And it's chimney-sweepers' dancing day.

For the chimney-sweeps of Cheltenham town,
Sooty of face as a swallow of wing,
Come whistling, fiddling, dancing down,
With white teeth flashing as they sing.
And Jack-in-the-green, by a clown of blue,
Walks like a two-legged bush of may,
With the little wee lads that wriggled up the flue
Ere Cheltenham town cried 'dancing day' ...

Alfred Noyes

In the Medway town of Rochester, present-day sweeps (and the local community) still keep the tradition alive. Their Sweeps' May Festival starts with a parade on the 1st May and finishes with a Sweeps' Ball on the last evening, 7th May. In 1992, The National Association of Chimney Sweeps (NACS) led the Rochester May Day Parade for the first time. Members of the association came from many parts of the country. Although dressed as their Victorian counterparts, monetary contributions collected by the sweeps were donated to local charities.

Bartholomew Fair

Ode on Bartholomew Fair

Behold, what crowds in every street are seen,
Some clad in yellow, others dres'd in green!

Chimney-sweepers, J Day (1791)

St Bartholomew's Fair began on 24th August and lasted 14 days. Until 1855, it was held every year on open ground known as Smithfield. Charles Lamb, *Essays of Elia* (1823) relates, that his 'pleasant friend Jem White' gave an annual feast to the chimney sweepers 'upon the yearly return of the fair'. On each occasion, James White, an agent of Provincial Newspapers, acted as both host and waiter. One week before the supper took place, cards were sent to master sweeps in and about the Metropolis, 'confirming the invitation to their young fry'.

A convenient place was chosen 'among the pens, at the north side of the fair', and when the guests arrived (about 7 pm) they found three tables 'spread with napery'. At each table was a 'comely hostess' with a pan of 'hissing sausages'. To accompany the sausages, the boys were given 'kissing crusts' – white bread with crust hard enough to break teeth – and plenty of ale. James White, as head waiter, took charge of the first table, and Mr Lamb and 'trusty companion Bigood' the other two. The young sweeps clambered and jostled to sit at the first table because their host was so popular.

When the festivities were over Mr White thanked the boys for coming. Then clasping the waist of 'old dame Ursula (the fattest of the three) that stood frying and fretting, half-blessing, half-cursing the gentlemen', he gave her a chaste kiss on the lips. Whereupon the boys 'set up a shout that tore the concave. While hundreds of grinning teeth startled the night with their brightness'. Then followed the toasts: 'The King', 'The cloth', and 'for a crowning sentiment that never failed: May the British supersede the Laurel'. Then with much 'standing upon tables', toasts were proposed to one another.

Eyre Arms

On Monday 1st May 1826 when the United Society of Master Chimney Sweepers celebrated their first anniversary, a grand dinner took place at Eyre Tavern, St John's Wood, Mary-le-bone. At 11 am that morning 200 apprentices and their masters met outside the Bedford Arms, Bedford Square, and paraded through the West End. When they reached Portman Square the climbing-boys danced outside Montagu House in commemoration of Mrs Montagu's past kindness to them. 'The clean and wholesome appearance of the lads',[17] was a credit to their masters and crowds of people followed them to Eyre Tavern.

The boys were treated to a feast of roast beef and plum pudding. Then the masters sat down to a 'very excellent dinner provided for the occasion'. After the toasts came the speeches. The masters had decided that instead of 'being permitted to loiter and dance about on the streets on the first of May, dressed up in tawdry apparel' soliciting money, their apprentices should in future be treated to 'substantial fare' on each forthcoming anniversary of the society.

The practice continued for many years. John Ogden, writing in 1840 refers to the apprentices' May Day dinners at Chalk Farm and Eyre Arms, where they ate 'an enormous rich plum-pudding, massy, large, and round'.[18]

195

Other feasts

Until the final Chimney Sweeping Act, wealthy London master sweeps subscribed to a fund to pay for their apprentices' annual supper. The feast took place at White Conduit House. The inn with its two tearooms and spacious gardens, was named after an ancient stone conduit which stood near by. White Conduit House in Islington (east of Penton Street) was one of London's most popular resorts. Mayhew tells how people used to 'flock to watch' the sweeps' festivities, and 'contribute towards the society'. Dickens also mentions this annual dinner.

Captain Budsworth from Clifton village (near Bristol) should also be remembered. His generosity to the sweeps began in 1809 when Bristol celebrated the Jubilee of George III. On an impulse, Captain Budsworth invited all the 'little Sooties' and their masters to dinner in his garden. Onlookers at the time were pleasantly surprised that the apprentices 'were so decently dressed', and 'looked so comely and well'. They were given all the beef, pudding and plum cake they could eat, and sixpence to take away. The boys behaved so well that the dinner was repeated every year on the King's birthday.

Chimney sweeps also celebrated the fifth of November. A London master told Mayhew that they received 'not only pence from the public, but silver and gold. One of his class, who got up a gigantic Guy Fawkes and figure of the Pope (5th November, 1850), cleared £10 over and above all expenses'.

Fable

Throughout most of the 18th and 19th centuries, an air of mystery surrounded the sweeps. It was commonly held that numerous lost or stolen sons might be found working as chimney sweeps. No one dared ill-treat a sweep, not knowing if he might turn out to be a nobleman's son.

Dickens, when writing an autobiographic account of *The First of May* recalls in his 'young days' seeing 'a little sweep' about his own age, with curly hair and white teeth, whom he 'devoutly and sincerely believed to be the lost son and heir of some illustrious personage'. One day before the boy began his 'ascent to the summit of the kitchen chimney', Dickens asked him about his parentage. The lad replied that he 'believed he'd been born in the verkis (workhouse) but he'd never know'd his father.' Dickens felt certain that from that time forth 'he would one day be owned by a Lord, at least'. To his disappointment

196

the boy was never claimed. In fact he eventually 'settled down as a master sweep in the neighbourhood of Battle Bridge' (present day King's Cross).

Rumours continued to perpetuate. Charles Lamb had written about 'a lost chimney-sweeper' at Arundel Castle who had somehow 'confounded his passage among the intricacies of the Lordly chimneys' and descending into a 'magnificent chamber' had crept between the sheets and 'laid his black head on the pillow and slept like a young Howard'. Whereupon he was discovered and restored to his right station in life. The fable is one of Arundel's present-day attractions.

Mayhew thought he had discovered the source of the fable when the middle-aged wife of a chimney sweep he had been questioning reported that she had 'often heard the story from her mother who passed a long life in the neighbourhood of Mrs Montagu's residence'. Lady Montagu had a son of tender years, who was supposed to have been stolen for the sake of his clothes. Some time after when the sweeps were necessary at Montagu House, a servant at first attracted by one of the boys' superior manner, then 'fancied a resemblance in him to the lost child'.

In this account, the connection with the Montagu family is nearer to the truth, though several facts are known to be incorrect. Lady Montagu's son (name unknown) died in infancy. The building of Montagu House was not completed until 1782; six years after 'young Montagu's' death at the age of 63. Then who was this young nobleman?

Edward Montagu (1713–1776)

Edward Wortley Montagu was born in May 1713 in Duke Street, London. His family was wealthy and well connected. His father[19] was British Ambassador in Constantinople (1716–18) and his mother was the celebrated Lady Mary Wortley Montagu, (eldest daughter of the Duke of Kingston). Lady Mary achieved recognition through her writings, and her introduction into Britain of inoculation against smallpox.

In 1718, when Edward was five years old and the family was living in Constantinople, smallpox was one of the world's most virulent diseases. Lady Mary discovered that the spread of smallpox in the Ottoman Empire had been curbed by means of 'engrafting'. In a letter to Sarah Chiswell, she explained how this was done. An old woman came 'with a nutshell full of the best sort of smallpox', and after 'putting into the vein as much venom as can lye upon the head of her needle', she bound up the little wound with a 'hollow bit of shell'.

Lady Mary had been left without eyebrows after catching smallpox

Young Edward Montagu with his mother Lady Mary.

shortly after her marriage, and her brother had died of the disease. In a second letter she declared: 'I am well satisfy'd of the safety of the Experiment since I intend to try it on my dear little son.' Another letter confirmed that Edward had been successfully 'engrafted'.

Following family tradition, Edward was sent to Westminster School. He ran away at least three times when he was 11 and 12. Edward's mysterious whereabouts caused much speculation. No specific dates are given in the Westminster School records, but in March 1725, Lady Mary, in a letter to her sister, the Countess of Mar, referred to her 'blessed offspring' having 'taken to his heels'. She reported that 'the young rake'... had transported his person to Oxford, 'being in his own opinion qualified for the University'. It was some time before Edward was found.

Edward inherited his mother's wit and vivacity. His good looks and easy charm, however, were deceptive; he was also a fluent liar. In August the following year, he ran away again. His truancy in 1726 lasted several months. His mother, annoyed that her son had made himself 'the talk of the whole nation', confided to her sister that Edward had gone 'knight-erranting, God knows where'.

The family placed an advertisement offering £20 for Edward's return. He was eventually found in the Port of Oporto, Portugal. Edward, having worked his passage on a ship, had found employment in a vineyard. When captured (in charge of a pack of mules) he was handed over to the Consul, who informed his parents.

His tutor, Mr Forster, reported Edward's escapades. Accounts about where he was found differ. Some say he went missing for almost a year and was discovered crying fish in Blackwall; others, (*Literary Anecdotes*, Nichols) that he had 'entered as a foremast man on board a ship bound for the Mediterranean'. However, the story of his sojourn with chimney sweeps was the most romantic by far.

During one of his escapades, Edward chanced to meet a young chimney sweep. As he and the boy were 'of the same size', Edward suggested that they change clothes. The boy liked the idea of Edward's garb and they swapped clothes in an empty house. The boy then dryly asked, 'did he also have a mind to try the trade?' 'Yes', replied Edward, 'if he's a good master'. 'You couldn't have a better', said the boy, 'he'll fill your belly, if he beats your back'. Undeterred and intrigued by the novelty of the situation, Edward accompanied the apprentice sweep to his master's house.

At first, the sweep and his wife were reluctant to employ Edward. Although dressed in the sable garments of a chimney sweep, with his fine hair covered by a dirty woollen night-cap full of holes, the 'comely youth ... with skin as fair as alabaster' still looked unconvincing. Their minds were changed by Edward's keenness. Giving their own apprentice another set of chimney-sweeping clothes, they promised that his 'finery' would be restored to him 'when he was out of his time'.

Edward, being too large to attempt narrow tortuous flues quickly adapted to wider ones, climbing them with scraper and long-handled brush. Edward's proficiency and cheerful disposition were soon put to other uses. A publican who was friendly with his master often enlisted Edward's aid to get rid of undesirable company. When drunken patrons (who had been gambling in the back parlour) refused to leave, Edward was instructed to 'ascend a chimney adjoining the room, then descend into the one they were in'. Creeping unobserved into their midst, he suddenly cried out in a loud voice, 'My master, Lucifer, has sent me for you all!' At his black appearance, they panicked and crowded out of the door in terror. Any winnings left behind on the table were then divided between the landlord and Edward as 'lawful money'.

While cleaning chimneys in Golden Square, Edward, out of curiosity, descended the flue of an adjoining house. Finding himself in an elegant bedchamber and tempted by the soft bed, he fell asleep. He made his escape later, when a timid chambermaid uncovered the bedclothes and fainted with shock.

A gold watch was Edward's undoing. It was nearing November 5th, and other sweeps had bought faggots for a bonfire. Edward, wanting to impress them but having no money, tried to sell his timepiece. The watchmaker became suspicious. He kept Edward talking while his man fetched a constable. When taken before a magistrate Edward was obliged to confess. His family, the headmaster, and the master sweep were all sent for. The master sweep was reprimanded and the magistrate profoundly thanked. Edward was forgiven, and even indulged, although he suffered temporarily with skin trouble caused by soot.

Edward resumed his studies. As he showed great aptitude for classical languages as well as French and Spanish, he was sent to the West Indies in the care of a tutor. (See Appendix notes for the rest of Montagu's biography.)

Memorial to Edward Montagu in Westminster Abbey, placed by his schoolfriend John English Dolben.

Gentlefolk, brought up by their nannies to fear chimney sweeps, refused to believe that a boy of noble birth should choose to associate with sooties. They presumed that he had been kidnapped.

Young Montagu's fame became legendary. In spring 1799, a report in *The Times*, stated that: as it was the first of May, Mrs Montagu would be giving her annual entertainment of roast beef, and plum pudding to the chimney sweepers of the Metropolis, in the court yard of her house in Portman Square, in commemoration of discovering her child among them, long after it had been trespassed away. Another report the following day repudiated the reason given for her benevolence, pointing out that it was 'wholly unfounded'. Despite this, the rumour persisted. Boz, in an article, *The First of May* (1836), wrote:

> Stories were related of a young gentleman, who having been stolen from his parents in infancy, and devoted to the occupation of chimney-sweeping, was sent, in the course of his professional career, to sweep the chimney of his Mamma's bedroom ... and was discovered and recognised wherein by his mother, who once every year of her life, thereafter, requested the pleasure of the company of every London sweep at half-past one o'clock, to roast beef, plum-pudding, porter, and sixpence.

It is now clear that the name 'Montagu' helped cause confusion. Elizabeth Montagu was indeed the benevolent lady, but she was Edward's distant cousin and his junior by seven years. Elizabeth's son had died in 1744 (when Edward was 31). The cousins did meet on a few occasions but made little impression on each other.

Elizabeth was mistakenly identified as Edward's mother because both she and Lady Mary were married to other cousins of the same name (Edward Montagu). It makes little difference; such misunderstandings led to myths that greatly enhanced the image of the chimney sweeping trade and inspired a rich amount of literature.

Climbing Boys' Cant (18th & 19th Centuries)

Chimney sweeps had their own cant (secret language). It was a mixture of 18th-century slang with adaptations used by (rogue) sweeps in order to deceive their customers. George Elson explains how it operated. When the boys needed food, clothing, or a higher fee, the oldest would tell the youngest which was the best to ask for, the right moment, and the right person:

> Now Jim, mang (beg) the rum mort (mistress) for a cant (piece) of panam or spreadham (bread & butter) or panam and fe (meat), cas (cheese).

The sweep boy was told to mang for a pair of stamps (shoes) or stockings, or any old tuggery (clothes). When a boy was sweeping a difficult chimney and the mistress refused to pay the fee demanded, the master would 'put his head under the cloth before the grate' and order the lad to 'pike the lew'. This meant 'burk' the top: leave the top section of the chimney full of soot (for a better-paid sweep to clear).

Some other cant vocabulary was as follows:

CLY ...	pocket	*CHIMNEY*	
DIVER ...	pickpocket	HOLE ...	chimney
GARNISH ...	bribe	FOGGY ...	foul
GENEVA ...	gin	NOTCHY ...	narrow
JAKES ...	privy (toilet)	EIGHTS ...	8″ square
KEN ...	house	NINES ...	9″ square
LAG ...	water		
MIZZLE ...	to run away	*MONEY*	
PANAM ...	bread	RINO/	
		READY ...	money
PROG ...	food	JACK ...	farthing
PUG ...	girl	MEG ...	halfpenny
SCORCH ...	beat with a brush	WIN ...	penny
SKUFTR ...	police	THRUMS ...	threepence
SPLORGER ...	owner	TESTER ...	sixpence
STAMPS ...	shoes	HOG ...	shilling
STINGO ...	strong ale	YELLOWBOY....	guinea
SWITCH ...	sweep's brush		
TUGGY ...	sooty cloth		

Family Tradition

Successful chimney-sweeping businesses remained in the family, passing from father to son or other family members.

Pearce family

Present day Pearce & Sons trading from 43 Upper Elmers End Road, proudly advertise as 'England's oldest family of chimney sweeps'. In the days of Charles William Pearce (1802), they established a permanent base in south-east London. Before this, the family were roaming sweeps travelling the countryside in horse-drawn caravans. Their favourite route was from Bristol to London where extra money was earned as prizefighters in boxing booths (see section on Henry Pearce, Chapter 5).

Percy Pearce, in his late 80s, is now the senior member of the family. He had been a sweep for 62 years. Percy and his younger brother Charlie, are the last of seven brothers and one stepbrother who all worked for their father, Alfred.

Alfred Pearce swept chimneys for 54 years. A photograph, taken in November 1937 shows him with six of his sons travelling to work on their motorcycles. Alfred had seven brothers, and his father before him was one of six sons. All were chimney sweeps. At one time there were 35 sweeps in the Pearce family operating in South London, Kent and Essex. The family used to supply 'nearly 5,000 sacks of soot a year to farmers for use as fertiliser'.[20] Apart from Percy and his son (who now runs his business) at Elmers End many other members of Pearce & Sons still operate throughout south-east London.

Dye family

The chimney sweeping business of Dye & Sons, 15 Green Street, Hertford, was well established by James Dye & Marian (Mary Ann Munns) in the 1830s and the business remained in the family. Marian, or Mother Dye, as she was known, appears to have been in charge of the business from the early days until her death in 1888. She had 11 children and outlived her husband by 26 years. Five of her children were boys; one died in a chimney accident (see Chapter 7), two chose other trades, and Daniel and David joined the family business.

We will follow the family of Daniel first. Daniel married twice and remained in the chimney-sweeping business all his life. When he was 92, he could still recall his climbing days.[21] His daughter, Clara, married a chimney-sweeping cousin (see later). His sons, Daniel (Dan) and William both became sweeps. An old photograph dating from 1885 shows 12-year-old William Dye being initiated into the trade. His father is dipping his face into a bag of soot.

In 1887, Dan Dye applied to Lord Salisbury for the contract to sweep Hatfield House and the Salisbury Estate Chimneys. His tender

Daniel and William Dye, Hertford, c,1885.

was accepted. In addition to the 83 chimney flues in Hatfield House (see Chapter 1) there were a further 199 chimneys on the estate. Even the stables had chimneys. Many of the flues were swept quarterly and Mr Dye was paid £40 per year. (The contract was still held by Dye & Sons in 1910.)

Dan married Elizabeth Ambrose and their two sons, Reginald & Eric helped in the business. In later years, the eldest son, Reginald, remembers accompanying his father to Hatfield House:

> When I was a young boy, me and my old dad used to get up very early, about 5 it was, harness the horse and get over to Hatfield House to sweep the chimneys. Not all of them in one go, some used to be done at one time, and others another time... I used to go upstairs to the trap-doors in the fireplaces, and wait till the brushes had got so far, and tell my dad, then he's come up and we'd do the next bit up. After we'd finished Lord Salisbury would give us breakfast. Then we'd go home again with the horse, we'd be back at about 8 or so, perhaps, then I'd get dressed proper and go to school.[22]

Every chimney in Hatfield House had a chimney-sweeping aid, and

Some of the chimneys the Dye family swept at Hatfield House. (Reproduced by kind permission of Lord Salisbury)

they can still be seen. At the base of each shaft, where it extends above the roof, is a small rectangular opening fitted with an iron door. Each chimney is numbered and inscribed with the name of the room containing the fireplace, e.g. No. 14 WEST ATTIC. Many of the chimneys are named after the wood used in room panelling: Maple room; Walnut dressing room; Hornbeam bedroom etc.

Apart from running a successful chimney-sweeping business Dan Dye made quite a name for himself. At the turn of the century, he was the first person in Hertford to use a motor-tricar for transport, the machine being the 'highlight of the procession formed to celebrate the relief of Mafeking',[23] May 1900. Mr Dye became Mayor of Hertford and served as alderman and member of the Hertfordshire County Council until well into his 70s.

Mother Dye's second chimney-sweeping son, David Dye, married Mary Jane Trundell and they had seven children. Of their five sons only the youngest, David Junior became a sweep. In the 1890s Dye & Sons consisted of the elder members; Daniel and David, Daniel's sons William and Dan, and their cousin David Junior.

David Dye Jnr. further strengthened family ties by marrying his cousin, Clara (Dye). They had one daughter, Joan, who still lives in her father's old cottage at No 28 Railway Street, Hertford. David Jnr. became head of the family business which he ran with Reginald's brother Eric Dye, then Peter Neal, Joan's husband. David Jnr. died in 1956 – the last of the Dye family sweeps.

Sherborne Street Sweeps

John Russell began his chimney-sweeping business at 15 Sherborne Street, Cheltenham, in 1826. He built up a good trade which his wife Ann (see Chapter 7) continued after his death. In the 1840s, Ann married her foreman James Short, and they moved to No 43 Sherborne Street in 1855. There is a remarkable trade sign in the Cheltenham Museum, which dates from the mid-19th century. It stands four foot high and represents James Short in every detail. The zinc figure of the sweep with his brushes used to stand on a shelf above the front doorway of No 43.

During his lifetime, James Short was known as 'the gentleman sweep'. His face had aristocratic features and he wore a top hat and frock coat. Details on the zinc replica show high cheekbones, hair around the ears, and a top hat, bow tie, and a row of buttons on a belted frock coat. Mr Short died in 1869 but his trade sign remained outside No 43 for almost a century. It was known locally as the 'old man'.

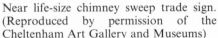

Near life-size chimney sweep trade sign. (Reproduced by permission of the Cheltenham Art Gallery and Museums)

The trade sign in situ at 43 Sherborne Street, Cheltenham.

James Short had employed several climbing boys. One of them, William Field carried on the business until 1888. Mr Field was immensely strong with such a bull-neck that he took to wearing a muffler instead of a collar. Because Sherborne Street was quite narrow, when farmers came to collect soot, Mr Field uncoupled the horses and was able to turn the cart himself. William Field's wife bore him 16 children. The eldest, Frederick, started working for his father when he was 12. Five years later, aged 17, he inherited the family business. Frederick married and had several children. When he retired from the trade, he had been working as a sweep for more than 70 years. A photograph (1950) shows him in waistcoat and cap, with his brushes and soot sacks tied to his bicycle.

The 'old man' trade sign was sold to the Cheltenham Museum, and Frederick Field's son, Arthur, donated his father's brushes and the brass name plate. The trade sign is now suspended over a doorway upstairs in the museum. It is an object of great curiosity, said to frighten children by its black appearance.

Notes

[1] *Irish Folk Ways*, E.E. Evans, 1957.
[2] Slate was inserted in some chimneys to improve damp proofing. It was known as 'flashing'.
[3] *England in the Age of Hogarth*, Derek Jarrett, 1974.
[4] Gentleman's Magazine, 1751.
[5] *Book of Days*, article, *Fabled Beasts*, Win Bennet, *Hertfordshire Countryside* magazine, October, 1995.
[6] *That Enchantress*, Book 1, (1698–1701) Doris Leslie, 1948.
[7] *Imperial Rome, Great Ages of Man*, Moses Hadas Jay, 1966.
[8] *The Graphic*, J.G., 3rd May, 1890.
[9] Reform of the British calendar 1752.
[10] *The Graphic*, J.G. 3rd May, 1890.
[11] *18th Century Journal*, John Hampden, 1776.
[12] *Every-Day Book*, William Hone, 1826.
[13] *London Labour and the London Poor*, Henry Mayhew, 1851.
[14] *Glimpses of Ancient Leicester*, Mrs T. Fielding Johnson, 1906.
[15] *Folklore of Hampshire*, Wendy Boase, 1976.
[16] Local Reminiscences of Evesham, *Notes & Queries*, G.M. Stratton, 1908.
[17] *Ibid*, William Hone.
[18] The Chimney-Sweep, *Head of The People*, John Ogden, 1840.
[19] Edward Wortley Montagu, Lord of the Treasury (1714–15), MP for Huntingdon.
[20] P. Pearce, *Solid Fuel Review*, July, 1991.
[21] *The Mercury*, 1940s.
[22] *Hertfordshire Civic Society*, Reg Dye, 1981.
[23] *Country Life*, letter, A. Knight Loveday, 24th Jan, 1957.

11

SWEEPS IN LITERATURE

I am Envy, begotten of a chimney sweeper, and an oyster-wife. I
cannot read, and therefore wish all books burn'd.

Christopher Marlowe, Dr Faustus, 1593

Introduction

Throughout the centuries, chimney sweeps have featured in a
surprising amount of literature. There are very few recorded facts
about the trade but sweeps are mentioned in every form of writing.
Tracts from the 15th, 16th and 17th centuries depict sweeps as part of
the bawdy humour of the times; whereas sentimental, religious and
moral literature referring to sweeps predominates in the 18th and 19th
centuries. Modern critics might consider that, apart from Dickens,
Blake and Kingsley there is little of literary merit overall; nevertheless
there was always an underlying affection shown towards the chimney
sweep.

Contrast and Heroics

Chimney sweeps are first mentioned in *Cocke Lorell's Bote*[1] (c1510), a
narrative poem of 400 lines. The poem was a popular English satire
about various people who sail a boat through England. Among the
London tradespeople whom Captain Cocke Lorell takes on board are
'Chymney Swepers and costerde Mongers.'

More than 80 years later, Shakespeare wrote a 'Pleasant conceited
comedy', *Love's Labours Lost*, which was presented before Elizabeth I.
In the play, Shakespeare's King of Navarre is repulsed by anything
black. Scornful of his friend's infatuation for Rosaline, a Lady-in-
Waiting, the king declares: 'To look like her are chimney-sweepers
black.' The very blackness of sweeps 'Besmeer'd with soot and Nasty
to the Sight ...' (poem, L. Meriton, 1696) was a recurring theme in
humorous verse, and sweeps were often allied with the devil.

John Gay[2] in *Trivia* (1716), refers to chimney sweeping as one of the 'sullied trades' that soils the clothes of others:

> The little chimney-sweeper skulks along,
> And marks with Sooty stains the heedless throng...

His observations were shared by Thomas Browne (1719), a contemporary writer, who, quoting the case of Sir John Toppington wrote:

> About two months ago he put on a milk-white suit, designing to show himself in it that evening in the park; ... Coming by Catherine Street, a saucy impudent chimney-sweeper daub'd his coat.

In the same year, a musical arrangement in four bars called *The Devil and The Collier* was commissioned by J. Tonson. In the scenario, while the devil is sheltering in a tree during a storm he talks to passing tradesmen:

> The next came by was a chimney-Sweeper,
> with his Poles and shackles;
> what tradesman art thou, the Devil then he said,
> thou usest all these tackles?
> I prithee gentle blande, come tell me thy trade,
> thy face is so besmear'd
> If thou hadst not been so black, with thy Tackles at thy back,
> thou hadst made me damnable afraid...

Eighteenth-century anecdotes about chimney sweeps can be found in the *Encyclopedia of Wit* (1819), and *Wit and Wisdom*, (1835).

> One day last week (1718) a gentlewoman unluckily stooping to buckle her shoe at a linen-draper's shop, her Hoop-Petticoat of a more than ordinary circumference, flew up, and an arch little chimney sweeper, passing by at that instant, conveyed himself underneath the machine and, with a loud voice cry'd out "Sweep! Sweep!" The gentlewoman being affrighted, leap'd back, the boy struggling to get out threw madam in the dirt and with much ado the young Devil got away and left the lady in no small confusion.
>
> *Daniel Defoe*[3]

On a more serious note, in 1732, the Rev. Dr Swift wrote:

> I am assured, and partly know, that all the chimney-sweepers

210

boys, where Members of Parliament chiefly lodge, are hired by our enemies to skulk in the Tops of chimneys, with their heads no higher than will just permit them to look round, and at the usual Hours when Members are going to the House, if they see a Coach stand near the lodging of any *loyal* Member, they call out 'coach, coach,' as loud as they can bawl, just at the instant when the Footman begins to give the same Call. And this is chiefly done on those Days, when any Point of Importance is to be debated. This Practice may be of very dangerous Consequence. For, these Boys are all hired by enemies of the Government; and thus, by the Absence of a few Members for a few minutes, a question may be carried against the *true interest* of the Kingdom, and very probably, not without an eye towards the Pretender.[4]

Chimney sweeps were portrayed as heroic and often amorous characters because they dealt with maids. Women – rather than men – applied to them to sweep their chimneys and their very trade took them into every room in the house including the bedchamber.

In a curious tract, *The Dutch Whore*, or *Miss of Amsterdam* (published, London, 1690) a chimney sweep takes on the role of a

The sweep was often believed to make the most of amorous opportunities! (Acknowledgements, Ken Bryant, chimney sweep).

211

romantic hero who rescues Doll, the heroine, from the Black Castle, a place of ill repute.

More heroics are found in Eileen Power's history of *Medieval English Nunneries*[5] when, in one 17th-century tale, a young girl is rescued from life in a nunnery by her lover who enlists the aid of a chimney sweep. When the sweep goes to the convent to sweep chimneys, he pretends to be ill with stomach-ache. While the Abbess hurries away to fetch medicine the sweep gives the girl a letter from her lover. A tryst is arranged. On his second return, the sweep carries the girl away in his sack.

Later, in the 18th century, Henry Fielding wrote a burlesque about contemporary playwrights called *The Tragedy of Tom Thumb*. It was presented at the Haymarket Theatre, London, in 1730. During the action of the play, the king and queen talk of love. The queen does not want Tom to marry her daughter.

TOM: So when some Chimney-Sweeper, all the day,
            Has through dark Paths pursu'd the Sooty Way
            At night, to wash his face and Hands he flies,
            And in his t'other shirt with his brickdusta Lies.

(When The Theatre Royal Drury Lane presented *Tom Thumb* as a burletta in 1806, Fielding's original speech for Tom had been altered slightly, becoming a two-verse 'air' which he sang.)

An original and amusing verse play, *The Chimney-Sweepers, A Town Eclogue* in which all the characters are chimney sweeps, was written in 1773 (printed for J. Ridley). The main characters are three young men, Grim, Dingy and Sooty-Dun. They sit round a fire engaged in light-hearted bragging about their girlfriends.

PLACE: Near Saint Martin's Church, by the statue of 'Martyr
          Charles'.
TIME: 1 o'clock in the morning.

          Three sable youths, of that illustr'ous crew
          Who clear the chimney's soot-encumber'd flue,
          Closely engag'd in pure and friendly chat,
          Round the dim remnants of a bonfire sat:
          And, while the dying embers they survey'd,
          Thus GRIM began, and DINGY answer made.

GRIM: Dingy, Saint Giles's boys with rapture tell
           Your feats in singing, since you sing so well:

212

Not Soot-Dun himself, if they say true,
Has half so loud, so shrill a pipe as you.

DINGY: Well have you heard, my equal is not found
From Holburn Corner down to Nibb's Pound:
And as to Soot-Dun – believe me, Grim,
Some says I sing more betterer nor him.

SOOTY
-DUN: Dingy, 'tis neither more nor less than spight:
You know where 'twas I cotch'd you t'other night,
Aks Moll Come-dusty – but, to end this strife,
I'll sweep a chimley with you for your life.

GRIM: Peace, Sooty-Dun, folks now are all asleep;
No chimleys for these next four hours to sweep.

SOOTY
-DUN: Coming from Chelsea t'other ev'ning late,
Jem Duffin stopp'd me at the turnpike-gate;
But when he knew me noddling on my ass,
"Ha! Clargymant! [*Clergyman*] says he, and let
me pass. [*Jem was a highwayman*]
The money sav'd I've in my pocket got,
And it shall buy my Bess a sup o'hot.

. . .

The Heroes rose, and each resumed his sack,
And hung his brush and shovel at his back;
Ambition fir'd each dauntless breast to soar
Through paths untry'd, new regions to explore,
And boldly mount to heights unknown before,
"The world was all before them where to chuse;"
So on they shuffled in their slip-shod shoes.

Writers in the earlier centuries treated chimney sweeps with respect;
trade for trade the sweeps were equal. Poets and dramatists used
themes where so-called 'black' trades (sweeps, coalmen, shoeblacks
etc.) were placed together, and 'black' and 'white' trades shown in
contrast to one another: sweep versus miller (white flour) or sweep
versus barber (ultra-cleanliness).

In an early example of burlesque humorous verse, Edward Ward's
Hudibras Redivius (1706), a sweep and a barber come to blows:

213

The contrast of black (sweep) and white (miller) was a popular one in pictures and dramas (Photograph by Frank Meadow Sutcliffe Hon. FRPS (1853–1941). Copyright The Sutcliffe Gallery, Whitby, by agreement with Whitby Literary and Philosophical Society)

Sitting by the kitchen fire [*of an inn*]
Two Toapers in a warm debate;
One was a sweeper of a chimney,
That dirty Rhime to Polyhimney,
With Negro Hands and Face, as Black
As was his Sooty Bushel Sack,
That hung across his sturdy Back.
The other was a Mealy Blade,
All powder'd o'er from Heal to Head;
One that prun'd fromsy Beards for two pence,
And therefore Master but of few pence,
Which sad misfortune caus'd a hot
Dispute between each Brother Sot,
About the payment of a Pot...

214

The barber, cursing vehemently, called the sweep (among other things) the 'picture of the devil'. This provoked the sweep. Both barber and sweep then engaged in a fracas in which the barber 'from White to Black' was 'truly dy'd'. The chimney sweeper was deemed the 'conqu'ror of the two' and the quarrel ended amicably.

More than a century later the sweep was still the victor in Michael Hall's comic song *The Doughey and Chummy* (1829):

> There was a bandy lass, and her name was Sal,
>
> . . . . . .
>
> Her Swell was a noted Chummy.
> On Monday nights together they'd go
> To the old Three Colts, the place you may know,
> No couple I'm sure could cut such a show
> As bandy Sal and her Chummy...[6]

18th and 19th Centuries

Of the numerous poets and writers of the 18th and 19th centuries who wrote about chimney sweeps (see Appendix) perhaps only William Blake and Charles Kingsley are remembered today.

> *The Chimney Sweeper*
>
> When my mother died I was very young,
> And my father sold me while yet my tongue,
> Could scarcely cry weep weep weep weep.
> So your chimneys I sweep, and in soot I sleep.
>
> . . . . . .
>
> And the Angel told Tom if he'd be a good boy,
> He'd have God for his father & never want joy.
> . . . . . .
>
> And so Tom awoke and we rose in the dark
> And got with our bags and our brushes to work.
>
> *William Blake*

In his youth, William Blake was apprenticed to James Basire, an engraver. When Blake published his *Songs of Innocence* (1789), their mystical themes of love and sympathy were hand-written and enchant-

215

ingly engraved by him. It is thought that William Blake had been inspired to write about chimney sweeps after learning about the early life of 18th-century architect, Isaac Ware.

Isaac Ware was a cockney. From the memoirs of a sculptor, Mr Nollekens, we read that:

A thin, sickly little boy, a chimney sweeper, was amusing himself one morning by drawing with a piece of chalk the street front of Whitehall upon the basement stones of the building itself, carrying his delineation as high as his little arms could possibly reach...[7]

He was noticed by an 'influential Nobleman' passing by in his carriage. The wealthy gentleman (possibly Lord Burlington)[8] stopped his horses and asked the boy where he lived. Isaac, alarmed at the thought of trouble, burst into tears and assured the gentleman that 'he would wipe it off'. After further questioning, the boy's master was found to be living in Charles Court, The Strand.

The master sweep was easily persuaded to part with his apprentice because the boy, although of good character, 'was of little use to him, on account of his being so bodily weak'. The sweep knew of the boy's fondness for 'chalking' and showed his visitor where Isaac had made a drawing of the front of St Martin's church on the wall of his business premises. On acceptance of an (undisclosed) fee the master sweep released Isaac from his apprenticeship and the boy began a life more suited to his talents.

Isaac Ware's benefactor paid for his education, financed a trip to Italy and introduced him to other patrons. Their faith in him was well rewarded. During his lifetime Isaac Ware designed many fine buildings, notably Chesterfield House (South Audley Street, 1749) and Wrotham Park (near South Mimms) for Admiral Byng (c1754). He published two notable books: *Designs of Inigo Jones and Others*, and his own work, *The Complete Body of Architecture*, as well as holding a number of official positions.[9] Ware died on 5th January, 1766, at 6, Bloomsbury Square; a house he had built for himself many years before. While a bust was being made of him by Roubiliac, Isaac had told him the story of his early boyhood.

> A little black thing among the snow,
> Crying "weep! weep!" in notes of woe!
> *The Chimney Sweeps, William Blake (1794)*

It was also believed that a young climbing boy named James Seaward was the role model for 'Tom' in Charles Kingsley's *Water Babies* (see later). At one time James was thought to have been employed in sweeping the rectory chimneys at Kingsley's home in Eversley (Hampshire).[10]

James Seaward, who lived at 31, Rose Street, Wokingham, Berkshire, remained a chimney sweep until his death in 1921. During his lifetime he was well liked and respected in the community. From 1892 Mr Seaward was a member of the Wokingham Town Council, later becoming an alderman. A staunch Baptist, he voluntarily cleaned the Baptist Church chimneys for more than 50 years. Unfortunately, the idea that it was James who so inspired Kingsley to write his allegorical tale has to be repudiated. *The Water Babies* was published in 1863, the year that James was born.

The Water Babies

Charles Kingsley's *The Water Babies* turned out to be the most influential and enduring work of fiction on the subject of chimney sweeps. Charles was born on 12th June 1819 in his father's vicarage at Holne, (Devon). In 1836, the family moved to Chelsea. Charles attended Cambridge University and became Professor of Modern History (1860–69). He took Holy Orders in 1843 and was rector of Eversley village for 32 years. Throughout his life, he sympathised deeply with the sufferings of the poor and his literary works were many and varied.

In 1863, Kingsley wrote *The Water Babies*, an allegorical children's story sub-titled *A Fairy Story for a Land-Baby*. The story was written to please Kingsley's wife. In her *Letters & Memories*, she wrote:

> One Spring morning, while sitting at breakfast I reminded him of an old promise "Rose, Maurice, and Mary have got their book (*The Heroes*), and baby (son, Grenville) must have his." He made no answer, but got up and went into the study, locking the door. In half an hour he returned with the story of little Tom – the first chapter of *The Water Babies*.

When first published, *The Water Babies* was highly acclaimed and aroused much public sympathy towards the climbing boys. The story humorously tells how Tom, a young chimney sweep, runs away from his unkind master, Mr Grimes, and falls into a river, where he becomes a water-baby. In the water, he meets many strange creatures. At the end of the story Tom meets up with his master, who has been imprisoned in a chimney top. Grimes tells Tom that he had run away from his mother when young and 'took up with the sweeps'. 'Foul I

Linley Samborne's illustration from *The Water Babies*, 1885. (Acknowledgements Armley Mills, Leeds.)

would be, and foul I am ...' said Grimes, 'and he cried so bitterly that Tom began crying too'. All ends happily, however. The good fairy forgives Grimes and he is released.

> So Grimes stepped out of the chimney, and really, if it had not been for the scar on his face, he looked as clean and respectable as a master-sweep need look.

The book is now a classic and has never been out of print. Armley Mills, Leeds contains over 30 editions of *The Water Babies*. Since 1863, Kingsley's story has undergone many changes; it has been reprinted by more than 12 different publishing houses, using a variety of illustrators (see Appendix). The latest publication; four little *Good Night, Sleep Tight* storybooks, published by *Grandreams Ltd* (1993) bears little resemblance to Kingsley's classic.

Sweeps in Dickens

Although chimney sweeps play no prominent role in Dickens's stories,

"He took up a live coal and put it to Grimes's pipe." A. E. Jackson, 1920.

they are mentioned to a greater or lesser degree in several of his most famous books, and three others, *Nicholas Nickleby*, *Dombey and Son* and *The Old Curiosity Shop* show illustrations of sweeps.

Charles Dickens began writing about life in London when he was 18 years old. His first series of *Sketches by Boz* was published on 7th February 1836 on his 21st birthday. In his observation *The Streets – Morning*, Dickens contrasts the 'boisterous mirth' of several school-boys as they 'rattle merrily over the pavement', with:

> The demeanour of the little sweep, who, having knocked and rung till his arm aches, and being interdicted by a merciful legis-lature from endangering his lungs by calling out, sits patiently down on the door-step until the housemaid may happen to wake.

Apart from Mr Gamfield in *Oliver Twist* (1838), Dickens's other master sweep was the celebrated Mr Sluffen, from Adam-and-Eve Court. In the following colloquial speech, Mr Sluffin mentions chimney-sweeping machinery.

> ...he 'ad been a chummy ... more nor thirty year – he might say he's been born in a chimbley, and he know'd uncommon vell as

219

'sheenery vos vus nor o'no use: and as to kerhewelty to the boys, everybody in the chimbley line know'd as vell as he did, that they liked the climbin' better nor nuffin as vos...

Sketches by Boz (1836)

In *Our Mutual Friend* (1840), Mrs Lammle tries to find out what her friend, Miss Podsnap most enjoys:

"Of course you like dancing?"
Miss Podsnap hesitates, and dimples "I can't say ... how I might have liked it if I had been a – you won't mention it *will* you?"
"My dear! Never!"
"No, I am sure you won't. I can't say how I should have liked it, if I had been a chimney-sweep on May-day."
"Gracious!" was the exclamation which amazement elicited from Mrs Lammle.

After attempting to convince Miss Podsnap that she could be a real friend and was not a 'frumpy old married woman' she concludes:

"...about the chimney-sweeps?"
"Hush! Ma'll hear!" [*She is assured she won't hear.*]
"...well, what I mean is, that they seem to enjoy it.".
"And that perhaps you would have enjoyed it if you had been one of them?"
Miss Podsnap nodded significantly.

A final reference to the trade is found in *David Copperfield* (1840). David is about 12 when he visits Mr Wickfield's very old house which bulged out over the road. David describes Mr Wickfield's office:

It looked into the garden, and had an iron safe let into the wall, so immediately over the mantel-shelf, that I wondered, as I sat down, how the sweeps got round it when they swept the chimney.

Other 19th-Century Novels

Other novels worth mentioning are *Jem Bunt* by Matthew Henry Barker (the Old Sailor), and *Valentine Vox, The Ventriloquist* by Henry Cockton. Both novels were published in 1840. *Jem Bunt*, subtitled *The Land & the Ocean* is a substantial novel illustrated with 23 etchings by Robert Crickshank. Jem, as a climbing boy features in many of them.

220

Jem (James Bunt) was an orphan assigned to the workhouse of St Leadenham. When he was 'above 6 years old' Jem's prowess at climbing made him a suitable candidate for the chimney-sweeping trade and he was 'bound' to affluent Master Sweep Theodore Fluewellin of Camberwell. Although Jem 'displayed marks of the corrector's hand' due to his stubbornness, the sweep was a good master, and Jem had a straw mattress and warm blankets at night. Nor was Jem's education altogether neglected. In winter, he went with other apprentices to an evening school, where he was taught to read, write, and cost accounts, for 4d a week. As for chimney sweeping:

The task of elongating his body, to force it through a chimney-pot, was, in his estimation, amply rewarded when, with the implements of his profession, he hung his arms over the brim, raised the cap of night from his head, gazed upon the surrounding scenery, felt himself above the cares of the world, and looked down upon his plodding fellow-creatures with a degree of pride and contempt.

Jem was engaged to sweep the kitchen chimney at the house of Sir Wentworth Weatherall, the brother of a sea captain. Sir Wentworth is 'dying in love' because he cannot get a letter 'to the object of his passion at the next house' – due to the barbarous treatment of her father. Jem comes up with a plan; he will 'dive down the chimbley' instead of going up it. The baronet is so keen to get the letter delivered that he suggests a fee of 20 guineas, and the task is accomplished. Jem eventually goes to sea in Captain Wentworth's frigate. At the end of the novel, Jem Blunt has achieved wealth and status.

Valentine Vox was described by *The Court Journal* as 'a clever Bozian work, very smartly and shrewdly written'. It tells the story of a youth who becomes a ventriloquist. S. Onwhyn illustrated the book with 60 engravings. Chapter 5 contains an amusing incident with a chimney sweep. 'An extremely humane and intellectual sweep who had become particularly knock-kneed in the profession', had been summoned to assist a constable at the nearby inn where burglars were thought to be hiding in the chimney. (Valentine had been practising his voices.) The situation had got out of hand when the constable ordered a fire to be lit. Shufflebottom enters with the machine upon his shoulder. Master Sweep Shufflebottom was a stout stumpy man 'who stood about five feet five, upon legs to which nothing stands recorded in the annals of legs.' Moreover, he owned a machine 'which was patronised by the nobility and gentry'.

221

In *Valentine Vox* a sweep is called in to help eject a burglar hiding in a chimney.

"I understand," said he, bowing with all the importance of which a master sweep is comfortably capable towards the fire – "I understand that you have certain burlarious burglars up the flue."

In the confusion which followed, the sweep's brush was 'captured' by another constable positioned on the roof, and everyone below, except Shufflebottom, 'deemed it expedient to crawl out on their hands and knees to avoid suffocation'.

In 1854 a sombre novel, *Tit for Tat* was first published anonymously in London, by Clarke and Beeton, then later in New York. *Tit for Tat* by a Lady from New Orleans[11] was sub-titled *American Fixings of English Humanity*. The story was about 'Totty', the young son of the Marquis of Hardfoot who is kidnapped by sweeps. The author, 'furious over the English public's enthusiastic reception of *Uncle Tom's Cabin*' (a story of slavery in the American South), in what he or she considered to be the first humanitarian novel devoted to climbing-boys, offered 'Tit' the climbing-boy of England, for 'Tat' the negro slave in the South. 'This race', the author said, 'is black, not from blood, but from Soot.' The novel, although re-published four times, makes uncomfortable reading, being little more than a series of stories of maltreatment taken from reports to the Parliamentary Select Committee (1852). (The situation in America in the mid-19th century was the same as in England, and white boys as well as Negro boys were still climbing chimneys.)

Amusing escapades with chimney sweeps can be found in *The Mimic*, a short story from *The Parents' Assistant* (Maria Edgeworth, 1897), and *Great-Uncle McCarthy* (Edith Somerville & Violet Martin, 1899), a story set in West Cork. In the Irish tale when the new magistrate, Major Yeates, is entertaining Mr Knox at Shreelane, the house where he is residing,

a shower of soot rattled down the chimney and fell on the hearthrug.

"More rain coming," said Mr Knox, rising composedly: "You'll have to put a goose down these chimneys some day soon, it's the only way in the world to clean them."

Early 20th Century

An unusual novel, *Climbing boy* by Esmond Quinterley, was written in 1900. Set in the year 1750 the novel details the last day in the life of Rob, who suffocates in a chimney flue. The story is told unsentimentally using continuous prose with no chapters or paragraphs. The following passage illustrates the contemptuous attitude shown by boys from wealthy families:

As he (Rob) bent to do more sweeping he heard the door being unlocked. In walked a young gentleman in peagreen coat and kneebreeches. "I heard you was here," he simpered, "An I came to see what you was like." Rob glared at the pampered boy with lace on his shirt, silver buckles on his shoes, a topwhip in his white hand. "I never saw a climbing boy close before," contin-

Little Jimmy is taken in by master sweep Grip. (Illustration by Enock Ward)

ued the young gentleman, "Heighho! what a filthy sight you are, to be sure!" Rob spat, turned his back, and started sweeping.

Early in the 20th century specially chosen books were awarded as school prizes. One such was *Little Jimmy* by D. Rice-Jones. In 1906, Oxford Education Council presented a copy of *Little Jimmy* to schoolboy William Grant for 'Regular Attendance and Good Conduct'. The novel contains 13 chapters and two illustrations by Enoch Ward. It tells how Jimmy Prior after losing his father in a busy London street, is befriended by a master sweep and taken back to the sweep's dingy house. The novel gives an insight into early 19th-century London.

"We'll give him a month," said Grip to his wife, "and if his father don't turn up before the end of that time, he'll never turn up, and the boy will be on our hands for good. Then I'll adopt him."

"Adopt him, Grip!" cried Mrs Grip in alarm "What do you mean? Adopt him as your own son?"

"No, not exactly that, Missus. I know a trick worth two o'that. I'll adopt him into my family of climbing boys, and learn him to earn his own living as I did afore I was his age. That's what I'll do."

Not everything turns out as planned, however, and there is an unexpected twist at the end of the story.

The Queen's Gift Book (1915), sold in aid of Queen Mary's convalescent Auxiliary Hospital, Roehampton, contains the story of *The Soot Fairies* by Beatrice Harraden. The book has a foreword by John Galsworthy, and paintings and drawings by Arthur Rackham.

"Where do you live?" asked Beryl.

The Soot-fairy laughed.

"Why up the chimney, to be sure!" she answered.

"You cannot think how beautiful and black it is up there. I am sure you would enjoy yourself with us, Beryl! There are no fairies so merry as the Soot-fairies..."

A final anecdote: In 1908[12] at Sutton Scarsdale Hall, Derbyshire, the home of Mr Arkwright, one of the chimneys was giving trouble. A sweep was called but was unable to remedy it. Mr Arkwright thought of the novel idea of hauling a cockerel up the flue by ropes, which were attached to a wire frame at the four corners.

The estate carpenter made the contraption, the cockerel was placed on it, and very slowly drawn up the chimney, but, alas, nothing happened. The bird, a black leghorn, simply sat down to enjoy the ride. However, the gamekeeper came to the rescue and put one of his gamecocks with the leghorn on to the wire frame. This was a great success; the two birds fought all the way up the chimney, dislodging the soot, which fell through the frame to the hearth below.

This was not the end of the episode; the gamecock was safely returned but the leghorn flew through a skylight and evading capture found its way into several bedrooms. Our 'feathered' sweeps conclude this history, leaving the last laugh to the birds.

225

The chimney sweep who became a gardener, with the help of the soot fairies, from *The Queen's Gift Book*.

Notes

[1]Similar theme to Sebastian Brandt's *Narrenschiff*, (*Ship of Fools*), 1494.
[2]John Gay, born Barnstaple, North Devon, was apprenticed to a London mercer. He remained in the capital and became popular with London audiences as a writer of comic operas. His operas – notably *The Beggar's Opera* – included folk songs and well-known tunes.
[3]*His Life and Recently Discovered Works* (1716–1729) William Lee, 1869.
[4]*City Cries or An Examination of Certain Abuses ... in London & Dublin*, Rev. Dr Swift, 1732.
[5]*Medieval English Nunneries, Folk Tales*, E. Power, 1922.
[6]*The Melodist* (songs), Vol III, 18.
[7]Told by Nollekens senior, *Life of Nollekens* J.T. Smith, 1828.
[8]*A Short History of British Architecture*, Dora Ware, 1967.
[9]Clerk of the Works, Windsor Castle (1729) and Greenwich (1733), becoming Secretary and Draughtsman (1736).
[10]*The Beast & The Monk*, Susan Chitty, 1974.
[11]Believed to be Marian Southwood or Matthew Estesis.
[12]Letter to *Country Life*, C.W. Dixon, April, 1957.

BIBLIOGRAPHY

Alexander, Ann, *Facts Relative to the State of Children who are Employed by Chimney Sweepers, as Climbing Boys*, William Alexander, York, 1817.

Baker, Rev. James, *The Life of Sir Thomas Bernard*, London, John Murray, 1819.

Bready, J. Wesley, *Lord Shaftesbury and Social Industrial Progress*, G Allen & Unwin, 1933.

Busse, John, *Mrs Montagu, Queen of the Blues*, Gerald Howe, London, 1928.

Caulfield, James, *Printsellers Chronicle*, Caulfield, London, 1814.

Chitty, Susan, *The Beast & The Monk*, A Life of Charles Kingsley, Hodder & Stoughton, 1974.

Clavering, Robert, Essay on *Construction & Building of Chimneys*, I. Taylor, London, 1779.

Cohen, J.B. & Ruston A.G., *Smoke*, a study of town air, Arnold & Company, London, 1925.

Court Leet Records. Southampton, Society Series, F.J.C. Hearnshaw, 1905.

Dashall, Hon. Tom, *Real Life in London*, 2 vols. Jones & Company, London, 1821.

Eckstein, George Frederick, *Practical Treatise on Chimneys*, London, 1852.

Ellis, William, *Modern Husbandman*, London, 1733.

Elson, George, *The Last of the Climbing Boys*, autobiography, John Long & Chandes, London, 1900.

Evans, E. Estyn, *Irish Folk Ways*, Routledge & Kegan Paul, London, 1957.

Fletcher, Valentine, *Chimney Pots & Stacks*, Centaur Press, 1968, 1994.

Gardner, H.W. *Survey of the Agriculture of Hertfordshire*, Royal Agriculture Society of England, Survey No. 5, London, 1967.

Glass, Joseph, *Chimney Sweeping Described*, S. Bagster, Jnr. London, 1815.

Grainger, Rev. James, *A Biographical History of England*, Vol. 2 part 2, 1769, London, 1820–1822.

Grey, Edwin, *Cottage Life in a Hertfordshire Village*, Harpenden & District Local History Society, 1977.

Hamilton, Lord Frederic, *The Days Before Yesterday*, *1920*, Hodder & Stoughton, 1950.

Hammond, J.L. & Barbara, *The Town Labourer 1760–1832*, Longmans 1917 reprint 1995.

Hampden, John, *18th Century Journal*, *1774–1776*, Macmillan & Company, London, 1940.

Hanway, Jonas, *Sentimental History of Chimney Sweepers in London and Westminster*, Dodsley, London, 1785.

Harper, Charles George, *Half-Hours with the Highwaymen*, Vol 1 Chapman & Hall, London, 1908.

228

Harrison, William, *Descriptions of England. Holinshed's Chronicle, 1577–1587, English Home Life*, Christina Hole, 1947.

Henning, F. *Fights For The Championship, 1856, Licensed Victualler Gazette*, Frederick, W.J. London, 1902.

Holland, John & James Everett, *Memoirs of Life and Writings of James Montgomery*, London Longman, 5 vols. 1855.

Hawkes, Jean, *The London Journal of Flora Tristan 1840–1842*, translation, Virago Press, 1982.

Hone, William, *Every-day Book* Vol 1, Hunt & Clarke, London, 1825.

Jarrett, Derek, *England in the Age Of Hogarth*, Granada Publishing, 1974.

Johnson, William Branch, *The Industrial Archaeology of Hertfordshire*, David & Charles, 1970.

Kay, John, Mrs. *The City Tron-men*, H. Paton, Edinburgh, 1836.

Keeling, Frederick, H. *Child Labour in the United Kingdom*, King & Son, London, 1914.

Kingsley, Frances Elizabeth, *Letters & Memories*, Friedrich Andreas Perthes, 1888.

Leslie, Doris, *That Enchantress, Book 1, (1698–1701)* 1948, Heinemann, London, 1966.

Marks, Percy Leman, *Chimneys and Flues, Domestic and Industrial*, Technical Press, London, 1935.

Mayhew, Henry, *London Labour & the London Poor*, 3 Vols. 1851, new impression, Frank Cass & Company, London, 1967. Mayhew's London, selections from *London Labour & the London Poor*, The Hamlyn Group Ltd, 1969.

Mills, Marian, *Your Most Dutyfull Servant, Eighteenth Century Chevening Recreated*, Sevenoaks, 1992.

Montgomery, James, *Chimney-Sweeper's Friend, Climbing-Boys' Album, 1823, 1824*. Second edition, London Longman, 1925.

Nichols John, *Literary Anecdotes, 1778*, Centaur Press, 1967.

Nokes, David, *Jane Austen*, Fourth Estate Ltd, 1997.

Platt, Sir Hugh, *A New Cheape and Delicate Fire of Cole-Balles, 1603*, Da Capo Press, New York, 1972.

Porter, David, *Considerations on the Present State of Chimney Sweepers, 1792*, London, another issue 1801.

Pott, Percival, *Chirurgical works*, London, 1775.

Prize Essays of the Highland & Agriculture Society, new series vvi (Vol xii p.535) 1839.

Pyne, William Henry, *The World In Miniature*, 4 vols, Ackermann, London, 1827.

Remains Historical & Literary, Cheltenham Society Vol xxxv, 1861 (Shuttle-worths).

Remembrancia, Records, The City of London, A.D. 1579–1664, iv 130 p.67,

Roberts Samuel, *A Cry From The Chimneys*, Longman & Orme, London, 1817.

Silvester Davies, Rev J., *History of Southampton, Court Leet Records, 1883*, 2nd edition, Hampshire Books, 1989.

Smith, John Thomas, *Nollekens & His Times 1737–1833*, 2nd edition, 1829. Oxford University Press, 1929.

Strange, Kathleen, H. *The Climbing Boys*, Allison & Busby, 1982.

Turner, Ernest Sackville, *Roads to Ruin*, Michael Joseph, 1950.

Walton, Mary, *Sheffield, Its story and Achievements, 1948*, 4th edition, Wakefield, S.R. Publishers, Sheffield, 1968.

Ward, Edward, *The London Spy*, 2 vols. J. Nutt & J How, London, 1698–1699.

Ware, Dora, *A Short History of British Architecture*, George Allen & Unwin, 1967.

Associations & Societies

Amalgamated Chimney Sweepers Society
Bristol Fire Office Engines, 1828
Hanley & Shelton Chimney Sweeping Association, 1855
Sheffield Association of Master Sweeps, 1809
Society for Abolishing the Common Method of Sweeping Chimneys, 1802
Society for Bettering the Conditions of the Poor, 1799
Society for Superseding the Necessity for Climbing Boys, SSNCB, 1803, 1838
Society for the Encouragement of Arts, Manufactures and Commerce, (now RSA) 1796, 1803, 1805, 21st December, 1807
Society for the Establishment and Support of Sunday Schools throughout the Kingdom. Gloucester
Society of Friends, America, 1803–1805
Society of Master Sweeps, Sheffield, 1809
Statute of Artificers, 1562
The Friendly Society, 1770, 1780, 1800
The Marine Society, 1756
The Master Chimney-Sweepers of Bristol, 28th June, 1817
The Mutual Instruction Society
The Patent Ramoneur Association, 1841 *The Ramoneur Company Ltd*, 1954
United Society of Master Chimney Sweepers, 1st May, 1826

Parliamentary Papers T. C. Hansard

Chimney Sweepers Regulation Bill, 16th June, 1834
Evidence before Parliament, 1834
Evidence before the Commons, 1840
Evidence, David Porter, House of Commons Committee, 1788
Evidence, Lords Committee, George Smart, 1818
Evidence, Parliamentary Committee, 1817
House of Commons Journal, 1st May, 1788
Parliamentary Papers, 17th May, 1817
The Chimney Sweepers Report, Commons Committee, 23rd June, 1817

APPENDIX

Chapter 1

Eleanor Cross

Known as the Great Cross, or Cheapside Cross, it was one of 12 crosses erected by Edward 1 in honour of his wife. Built in stone by Italian artists, it stood in the centre of Cheapside for 353 years. The original cross consisted of three tabernacles; each supported by eight delicate columns; the first, probably 20 feet high; the second 10; the third, 6. In the first, the effigy of a Pope was installed; around the base of the second stood four figures of the apostles, their hands each encircled by a nimbus. Immediately above them stood a Madonna, with the infant Jesus in her arms. The third was occupied by five standing figures, and above it rose a cross (all the limbs of it were equal), surmounted by the celestial dove.

The cross was re-edified many times, usually to commemorate coronations or visits by reigning monarchs. In 1441 and 1485 it was rebuilt and combined with a drinking fountain.

Resolution of the Maidens of London (authentic spellings)

'We the maidens and Virgins of the famous City of London, ... do declare, that we are fellow felers of your great sufferings, ... and that we are willing to ... help forward with your design according to our powers, not withstanding the weakness of our sex, always provided that you be in readiness upon call to sweep, cleanse, and brush away the sut, dust and cobwebs, which (through your absence) hath ingendered in our nooks and private corners; and we shall according to our abilities contribute quarterly (out of our wages) towards the propogating that good work; our selves confessing that we have been at a loss through your want of a constant standing, whereby you have been forced to keep at a distantial posture from us; we being compelled with great pain and labour to look you up in Pick Hatch, Rotten Row, and Old Street. Therefore we beseech you to go and prosper, and our hands and hearts (who are well wishers to your occupation) shall attend you...'

Signed by the many thousand Maids
in and about the City of London. 1663

Chapter 2

Horne, Wright, Dale, Wood and Sells

When 21 year old Benjamin Horne started his coal business at Bankside in 1719, he became one of the first coal factors. Joseph Wright came from Newcastle in 1731 and went into partnership with Henry Ridley Dale at Lower Thames Street. Both the Horne and Dale family businesses lasted through many generations.

John Wood's business was established at Wapping in 1737. Old ledgers from his firm contain addresses of customers who lived in the wooden houses on Old London Bridge. John's son Richard became coal merchant by Royal Warrant to George III (a tradition held by one of the old Charrington firms through successive reigns and still carried on today). Richard Wood and his sons had their wharf at 19 Northumberland Street, near Hungerford Bridge.

In 1738, Edward Sells became an apprentice to lighterman and coal merchant, Samuel Price. Price had his business premises at Dowgate dock (between Canon Street Station and Southwark Bridge). The dock – an outlet for Walbrook River – was also a laystall, where carts full of nightsoil from London privies were discharged. Edward would have known the chimney sweeps who were engaged there as nightmen.

After completing his seven-year indenture, Edward moved to Lambeth. On 7th May 1754, he leased 'a wharf, shed, backyard and house at Masons Stairs, Bankside'. In the yard at the back were a pavement of Newcastle stone and a door leading 'to the Necessary house in the shed over the wharf'. Edward bought his coal from ship owner Henry Fowles. A bill of sale for Pontop coal (September 1755) shows that it cost 30s.6d. a caldron. Edward Sells died in 1793. He was succeeded by seven more generations of Sells, who all kept the family name Edward. The property with its convenient privy was bought by the Sells family and remained in their ownership until the late 19th century.

[Quotes: *Two Centuries in the London Coal Trade*, Elspet Fraser Steven, 1952]

Chapter 3

Flues

Rumford's improvements to the fireplace opening (to be used in internal chimneys) included the following specifications:

(a) The front opening should be square.
(b) The depth approximately half the width of the front.
(c) The sides should be splayed.
(d) The upper two thirds of the fireback should slope outward.
(e) Above, 4″ in depth, should be a restricted 'throat' and 'smoke shelf'.

232

(f) Higher still, a 'smoke chamber' with tapering sides of 60° leading into the flue.

(g) The area inside the flue should be one tenth the area of the front opening.

Other 18th-century London Master Sweeps

1749	Samuel Bean, Little Shire Lane
1749	John Bagley, Swallow Street
1749	John Connel, Angell Street
1749	Henry Harrison, James Street
1749	Thomas Stuckley, Grosvenor Mews
1763	John Bates, St Lukes, Nr. Old Street
1780	Samuel Collins, Tothill Street
1770	Francis Hallmarke, Oxford Road
1770	W. James, Grace-church street
1784	George Cordwell, Grosvenor's Mews

18th-century London Masters Trading as Nightmen

1745	Robert Stone, White Cross Street
1750	Webb and Lawless, 1 Mutton Lane, Clerkenwell
1770	John Bates, White Cross Street
1779	Philip Page, Golden Lane
1786	Smith, St Dunstan's Alley
	William Hall, No 1, Small-Coal Alley, Norton-Falgate
	Jonathan Crow, No 37, Cross Street, Islington
	Joseph Lawrence, Grosvenor Mews
	Benjamin Watson, No 2 Great Portland Street

Chapter 4

Other 18th-Century Indentures:

5th December, 1791, Birmingham, Thomas Saunders apprenticed to Master Sweep Daniel Seaman.

15th January 1824, widow Elizabeth Joules of Adam & Ave Court, St Pancras bound her 9-year-old son, James Joules to St Pancras master sweep George Hardy. Nearly four years later the same master sweep, now operating in St Marylebone, took on apprentice Thomas Stirling aged 9 from St Giles in the Fields.

Reasons for Flues Branching Off
Allowance made for a fireplace above.
Flues meeting to share the same chimney.
Avoidance of end beam or girder

233

Chapter 5

William Watson's apprentices

Charles Brooks ...	Hatter
Frederick Mochford ...	Tailor
William Smith ...	Scaleboard Cutter

Cancer Cases

In 1921, Dr Sidney Henry, a London Medical Officer found that there were 121 fatal cases of cancer in chimney sweeps.

A Comic Song

Duck-Legged Dick

Duck-legged Dick had a donkey
And his lush loved much for to swill,
One day he got rather lumpy,
And got sent seven days to the mill.
His donkey was taken to the green-yard,
A fate he never deserved.
Oh! it was such a regular mean year,
That alas! the poor moke got starved.
Oh! bad luck can't be prevented,
Fortune she smiles or she frowns,
He's best off that's contented,
To mix, Sirs, the ups and the downs.

Chapter 6

How to Make and Use a Traveller (Wood Heat, John Vivian, 1976)

1. Obtain a bag of heating contractor's furnace or fireclay cement.
2. Fashion a square board 1" smaller all round than the narrowest part of the flue.
3. Drill holes in each corner and attach short ropes so that they can be held up by a main rope (to stop the board from tipping).
4. Place the board in a strong cloth bag that has been filled with loose pliable stuffing, such as straw or rags etc.
5. The rock-hard cement mixture can now be placed on the board inside the bag, and the top of the bag tied tightly.
6. Attach second rope to top of the bag, to hang down the flue in case the traveller gets stuck.

234

7. A thick cream of cement can now be poured down the flue.
8. As the traveller is slowly pulled up the chimney, cement adheres to the sides of the flue and fills in the gaps leaving a smooth passage.

Soot-doors

The London Building Act (1930) specified that 'chimneys and flues having proper soot-doors of not less than 40" square may be constructed at any angle, but in no case shall any flue be inclined at a less angle than 45° to the horizon. All soot-doors shall be at least 15" distant from any woodwork'.

Jonas Hanway

In 1743, Hanway went abroad after having accepted a partnership with Mr Dingly, a St Petersburg merchant. Hanway became familiar with the Caspian wool trade and travelled extensively in Persia and China. Perhaps, as a result of learning in China that no action was taken by authorities if a newborn baby was killed by its parents, Hanway took a particular interest in abandoned children. He was equally horrified that out of 100 children admitted to English orphanages, only 7 survived.

Additional Chimney Sweeping Machines Ordered (1838)

Belfast 1, Cork 3, Dublin 1, St Albans 1, Barnstaple 1, Brighton 3, Lord Ebrington 1, London 11, Upper Canada 1. One each; Ackworth, Aversham, Egham, Canterbury, Cheltenham, Derby, Egham, Northampton, Ramsgate, Reading, Richmond, Sheffield, Taunton, Isle of Thanet, Uckfield, Worcester and Worthing.

Chapter 7

Girls: Working Conditions in Other Trades

Sarah Goodyer, aged 8, from the West Riding of Yorkshire worked a 14-hour day, in the dark, as a trapper in the Gauber coal pit. Young girls like Sarah, who sometimes sang when she had a light, 'but not in the dark', were employed in the mines (Staffordshire, Lancashire and the West Riding) to open and shut the doors which controlled the mine ventilation. They also filled skips with coal, then either pushed or dragged the trucks along to the foot of the shaft. During their 12-hour working day they were completely in the power of the overseers or 'Butties'.

Lucy Luck was born in 1848 and she started working in the silk mills at

Tring (Hertfordshire) before she was 9 years old. Her wage at the mill was 2s 6d per week, and she was so small she had to stand on a wooden horse. In the evenings, to increase her earnings, Lucy plaited a set amount of straw (5 yards), for the straw hat industry.

Perhaps the worst job of all was agricultural labouring in the Fen districts where 'Gangs' of women and children (who were cheaper to employ than men) worked all day from early morning until night, throughout all seasons. They were needed to clear the fields of gorse, thistles and stones.

Montagu House

Designed by James Stuart, it was sumptuously decorated; the 'Feather Room' displayed hangings made by Elizabeth from the plumes of many hundreds of birds. The room became the subject of a poem by Cowper.

Chapter 8

Jack Hall Ballad (Continued)

2
I've twenty cows in store, that's no joke, that's no joke...
I've twenty cows in store, and I'll rob for twenty more.
My neck shall pay for all when I die.
Chorus

3
I've candles lily-white, that's no joke, that's no joke.
I've candles lily-white, Oh I stole them in the night.
For to light me to the place where I lie.
Chorus

4
They tell me that in gaol I shall die, I shall die.
They tell me that in gaol I shall swallow no brown ale.
But be damned if ever I fail till I die.
Chorus

5
I rode up Tyburn Hill in a cart, in a cart...
I rode up Tyburn Hill and 'twas there I made my will
Saying the best of friends must part, so farewell.
Chorus

6
Oh I climbed up the ladder, that's no joke, that's no joke.
Oh I climbed up the ladder, and the hangman spread the rope.
And the devil of a word said I, coming down.

The Ballad of Sam Hall

My name it is Sam Hall,
Chimney-sweep, chimney-sweep; (repeat)
And I robs both great and small
And now I pays for all,
Chimney-sweep.

2
Then the Parson he will come,
Chimney-sweep, chimney-sweep; (repeat)
With looks so bloody glum
And talk o' what's to come,
Chimney-sweep.

3
Then the Sheriff he'll come too
Chimney-sweep, chimney-sweep; (repeat)
With his bloody crew,
Their bloody work to do,
Chimney-sweep.

4
Then up the drop we'll go
Chimney-sweep, chimney-sweep; (repeat)
While all the people down below
'll say, "Sam Hall, I told you so,"
Chimney-sweep.

Areas in London built by David Porter

Dorset Square, Upper Baker Street, Great Cumberland Place etc.

Family details: David Porter's illegitimate son David Charles was born to a Mary Bates, and baptised on 30th January 1802. Brought up in the Porter family and well provided for in his father's will, he became a man of property. In 1850–51 three of his sons emigrated to New Zealand. They were among the first settlers in Canterbury and Wanganui, where their descendants have established a large 'Porter clan'. Porter's Pass commemorates their name on land known as Castle Hill Sheep Station.

St Bernard's Monastery

The monks had established their monastery in 1835 and moved into their impressive new buildings, which they helped to build, in 1844, by which time there were 30 monks and novices. Four years later the monastery was designated an Abbey – the first in England Since the Reformation – and Bernard Palmer became its first Abbot.

237

Chapter 9

Chimney Sweeping Machine Patents

No 4225, 1818 ... Zachariah Barratt, carpenter, 27 Windmill Street, Tottenham Court Road
No 4744, 1822 ... George Richards, architect, Truro, Cornwall
No 7777, 1838 ... Samuel Stocker, machinist, Bristol
No 9284, 1842 ... Sir Francis Desanges, Upper Seymour Street, Portland Square
No 9284, 1842 ... A.H.A. Durrant, Long Castle, Shropshire
No 9343, 1842 ... George Hawe, Manchester
No 9921, 1843 ... David Evans, engineer, Coleshill Street, Eaton Square
No 10136, 1844 ... John Parsons, Selwood Terrace, Brompton, Middlesex
No 10164, 1844 ... William Jeffries, Little Sussex Place, Hyde Park Gardens
No 10273, 1844 ... James Kite, coal merchant, Hoxton, Midx
No 11440, 1846 ... Robert Teagle, plasterer, Hammersmith
No 11667, 1847 ... Osman Giddy, gentleman, Hereford Lodge, Old Brompton
No 11686, 1847 ... Lemuel Wellman Wright, engineer, Chalford, Gloucester
No 11961, 1847 ... George Taylor, gentleman, No 2 Bartholomew Pl. Kentish Town
No 12090, 1848 ... Alexander Alliott, bleacher, Lenton Works, Lenton, Nottingham

SSNCB Recommendations

Robert Day, 21 Newton Street, High Holborn
Edward Raven, 64 Lant Street, Borough
John Shepherd, 19 Kinnerton Street, Knightsbridge
Thomas Peacock, Chester Mews North, Grosvenor Place

London Gentlewomen Who Made Donations Towards the Purchase of Machines

		£
1828	Lady Ann Hamilton	5
1828–1835	Miss Angerstein	63
1830–1834	Mrs Holland	40
1832	Duchess of Kent	20
1834	Mrs G.F. Young	6
1835	Miss Preston	5
1835	Mrs Butlin	6.10s
1835–1838	Mrs Burlingham	8
1838	Sarah Adams	5

Chapter 10

Edward Montagu Biography (continued)

In 1733, Edward returned to England. While still under age he began the first of many amorous liaisons. He married a handsome washer-woman many years his senior, then abandoned her two weeks later. (She lived happily enough – maintained by Edward's father – and died in 1756.)

Edward had no idea of the value of money and was constantly in debt. Given an allowance of £300 a year in the hope he might reform, he was sent by his father to Holland, supervised by a 'Governor' (tutor). Enrolling at Leyden University on 6th September, 1741, he studied Arabic and European languages. His good intentions evaporated, however, and his parents were constantly harassed for money. When Lady Mary paid him a visit, she reported to her husband that 'their son had entirely lost his beauty and looked seven years older than his real age'.

To his credit, Edward joined the army in Flanders where he obtained a commission. He survived active service in the Battle of Fontenoy (his letters make entertaining reading) and was captured by the French. On his return to England, he astonished London society by his extravagant dress, which included a wig of iron wire.

His father, pleased with a satisfactory report from General Sinclair, was influential in helping Edward became an MP for Huntingdon in the 1747 general election. But by the time of his father's death in 1761, Edward had become an embarrassment to his family, who considered him insane. Despite the publication of a number of historical essays, and a Fellowship of the Royal Society, he was disinherited by both parents. The bulk of his father's fortune went to his sister, and Edward received an annuity of £1000 per year.

For the next 16 years, Edward led an adventurous life abroad, eventually becoming a Mohammedan and adopting Turkish dress. In Venice in 1775, George Romney painted his half-length portrait. When Edward heard of the death of his first wife (there were several others) he decided to return home. He never reached England. An extraordinary linguist and an extrovert to the end, he died on 29th April 1776 after swallowing a fishbone. He was buried in the cloister of the Erenietani, Padua.

Edward's son was also named Edward Wortley Montagu. Aged 12 (1763) he was a King's Scholar at Westminster School.

Chapter 11

Additional Works About Chimney Sweeps

1720   *The Chimney Sweeper*, two songs with music
1732   *John Cole*, W. Oldirworth
1750   *Wits & Beaux of Society*, George Selwyn
1798   *Tales of the cottage*, Madame la Comptessa de Genlis

1804	*London Cries, Sweep! Sweep!*
1808	*Sweep O!*
1808	*Chimney Sweeper riddles*, Library of fiction
1811	*Cries of York*
1819	*A Case of Privilege*, Encyclopedia of Wit
1828	*Striking a Balance*, Encyclopedia of Wit
1830	*George and The Chimney Sweep*, Jane & Ann Taylor
1830	*The Climber's Complaint*, James Montgomery
1830	*The Young Chimney Sweepers*, Religious tracts
1835	*A Chimney-Sweeper No Bishop*, Encycl. of Wit & Wisdom
1839	*The Poor Little Sweep*, Samuel Roberts
1877	*The Sweepers & The Thieves*, D. Lewis
1878	*Friendship*, Ouida
1880	*The Three Clever Kings*, Mary De Morgan
1884	*The Little Chimney Sweep*, W.B.F.
1897	*The Massarenes*, Ouida
1937	*And So – Victoria*, Vaughan Wilkins
1967	*Smith*, Leon Garfield

Water Babies, Charles Kingsley

	First published *Macmillan's Magazine*, (August 1862–March 1863)
1863	*Macmillan & Company*, illustrations, J. Noel Paton
1885	Second edition, illustrations, Linley Sambourne
1908	*Oxford University Press*, illustrations, A.E. Jackson
1908	*Blackie and Son*, school reader, illustrations Alice Woodward
1909	*Macmillan & Company*, paintings, Warwick Goble
1910	*Macmillan & Company*, paintings, Warwick Goble
1915	*Raphael Tuck & Sons*, illustrations, Mabel Lucy Attwell
1915	*Constable & Company*, illustrations, W. Heath Robinson
1917	*Oxford Clarenden Press* abridged annotated, J.H. Smith and M.L. Milford, illustrations, Janet Robertson
1920	*Oxford University Press*
1948	*Oxford University Press*
1948	*Ward & Lock Co. Ltd*, illustrations, Harry G. Theaker
1984	*J. Coker and Company* large print 'in easy words of one syllable', illustrations, G.E. Breary
1984	*Puffin Classic*, abridged
1993	*Grandreams Ltd*, four *Good Night, Sleep Tight* storybooks, abridged with addition to text, Beryl Johnston, illustrations, Dorothea King

INDEX

242

243

St Bartholomew's Hospital, 90, 92
St Bernard's Monastry,
  (Acknowledgements), 78, 152,
  (Appendix), 237
St George the Martyr Church, 115
St George's Church (Hanover Square),
  42
St George's Hospital, 92
St George's Square, 141
St James's Church, 102
St James's Chronicle (1802), 134, 161
St Martin's Church, 140, 216
St Martin's Lane Academy, 84
St Martin's-le-Grand, 22
St Mary-le-Bow, 139
St Pancras, 29
St Peter's Chains, 193
St Swithin's Church, 168
St Thomas's Hospital, 170
Stanhope family, 35
State of Chimney Sweepers' Young
  Apprentices, The, (1773), 113
Statute of Artificers (1562), 56
Steer, James, 38
Stevens, John, 133
Stevens, Robert, 47, 116, 117, 120, 127,
  170, 176
Stirling, Thomas, (Appendix), 233
Stockton-on-Tees, 170
Stone, Robert, (Appendix), 233
Strawson, (notes), 55
Stubbs, Phillip (1583), 189
Suffolk, 177
Sunderland, 21
Surrey, 22, 41
Sutton Scarsdale Hall, 225
Swallow Street, 122
Sweeps' Wedding, The, 188
Swift, Jonathan, 34, 210
Sydney Hotel (Goole), 77

Taylor, Elizabeth, 126
Taylor, James, 110
Taylor, Mary, 128
Taylor, Mr, 37
Taylor, Robert, 128
Teddington, 156
Tempell, Jeane, 121
Tennants' Chemical Works, 70
Tenniel, Sir John, 84
Thackeray, William, 39

Theatre Royal, Drury Lane, 212
Thomas, Edward, 98
Thornton, 69
Times, The, (1785) 114, (1799, notes) 138,
  187, 201, (1847) 70, (1864) 112,
  (1875) 173
Tinson, Robert, 77
Tit for Tat (1854), 223
Tomkinson, Albert, 43
Topham, William, 77
Tooke, William, 72, 116, 161, 169
top hat, 47, 155, 187, 188, 206
Topham, George, 77
Trade signs/cards (see advertising)
Tring, 185, 186, 192, (Appendix), 236
Tronmen, 105
Tuff, 52
Tunbridge Castle, 3
Tyburn, 144

umbrella, 113, 162
Union School, 120
United Society of Master Chimney
  Sweepers, 195, 196, 230

Victoria Theatre, 99
Victoria, Queen, 67, 117
Victorian Low Life, 97, 98
Vinson, Mary, 122
Vinson, Richard, 122
Voyer, Mrs, 125
Vyse, Worthing, 75, 149, 151

Wages (see fees)
Walker, D, *General View of Agriculture in*
  Hertfordshire, 25
Walker, Fowles, 113
Wales, 4, 40
Wales, Prince of, 115, 162
Wales, Charlotte, Princess of, 63
Waller, Jamesina, 82
Wapping, (Appendix), 233
Ward, Edward 'Ned', *Hudibras Redivivs*
  (1706), 213
Ward, Enock, (illustration), 224
Ware, Isaac,
  Complete Body of Architecture, The,
    (1754), 216
  Designs of Inigo Jones, 216
Warwickshire, 127
Watson, Benjamin, 87, 89, 172, 176

Watts, Henry, 127
Webb, (Appendix), 233
weddings, 186–188
Welbeck Street, 114
Wellington, Duke of, 129, 156
Wensleydaie Advertiser, (1845), 61
Werneth, 57
West Horndon, 7
West Indies, 28, 64, 65, 200
Westdown (N. Devon), 95
Western Gazette, (1907), 188
Westminster, 36, 87, 107, 114, 140, 143
Westminster Abbey, 114, 156
Westminster Baths, 93
Westminster Bridge, 162
Westminster Hospital, 165
Westminster School, 198, (Appendix), 239
White, James, 'Jem', 194, 195
White Conduit House, 196
Whitfield, Mrs, 128
Whitney, John, 38, 122
Wiggett, Mary, 122
Wilberforce, William, 107, 147
Wilkins, Harriet, 126
Wilkins, William, 170

Wilson, Ann, 128
Wilson, Mrs, 125
Winborne St Giles, 119
Windsor Castle, 38, 130
Wit & Wisdom, (1835), 210
Wizeman, Alfred, 21
Woburn, 154
Wokingham, 217
Wolverhampton, 78
Wood, John, & Richard, 22, (Appendix), 232
Wood, William, 37, 116, 117, 130, 178
Woodward, William, 37
Wright, Joseph, 22, (Appendix), 232
Wright, William, 29
Wrotham Park, 216
Wyndham Club House, 172

Yates, Robert, 124, 125
Yeoman, John, 22, 38
Yeomanry Cavalry Barracks, 37
York, 116, 136, 156, 170, 177
York Castle, 70
York, Dean of, 116
Yorkshire, 61, 185
Young, T, (Dublin), 96